Praise for David Teems' writing in his previously publis~~hed b~~

"David Teems is one of the most t[...] have encountered in the Christian [...]

[...] ~~on~~ Buseck, D.Min., Director of Ministries at CBN.com, author, *Praying the News*

"Favorite read of the year! Crammed with research and brilliantly penned. Smart book for the discriminating reader."

— Patsy Clairmont, author of *Kaleidoscope*

"One of the best written books I've ever read. It's a page turner."
"More exciting than any movie I've seen in recent years."

— Jim Cantelon and Moira Brown, hosts of *100 Huntley Street*, Canada's longest running daily talk show

Tyndale

The Man Who Gave God an English Voice

David Teems

THOMAS NELSON
Since 1798

NASHVILLE DALLAS MEXICO CITY RIO DE JANEIRO

Published in Nashville, Tennessee, by Thomas Nelson. Thomas Nelson is a trademark of Thomas Nelson, Inc.

Published in association with Rosenbaum & Associates Literary Agency, Brentwood, Tennessee.

Thomas Nelson, Inc., titles may be purchased in bulk for educational, business, fundraising, or sales promotional use. For information, please e-mail SpecialMarkets@ ThomasNelson.com.

Library of Congress Cataloging-in-Publication Data

Teems, David.
    Tyndale : the man who gave God an English voice / David Teems.
        p. cm.
    Includes bibliographical references.
    ISBN 978-1-59555-221-1
    1. Tyndale, William, d. 1536. 2. Bible. English—Versions—Tyndale. I. Title.
BR350.T8T44 2012
270.6092,dc23
    [B]   2011028649

Printed in the United States of America

12 13 14 15 16 QGF 6 5 4 3 2 1

To Ward Allen

Where the Spirit is, it is always summer.

—William Tyndale

Contents

Contents

Prologue

Do You Not Know Me? My Name Is Tyndale.

O for a muse of fire, that would ascend
The brightest heavens of invention,
A kingdom for a stage, princes to act
And monarchs to behold the swelling scene!

—William Shakespeare, *Henry V*

THE OLD WORLD WAS DYING, AND WITH AN INCH OF POISON AROUND its heart. The Middle Ages was coming to its slow climactic end, and in a blaze of flesh and madness. It would not give up without a fight. Otherwise good men were swept up in a kind of collective psychosis. The times were treacherous. And H8 was king.

Church and state tolerated a kind of shared headship—often a troubled or aggravated headship, but a league nonetheless. Rulers were validated with a nod from Rome, and the papal court was not unlike that of royalty. The apparatus was long in play. The Englishman "became as much an outlaw by disobedience to the one as by disobedience to the other."[1]

Christianity was indeed the "matrix of medieval life." You could do very little without the blessing of the Church. The Catholic Church "governed birth, marriage, death, sex, and eating, made the rules for law and medicine, gave philosophy and scholarship their subject matter."[2] It taught the faithful how to spend their money, how to sweat their tithe, what to believe, what to think.

Culture grew within and around the Church. She was the watchful parent. And membership was not optional, "it was not a matter of choice; it was compulsory and without alternative, which gave it a hold not easy to dislodge."[3]

The Renaissance, however, with its discovery of the New World, with its reinterpretation of the cosmos and man's reassigned place within it, with the downsizing of the great myths that had driven culture along, allowed man to reimagine himself. And becoming self-aware, he didn't necessarily need nor want a demanding mother. Such an evolutionary state in the progress of man could not help but create a powerful tension. It is within this tension that our story lives.

Myopia

The aggravation was an old one that went as far back as John Wycliffe (1328–1384), who argued that temporal matters belonged to the civil powers alone, that the monarchy was superior to the priesthood. And while his angels-dancing-on-the-head-of-a-pin contemporaries were asking questions like "Does the glorified body of Christ stand or sit in heaven?" or "Is the body of Christ, eaten in the sacrament, dressed or undressed?" Wycliffe started asking better questions. His questions, as well as the answers he gave them, were incendiary.

Revenues were flooding into the Church from all compass points and from a variety of cleverly invented streams. Wycliffe, however, could find no justification in Scripture for the "organization of the church as a feudal hierarchy, or for the rich endowments the Church enjoyed."[4] He felt that the Church should be stripped of its coin and that it should distribute its wealth among the poor. "God gave his sheep to be pastured," he wrote, "not to be shaven and shorn."[5]

The Church was incensed at Wycliffe for his ideas, for his audacity, for his objection to the doctrine of transubstantiation among other things, and for his insistence on a vernacular Bible, which he and his associates produced in 1382. Had he not died of a stroke two years later, he would have burned for his trouble.* Still, Wycliffe's impassioned rant is useful to this prologue. It expressed "both national interest and popular feeling."[6]

But John Wycliffe died of natural causes. William Tyndale did not. There is hardly anything natural about condemning a man to burn alive and finding contentment in the act, a pious contentment at that, as if Christ had been done some honorable service.

At the heart of medieval Christianity, if indeed it had a heart, was a reliance on fear and manipulation. The capacity to inspire terror in its faithful was the first rule of order and dominion. The only modern analogue might be radical Islam, with its commitment to *jihad*.

This particular spirit is a very old one. It changes names often and it is not limited to any one ethnic or religious persuasion. While it may vary in its method—and certainly belief—among the most common identifying marks are blind devotion and ritual murder.

One hundred years before William Tyndale was born, the Church claimed that many "false and perverse people of a certain new sect . . . do perversely and maliciously in divers [many] places within the said realm, under the color of dissembled holiness, preach and teach these days openly and privily divers new doctrines, and wicked heretical and erroneous opinions contrary to the same faith and blessed determinations of the Holy Church."[7]

There was only one answer. Fire.

In 1401, Henry IV made the burning of heretics policy in England, a policy that was not rescinded until the reign of Elizabeth I more than 150 years later (1559). The following excerpt must be weighed against

---

* Wycliffe was eventually burned at the stake, but only after being dead for more than forty years. In the most bizarre little ceremony in 1428, his body (or what was left of his body) was exhumed and marched around the town of Lutterworth; he was defrocked, then turned over to the secular authorities for "execution." It was Wycliffe's denial of transubstantiation that got him in the most trouble. For this he was labeled a heretic.

the Church's need for spectacle. By a consideration so very English, the condemned were to be led onto a stage.

> Before the people in an high place cause to be burnt that such punishment may strike fear into the minds of others, whereby, no such wicked doctrine and heretical and erroneous opinions, nor their authors and fautors [agents], in the said realm and dominions, against the Catholic faith, Christian law, and determination of the holy church, which God prohibit, be sustained or in any way suffered.[8]

The strategy was simple. "Strike fear into the minds of others." Salvation was perceived more as an escape from the flames of hell than divine citizenship with a God of love—avoiding the torments of the damned rather than the embrace of a warm human Christ, a loving Savior. There were exceptions to this general idea of God, certainly, and among faithful Catholics, but they stood in contrast to the general mood of the times and the corruptions of its leadership.

The claims of the Church for the mysteries of the faith were absolute, final. Nothing was open for discussion, and because religion so mingled with everyday life, because the Church could not err, or so it was taught, they did not question. Oddly, because the hypnosis was so thorough, the burning of a heretic received little sympathy from the people, only "morbid curiosity, from citizens shrewd enough to avoid getting involved in such dangerous questionings."[9]

It was into this angry, unjust, and conflicted world that the English Bible was born.

Food for Lions

William Tyndale translated the English New Testament (and the Old) under severe external pressure. He was exile. He was hunted. He was continually under the threat of death. His life was reduced to a kind of living martyrdom.

Christianity itself was born under similar conditions. Like Tyndale's

English Bible, it was born in defiance. Christianity materialized under intense pressure, under severe persecution and the threat of death. She was exile, outcast, excommunicate.* And she thrived in it.

> They were food for lions and for the dark entertainments of the Caesars. Desperation imposed itself upon them in swift running tides. It distilled into the blood, writing itself deep into their code of life. It mingled together with love to give them a beginning, a beginning that could have only happened in such a time, when every hour and every minute was precious. It sifted the heart of debris. It made love authentic, immediate, relevant. They knew heaven was close, one step, one martyrdom away. Love bound them together, love that was larger than their disputes or differences. It was currency among them, the gold by which they traded among themselves, the coin that purchased heaven.[10]

Christianity is always at its best when under fire. I am not sure it could have come together any other way. The blood that was spilled in its nativity served only to strengthen its resolve.

As the rhapsody above might suggest, to William Tyndale "every hour and every minute was precious." The danger that stalked him "sifted the heart of debris." Economy and brilliance are the result.

Created in the same heat as that of its true mother, the Bible Tyndale bequeathed us could have been translated no other way. Under more peaceful conditions or in more reasonable times, it would not have been the same Bible any more than

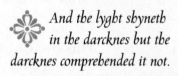 *And the lyght shyneth in the darcknes but the darcknes comprehended it not.*

–JOHN 1:5, WILLIAM TYNDALE
NEW TESTAMENT

Christianity would have become the lovely creature it became without the agonies of its birth. Only someone with Tyndale's peculiar gifts and

---

* *excommunicate*—Ironically, this word was a Tyndale innovation. The *Oxford English Dictionary* credits Tyndale with its first usage (1526 Tyndale Bible, John ix. 22 "He shulde be excommunicat out of the Sinagoge").

sensibilities would have been able to metabolize all of this effectively and with such pure results.

We will explore this in some detail, but exile had a profound effect on Tyndale. By being absent from his native England, she was more present to him, more immediate in his thoughts. Exile was his making, and it lies at the soul of all he wrote and translated.

The conditions of a brutal, tyrannous culture, the imperium the Catholic Church seemed to have over the conscience of the Western world, the severity of the age and the conditions under which Tyndale lived and worked, the toiling of his great mind and spirit against the mood of the times and the pitiless thing in its heart; these things came together to give the English world something it had never seen before, or had hardly imagined. No other English Bible or translator would ever suffer these conditions again.

The Bible William Tyndale gave us was the first of its kind. It was organic, proof that nature's first green is gold. Its first vitality was its finest vitality—its first life its best, its biggest life. His Bible was not the mere result of a linguistic evolutionary process. There was no precedent, no antecedent English Scripture. The only comparison might be to imagine the very first English poems or plays being written by William Shakespeare, and that all future poems and plays were either a mimic or some argument with his great work.

This Book Must Grit Its Teeth

My book *Majestie: The King Behind the King James Bible* is a very different book from this one. *Majestie* was allowed to laugh. James I of England, with his odd psychology, his waddling gait, his quirky humor, and all his numerous, grand, and lovely contradictions seemed to demand it. James Stuart was "an amusing mix of bombast and imperium, of sparkle and grime, of visionary headship and blunder." He was the "unscrubbed child who never grew up, nor had any mind to."[11]

This present book, however, asked things of me that *Majestie* did not. To be honest, I hesitated at first. I was not sure how to begin. I enjoyed what the Elizabethans and the Jacobeans brought out in me, and thought it might be the same with their grandparents. I was wrong.

The age of James was indeed an enlightened age—intellectually, artistically—and it had permission to laugh. There were laughable things. The playhouses and the taverns swelled with mirth, as did the court of its monarch. James loved to laugh, as did Elizabeth.

England was prosperous. She had replaced Spain as the most powerful country in the world. Gloriana left a beatific glow on everything it touched. After the great tension of the age that preceded it—the age of Henry VIII and his tragic Anne, of Luther and Tyndale, even the homicidal Mary I, the bloody queen—it was as if some large bound thing had been emancipated.

In the age of Tyndale, there was very little that was laughable. It was a rather humorless age. C. S. Lewis used the word *drab*, but he was lamenting the poor state of its literature (which in itself is evidence of a repressed artistic subculture), so he understated the age, which was a bit more savage than his words imply.

In the midst of all this generally bad behavior, you may actually welcome, as I did, what humor you find, which comes from the players themselves—Thomas More, Martin Luther, and William Tyndale. In the midst of all the heaviness, all the growl and snap, each of these men have their lighter moments. With all the destruction and cruelty of the age, with H8 in the seat of English power, a little joke now and then—even Martin Luther's flatulence—is a refreshing change.

But, ultimately, where *Majestie* laughs, this book must grit its teeth. It will inform. It will amuse, and perhaps even entertain. It will certainly bewilder. But the age itself is deadly and there is hardly anything funny about that.

Reading Tyndale

The only explanation for William Tyndale is a spiritual one. All other explanations fail to satisfy or convince. What history we have of him is patchwork and unstable. Even a literary consideration of Tyndale fails to explain. He was an exceptional writer—gifted, instinctual, intuitively spare. He was a bit of an anarchist (as the best writers often are). But his genius was useful to him only as it served a greater purpose, which for Tyndale was *always* spiritual.

The suitable treatment of Tyndale, therefore, is always on his terms. We must meet him when and where he chooses to be found. This is not as fanciful or obscure as it might sound. Against what limited history we have, we are forced to look at what he wrote. But we are hardly at a disadvantage. His work bears all his true marks, and renders a sufficient likeness.

While tangibles are limited, the bigger picture lies in the work itself. There are fewer shadows to chase, fewer leaves to unturn or uncertainties to tolerate. In reading Tyndale, instead of being frustrated at the lack of biographical information, I found it best to be content with what was important to him—to note how he thinks, to trace the patterns of his thought life, his preoccupations, his distractions, the movement of his passion.

> *A writer of imaginative prose (even more than any other sort of artist) stands confessed in his works. His conscience, his deeper sense of things, lawful and unlawful, gives him his attitude before the world.*
>
> – ROBERT CONRAD,
> *A PERSONAL RECORD*

This method is ineffective with some writers, Shakespeare included, but it works with Tyndale. It is in his great body of work that he materializes for us, that he steps to the foreground and smiles for the camera.

He writes with tenderness, with paternal authority and warmth. His voice is immediate, scintillate, penetrating, translucent. His text has a like-there-is-no-tomorrow kind of desperate charm that is both intense and weightless at the same time. He can write intelligently about eternity, and yet with aesthetic restraint. Death and treachery provide a kind of muse.

He is always moving. He has little choice. The threat level suspends between orange and red. The heat is never off. He is nomadic. And as we might expect, his work reflects this condition. His nontranslation text has a kind of epistolary character, not unlike the letters of the New Testament. Tyndale must think and write while on the run. His text, therefore, has a modern economy and a pace that moves it along evenly. And though he is neither truculent nor combative by nature, he is not afraid to strike when that is all that is left to him, when the bullies rant.

Even his Englishing of the Scripture has something to tell us. To William Tyndale, the Word of God is a living thing. It has both warmth and intellect. It has discretion, generosity, subtlety, movement, authority. It has a heart and a pulse. It keeps a beat and has a musical voice that allows it to sing. It enchants and it soothes. It argues and it forgives. It defends and it reasons. It intoxicates and it restores. It weeps and it exults. It thunders but never roars. It calls but never begs. And it always loves. Indeed, for Tyndale, love is the code that unlocks and empowers the Scripture. His inquiry into Scripture is always relational, never analytic.

A Portrait of a Much Truer Kind

If it is our business to discover William Tyndale at least in part by what he has written, we will look at the imprint he left upon those men who were close to him, those indelible marks that go much deeper and are more telling than any printed page. It is often a portrait of a much truer kind.

Tyndale was not shy about what or who he loved. There, too, he left a kind of trail we can follow.

The letters he wrote reveal a gentle spirit, artless and without guile. Even those men who arrested Tyndale "pitied to see his simplicity" when they took him. According to a friend, he lived but "a poor apostle's life" and possessed "a faithful, clear, innocent heart."[12] For all the malevolence that threatened to cut him off, these qualities offer refreshing pause against all the smoky horrors of the age.

Even Thomas More, who made an enemy of Tyndale, once said he was "well known, before he went over the seas, for a man of right good living, studious and well learned in the Scripture, and in divers places in England was very well liked, and did great good with preaching."[13]

Tyndale's work reflects an absolute clarity of mind and conscience. There is little that could be considered leisurely about his writing. His text does not lope or stroll. He gets right to the point. David Daniell used the word *startling* to describe Tyndale's "everyday immediacy."[14]

William Tyndale loved Scripture most of all. It was sanctuary. There is a portrait of Tyndale that currently hangs in the dining hall at Hertford College (Oxford). In the portrait he is pointing to a book, which we may assume is his English Bible.* And though it is doubtful that the likeness comes close to being Tyndale's, it is a fair appraisal of his nature. It is never about himself. Perhaps overmodest, Tyndale once wrote to his friend John Frith, "God hath made me ill-favoured in this world, and without grace in the sight of men, speechless and rude, dull and slow-witted."[15]

He was somewhat of a loner. He was warm, generous, selfless, and he kept his own counsel. He was kind, and he was intensely focused. He could be a difficult piece of work at times. If he was innocent, he was also outspoken (which in Tyndale is not a contradiction). The English Paul he might have been, he had his share of Timothies, as well as the occasional John Mark, that is, the dissenter.

He was not moved by the usual attractions of early modern culture. By the leaning of his own nature, by the obligations of his calling, by the demands of his particular genius, William Tyndale was exile long before he left England.

And once he leaves England, he is outlaw. His translation is outlaw. All his works are outlaw. His thoughts are outlaw. He has a bounty on his head, a target on his back. The story cannot help but fascinate.

---

* Above the image of Tyndale are the words *gulielmus tindalus martyr, olim ex avla magd,* which mean "William Tyndale, Martyr, sometime [formerly] from Magdalen Hall." Just below the pointing finger is a Latin couplet that reads, *ha cut suas dispergam roma tenebras, sponte ex terries ero sponte sacrificium* (To scatter Roman darkness by this light, The loss of land and life I'll reckon slight). Had the artist known Tyndale a little better he would have forgotten the rhyme and might have framed his praise in English. No portrait of Tyndale was made in his lifetime.

Call a manhunt, throw in a villain (a real slimy one, a Dickens character), mention the word *conspiracy*, set the world against a single unsuspecting Englishman, betray him into the hands of the local authorities, cast him into the dank bowels of an old flinty castle, deny him any kind of light, have him speak in his own defense at a sham trial, call him an arch-heretic, condemn him to an eternity in hell, stand him upright in the midst of dry kindling and gunpowder, let him utter some memorable last words, strangle the life out of him, set him ablaze, and what you have is a great story.

It's just not *our* story.

This present treatment of Tyndale departs from the usual "champion of the faith" treatment. As compelling as such stories are, as convincing, and often as true as they may prove to be, when his martyrdom alone is at the center of the argument, we stray wide of the point. By some cognition, Tyndale seemed well aware of how his life would end. You can hear it in the quiet resolve in which he often speaks, as in his letters to his friends. He is almost palpable.

We will address those elements of his life, certainly. When patched together they are too colorful, and too outrageous to omit. But Tyndale's contribution to the English-speaking world was far greater than the price he had to pay to achieve it. Of the unkindness that would eventually take his life, he said, "It is swallowed up as a little smoke of a mighty wind, and is no more seen or thought upon."[16]

Emancipation

Today, in our common English, we speak Tyndale more than we do Shakespeare. And the King James Bible with its high step and its lovely old voice gets the applause that rightfully belongs to William Tyndale. Yet what is dumbfounding to me is how hidden he remains, how misprized, and how thoroughly uncelebrated.

If you have ever bid someone a warm *Godspeed*, you have William Tyndale to thank for the blessing. And *network* is not a word you might have expected to hear in 1530. Tyndale set these two words adrift into the English language almost five hundred years ago, and with them words like *Jehovah, thanksgiving, passover, intercession, holy place, atonement, Mercy seat, judgement seat, chasten, impure, longed, apostleship, brotherly, sorcerer, whoremonger, viper,* and *godless.** This is just a start. An impressive start, certainly, and there are literally hundreds more.

The following expressions made their first appearance through Tyndale. And while old and well rehearsed to you and me, to the English believer in 1526 they were astonishingly new.

Behold the lamb of God

I am the way, the truth, and the life

In my father's house are many mansions

For thine is the kingdom and the power and the glory

Seek, and ye shall find

With God all things are possible

In him we live, move, and have our being

Be not weary in well doing

Looking unto Jesus, the author and finisher of our faith

Behold, I stand at the door and knock

Let not your hearts be troubled

The spirit is willing, but the flesh is weak

For my yoke is easy and my burden is light

Fight the good fight

Imagine hearing these words for the first time, especially after being denied this most primary exchange for centuries. God is no longer hoarded or kept at a distance. He is flush, lucent. And he sounds like you sound. He uses your words, your patterns and rhythms. There is no

---

* The words in this sequence (italics) are listed in Appendix B: First Usage from the *Oxford English Dictionary*.

longer a wall, or a divide, at least not by way of speech. The generosity alone is overwhelming.

We will explore these first impressions, but the presence of Tyndale's New Testament in 1526 was electric. It was also forbidden, which only added to the enchantment.

Considering his impact on the English language and Englishness itself, Tyndale has only one rival. But even the great playwright himself must concede that he is but heir to what the translator left behind. To quote an English Scripture brought new pleasure, put a new taste in the mouth for the English word. It ennobled the tongue, and long before there was a *Hamlet* or a *Lear*. That same nobility is traceable throughout the Shakespearean canon. Tyndale is inescapable.

Then there is the lovable malaprop, Bottom the Weaver, musing on his dream and botching the old text so magnificently.

> *The eye of man hath not heard, the ear of man hath not seen,*
> *man's hand is not able to taste, his tongue to conceive,*
> *nor his heart to report, what my dream was.*
>
> (WILLIAM SHAKESPEARE,
> *A MIDSUMMER NIGHT'S DREAM*, IV, I, 216–220)

> *The eye hath not seen, and the ear hath not heard,*
> *neither have entered into the heart of man,*
> *the things which God hath prepared for them that love him.*
>
> (I CORINTHIANS 2:9,
> *THE WILLIAM TYNDALE NEW TESTAMENT*, 1526)

Phrases like "be not deceived" (from *Julius Caesar* and the Epistle to the Galatians) or "get thee to Nineveh," which has an aural likeness to "get thee to a nunnery." Mistress Quickly's complaint about the fat knight, "he hath eaten me out of house and home" (*Henry IV, Part One*), echoes Tyndale's "eat the poor out of house and harbor" (*The Parable of the Wicked Mammon*) and a thousand other touches.

Even without considerations like sound, weight, movement, syntax,

Without Tyndale's New Testament, and Cranmer's prayer book, it's difficult to imagine William Shakespeare the playwright.

— STEPHEN GREENBLATT,
RENAISSANCE SELF FASHIONING

and other essentials Shakespeare inherited from the translator, there is perhaps some truth to the maxim "without Tyndale, no Shakespeare."[17]

The following exercise shows just how current Tyndale is. The account itself is a rather silly one, but the point is made. Tyndale words are in italics.

If you have ever been to the *sea-shore* just because the *waves* somehow enchanted you, or if on a particular visit someone kicked sand in your boyfriend's face (an outdated and *inexcusable* act) thinking him a *weakling*, though you *refused* to believe it because you happened to be wearing *rose-colored* glasses and because of a *long-suffering* faith in your *dearly beloved*, or simply because you consider him a *godly* man, *unbeliever* that he used to be, William Tyndale gave you the words to tell your story.

If, by some act of *childishness* on the part of one of your friends (some particular *busybody*, though you once thought them the *salt of the earth*) you have ever been used as a *scapegoat*, or if that bad grade you got in English caused an *uproar* in your home, in spite of how *zealous* you were about Keats, how much time you spent at your *writing-table*, or how that *stiff-necked* teacher, that *taskmaster*, Mr. Jones, *grossly* misunderstood it when you said you *lost* your homework or that the dog buried it in some *ungodly* place. The *peace offering* you made him hardly moved him a single *jot*, which I am sure left you disillusioned and *brokenhearted*.

The English-speaking world owes William Tyndale a debt it is hardly aware of. Following the advent of Tyndale's English Bible, a single generation later, from 1570 to 1630 more than thirty thousand new words entered the English language, more than any other time in history.

The Bible is certainly not the only reason for such a heady infusion of words. The advent of the English theater in the late 1570s generated its own profuse word mill. But the currents were swift and powerful and they ran together, pulpit and stage.

Even so, it was a vernacular Scripture that liberated the English voice, and the English conscience along with it. It had the effect of an awakening. It came upon the English spirit with arousal, the way perhaps only great art can—an intrusive, meddling art (though the word *art* itself cannot explain).

An English Scripture not only kindled a new English pride, it created a new English citizenry. In Tyndale, the old world was finished.

Thomas More used English with condescension. It was a lesser creature. English was "at the bottom of the pond." Latin being the rule at the academy, students were discouraged from speaking English. And to allow God to speak anything other than Latin was unimaginable, not to be tolerated.

Tyndale changed all that. He was the liberator, the broker between the Englishman and his God, if not between the Englishman and himself. Tyndale's Bible not only validated the English language, it did so grandly. "Tyndale gave to English not only a Bible language, but a new prose. England was blessed as a nation in that the language of its principal book, as the Bible in English rapidly became, was the fountain from which flowed the lucidity, suppleness and expressive range of the greatest prose thereafter."[18]

The loosening of all the old tensions and the unmuzzling of God in the common tongue had the effect of a great emancipation. All those things that caught in its throat were suddenly unbound. The momentum the English Bible created, the hunger for the English word, the readership and its consumption was too thorough and too deep. The English became *a people of the book* (the Bible). "As though all England," Thomas More once mocked, "should go to school with him [Tyndale] to learn English."[19]

The Great Wound

In fairness, the Catholic Church today is not the same Catholic Church it was in 1500. I hope this might serve as an apology. It is difficult to write about religion and not offend. And there is nothing more unattractive in a text than the envenomed hiss, the invective one party directs toward another. To the Catholic hierarchy of 1528, William Tyndale was a heretic, a most loathsome enemy of the faith. To Tyndale, the pope was Antichrist, and purgatory a dark imagination. Nobody wins. That's the whole point of an age that cannot laugh. The only effective way to perceive the age of Tyndale is by the severity, the injustices, by the great wound in its heart.

Do You Not Know Me?

In January 1531, after Tyndale had been living in exile for seven years, Henry VIII sent an emissary, Stephen Vaughn, to the continent to find the translator, to persuade him to return to England and on promise of safe conduct.

Vaughn sent letter after letter to Frankfurt, Hamburg, and other cities where he suspected the translator might be. He wrote back home of his doubts and his lack of success. In Vaughn's correspondence to the king we are given something about Tyndale and from a close and indifferent observer. Weeks into his search, Vaughn was approached at last by a messenger sent by the translator himself.

"What is your friend," Vaughn asked, "and where is he?"

The messenger replied, "His name I know not, but if it be your pleasure to go where he is, I will be glad thither to bring you."

Describing the event some time later, Vaughn wrote, "I concluded to go with him, and followed him till he brought me without [outside] the gates of Antwerp, into a field lying nigh unto the same; where was abiding [waiting on] me this said Tyndale."[20]

Emerging from the shadows of the approaching evening, the expatriate translator spoke first.

"Do you not know me?"

"I do not well remember you," Vaughn said.

"My name is Tyndale."

Vaughn, not knowing just what to expect, was soon awed with his new acquaintance—so much so that he was warned later not to defend Tyndale with too much enthusiasm. He could burn for his affection.

Vaughn wrote to Thomas Cromwell, the mediator between himself and the king, and said, "It is unlikely to get Tyndale into England, when he daily heareth so many things from thence which feareth him [makes him fearful] . . . The man is of a greater knowledge than the king's highness doth take him for; which well appeareth by his works. Would to God he were in England!"[21]

The events that followed are reserved for another chapter, but Tyndale's first question "Do you not know me?" provides a useful context for our inquiry. It struck me as odd how he put the question, as if Vaughn should somehow know him already.

At first glance we, too, may not recognize Tyndale. But as we explore his body of work, the translation particularly, we may come to admit that perhaps we know him already, as his question to Vaughn implies. Either way, it makes my task rather clear. Again, we will meet with Tyndale, but only when and where he chooses. That is, on his terms. And if it be your pleasure to go where he is, I will be glad to bring you. Thither.

David Teems
Franklin, Tennessee

1
Translating Tyndale

Comerado, this is no book;
Who touches this touches a man.

—Walt Whitman, *Leaves of Grass, 1855 edition*

SIR THOMAS MORE ONCE WROTE THAT WILLIAM TYNDALE "SEEMS to be everywhere and nowhere." While his tone was anything but friendly, it may be one of the better assessments of Tyndale. The statement is as true today as it was when More said it to his friend Desiderius Erasmus five hundred years ago. What he meant was that the words of William Tyndale, that is, his translation of the Bible and other writings, were spreading widely and infectiously, and yet the man himself was a ghost.

Indeed, to More, it was a kind of haunting.

Of course, Thomas More's pursuit of Tyndale had an altogether different motive than yours and mine. He wanted nothing more than to "find him [Tyndale] with a hot firebrand burning at his back, that all the water in the world will never be able to quench."[1]

Tyndale had little choice but to remain hidden. It was a necessary craft for his survival. And his art reflects this economy of movement—the subtleties, the phantom light-footedness, the acuity. The translation he bequeathed us is as articulate and precise as he was elusive and absent.

We know more about the sound of his last name than we do the year he was born, who his parents were, where he grew up, how old he was when he attended Oxford, and whether or not he attended Cambridge as certain histories imply, or why there seems to have been two family names.

Unfortunately, against our current appetite for biography and memoir, we are just not allowed anything solid or filling. Reading what relatively few biographies there are, and even what primary sources are available, I easily tired of "it *could have been* this way," or "he *might* have lived here," or "we are *almost* certain he lived in this place or that one over there, that he did *this* or *that*."

Reading Tyndale biography you have little choice but to labor through all the qualifiers, those conditionals that weaken a text, that soften its resolve—words like *maybe*, *might*, *perhaps*, *possibly*, and so on.

No Complete Memory of Him

His name rhymes with *spindle*. The second syllable was often spelled *dal*, *dalle*, or *dall*. The Latin form, which William Tyndale used often, was *Tindalus*, and he was known to spell it Tindale or Tyndale. Though convention favors the latter, it was of little concern to Tyndale himself. English was years away from any standardization, so the only rule was indifference, or taste. He just as often spelled his name Tindal or Tindall. The *Oxford English Dictionary* spells his name Tindale.

Nor is there any explanation for the presence of the extra surname. Hutchins (Hutchyns or Hychyns) may have been an alias created by an uncle during the War of the Roses, a Yorkist who fled from northern England (possibly Northumberland, location of the Tyne River[*]) to Gloucestershire at the rise of the Lancastrians. One biographer has called this story a "romantic invention."[2]

Thomas More was convinced that there was something shameful about

---

[*] The name Tyne-dale has a geographical implication, literally a dale along the Tyne River.

the name changing, that it smacked of something criminal. The presence of an alias, so he thought, carried with it "the reek of dark deeds."[3] When Sir Thomas meant to be particularly nasty, he called Tyndale "Hutchins."

Whatever information we have comes as a result of a kind of crude sifting. We are forced to imagine. There is nothing at all on Tyndale's childhood. Estranged mother that she became, England has no complete memory of him. In the end, the shapes we might assume of Tyndale's childhood are elusive. Mozley said it best: "We have certainty of nothing."[4]

Though we have no date of birth, Tyndale would have been baptized into the Catholic Church as an infant, an event he denounced later in life. On the chrism, or the anointing oil, he wrote, "They think that if the bishop butter the child in the forehead that it is safe."[5]

It was preferred that the child be baptized on the same day as its birth, or at least within a matter of days. Infant mortality was common, so haste to church was just as common. It was thought that if the unbaptized child died, it went to *Limbo* (*Limbus puerum*, a child's paradise, a holding place between heaven, hell, and purgatory for the child not vindicated or freed from a state of original sin). *Limbus patrum* (Limbo of the fathers) was reserved for the older pre-Christ unbaptized—Moses, David, the prophets, individuals who were righteous but without Christ.

Limbo has since been closed, due to reconsideration.

Tyndale thought the notion absurd, and purgatory merely an invention to squeeze coin from the masses.[6]

Certainty of Nothing

The accepted year of Tyndale's birth is 1494. This number varies from source to source and is calculated primarily on the receipt of his Oxford University degrees.[7] The year 1495 is the latest he may have been born. He received his Master of Arts degree in 1515, a degree that could not be legally taken until a candidate was twenty years old.

According to John Foxe, William Tyndale was born "about the border of Wales," in the western part of Gloucestershire "where the range of the Cotswolds fall into the vale of Berkeley, with the River Severn flowing beyond." Idyllic, pastoral, lush, verdant, the region incites a kind of rhapsody from its close observers.

> ✿ *{Tyndale} was born*
> *near the borders of*
> *Wales and perhaps there*
> *absorbed the thrilling poetic*
> *cadences of language that even*
> *today can make unbelievers*
> *weep at the united voices of a*
> *Welsh choir singing old hymns*
> *in a thunder of feeling.*
>
> – RICHARD MARIUS, *THOMAS MORE*

The most promising candidates for Tyndale's birthplace seem to be the villages of Slimbridge or North Nibley, possibly even Dursley or Stinchcombe, all located between Gloucester and Bristol, and all on the western edge of the Cotswold hills (Southwest England) by the river Severn.

The name *Cotswolds* means "sheep enclosure in rolling hillsides." Indeed, sheep fattened the land with industry. Cloth was big business and the area prospered, creating a new kind of English nobility, fashioned out of new money. So much so, that the region, which includes Gloucestershire, was "precociously early modern."[8] It is generally thought that the Tyndales of and around Gloucestershire were landowners and successful merchants, possibly yeoman farmers. Either way, the name seemed to carry weight. This could explain his tuition at Oxford.

William had two brothers: John, the younger, and Edward, the older.[9] Edward was capable and enterprising, well known in the vale of Berkeley, particularly around Slimbridge. He lived at Hurst Farm (Slimbridge) and was buried in Slimbridge churchyard in 1546. For years he held the honorable post of receiver (a collector of rents) for the lordship of Berkeley. He also became the steward and auditor of Tewkesbury Abbey.

The will of Edward Tyndale still exists. He married twice and had thirteen children. A man of sufficient means, he left his "great lute" to his son, and his "best bow" to the vicar of Tewkesbury.[10]

Edward did not seem to bother himself in his brother William's business, though the association was hardly avoidable. In a letter written in 1533 by John Stokesley, bishop of London, to Thomas Cromwell, begging that a certain piece of land in Gloucestershire be given to a servant of his (the letter was padded with cash), Stokesley, once a rector of Slimbridge, did his best to frustrate the efforts of another suitor for the land who "hath a kinsman called Edward Tyndale, brother to Tyndale the arch-heretic."[11]

Edward, like his translator brother, seemed able to move quickly. But unlike his translator brother, he avoided trouble. John Tyndale, however, was closer to his brother William's affairs, and therefore seemed to invite trouble. Leapfrogging a bit in time, in November 1531 the same Bishop Stokesley arrested John, a London merchant, and brought him before the new chancellor, Thomas More. Stokesley charged him and those with him for "receiving of Tyndale's testaments and divers other books, and delivering and scattering the same" about London. The name Stokesley will come up again—an angry little man with a fixation for the Tyndales.

After a night in jail John was paraded through the streets of London faced backward on a horse. He was also forced to wear a counterfeit mitre (a headdress worn by a bishop) made out of pasteboard. On what looked more like a dunce cap were the words *peccasse contra mandata Regis* (I have sinned against the commandments of the king). A copy of the New Testament and other outlawed books (among them *Practice of Prelates*, a book of Tyndale's that H8 particularly disliked) were fastened about his neck, "pinned and tacked" to his gown. John was forced to throw the books into a fire prepared for the little spectacle, and had to pay a sizable fine.

A letter from the Venetian ambassador provides a context for the moment. Histories come alive in such letters. Henry VIII wants a divorce from his queen, Catherine of Aragon. The stir is a large one, and Henry has little choice but to involve the pope and most of Europe in his business (at least at the beginning). William Tyndale has voiced his complaint against it, and three thousand copies of his *Practice of Prelates* are circulating among the British public. The following letter, dated December 1530, is from Augustino Scarpinello to Francesco Sforza, Duke of Milan.

The author of the aforesaid work, entitled "Practyse of Prelates," (*Pratica di Prelati*) by name Tyndaro *sen* Tindal, is an Englishman, and for some while (*et he parechj giorni*) has lived, and is at present living, in Germany, and is said to be a man of *magnae doctrinae* [great learning]. His brother, together with certain other persons, who went about circulating this work *in vulgus* [to the general public] were lately paraded through London, along the public thoroughfares (*per plateas publicas*) with pasteboard mitres on their heads, bearing an inscription, thus, *Peccasse contra mandata Regis* and the book suspended from their necks; and having completed the circuit of the thoroughfares, they were ordered to cast the pamphlet [*Practice of Prelates*] into the fire prepared for that purpose.[12]

England, the land that gave us Shakespeare, knew by instinct, by some inwardness peculiar to itself, and still does, how to put on a great show.

As Sure as God Is in Gloucester

Though no record exists, young Tyndale would have attended an elementary school of some kind, an ABC as they were called. He may have met with a nearby priest for private instruction. There was a grammar school within a few miles of where he was raised, at Wotton-under-Edge, a school founded in 1384 by Lady Berkeley. The holidays and school times were not so different as they are today. Judging by the young age Tyndale went to university, his instruction in grammar may have begun at Magdalen Hall (Oxford).

A single line in one of his writings gives us a glimpse of a precocious memory (the first intimation and evidence of a literary soul). Defending the Scriptures in English, in *The Obedience of a Christian Man*, Tyndale said,

Except my memory fail me, and that I have forgotten what I read when I was a child, thou shalt find in the English chronicle, how that king Athelstane[13] caused the holy scripture to be translated into the tongue that then was in England, and how the prelates exhorted him thereto.[14]

I am not going to make the error of assuming when his powerful attraction for linguistics began, or even his love of Scripture, but at least we have here a memory recalled, a place marker from early childhood.

In Gloucestershire, where he grew up, the church was in a state of decay. The complaint was old, and the annoyance generations deep. From around 1476, pastors in the diocese of Worcester, which included Gloucestershire, were "almost non-resident." It was at best a distracted spirituality.

> Ecclesiastical orders had amassed to themselves, in the name of God, enormous riches and a great proportion of the land, and on this they claimed to be exempt from taxation . . . Gigantic fortunes were built up by favored ecclesiastics, while the poor people went unshepherded. An open scandal also was the unchastity of the clergy and of the monastic bodies. While claiming to be too pure for holy matrimony, they were at liberty to keep concubines . . . Yet in this general decay of the Christian spirit the rites and ceremonies were carefully observed. Never were there more services, more holidays in honor of saints, never were relics and shrines more venerated, never were pilgrimages more splendid. The outward form was there, but the spirit was lacking.[15]

The diocese of Worcester was the most neglected of all dioceses in England. It was bishoped by three Italians, men who never set foot in England (and yet drew their stipends regularly). Gloucester was also the site of a highly venerated relic of the blood of Christ, vouched for by an individual who eventually became pope. Later exposed as a fraud, it was legend enough to generate the proverb, "As sure as God is in Gloucester." (Perhaps more germane to our study than the slogan itself is the proverb-generating vitality of Gloucestershire from which the slogan materialized, the vitality Tyndale was weaned on as a child.)

John Hooper, a fellow student with Tyndale at Oxford, became a bishop some years later. To get an idea of how deep the neglect was, Hooper conducted a survey of 311 members of his clergy. Nine priests did not know there were Ten Commandments; thirty-three had no clue where they were in the Bible (most of them suggested the New Testament); ten could not recite the Lord's Prayer; and thirty did not know Jesus had said it in the first place.[16]

Hooper burned at the stake during the reign of Mary Tudor.

Parish priests in the Middle Ages were often uneducated and could not understand a word of Latin, yet these same priests intoned the Mass regularly. And it didn't matter. According to Catholic doctrine the sacraments operate *ex opere operato*, that is, entirely on the work of Christ, "and thus do not depend on the worthiness or education of the priest."[17] As long as a duly ordained priest performs the ritual correctly, the sacrament is valid. Being there is enough.

Because Church Latin was beyond the general believer, there were many who considered the Mass a form of magic. "Hocus-pocus," the incantation we learned as children, is thought to be a corruption of the phrase heard in the Mass, *hoc est corpus meum* (this is my body).

As far back as the fourteenth century, the chafe between the people and the priesthood was evident. "When a priest could purchase from diocesan authority a license to keep a concubine, how should he have better access to God than the ordinary sinner?"[18] Even in Wycliffe's time, when a man confessed adultery, his confessor (priest) was not allowed to ask the name of the woman involved. This was a safeguard to insure the priest would not be tempted to go after the woman himself. The presence of such a rule implies that the offense was common enough to demand restraint.

The Catholic priest was required by canon law to be celibate. But many of them were living openly with women in unofficial common-law relationships that could not be regularized by marriage. This practice, far from being condemned, was actually welcomed both by the bishops and, oddly, by the locals. To the bishop, it provided a stream of income due to the annual fines imposed on the miscreant priests. To the locals, they assumed their own wives and daughters were safer.

Luther once claimed that certain cardinals were thought of as living saints because they confined their sexual activities to adult women.

Monks had an even worse reputation for sexual mischief.

A Renegade Theology

Lollard was the name given to a follower of John Wycliffe. It was derogatory, descended from the Middle Dutch *lollaerd*, meaning "a mutterer, a mumbler." The word "was taken to connote great pretensions to piety and humility, combined with views more or less heretical."[19] Lollards were often itinerant preachers, and considered heretics. Many of them burned for their convictions.

With the void created by the absent bishops, an absentee priesthood, not to mention the general stench such neglect often leaves, Lollardy, with all the daring in its voice, all the challenge, became quite popular.

Lollardy was not an organized sect. Though belief among them was consistent and aimed in the same general direction, there was no single creed. Individual Lollards were distinguished by a "critical, almost puritanical approach to established Christianity, a deep hostility to the Papacy, an enthusiasm for Bible-reading, and the assertion of the religious independence of the individual."[20] It is not unlikely that the boy Tyndale would have heard, and often, sermons preached by their kind.

Tyndale grew up in the complaint. It was the meat he fed upon.

With some justice, the Lollards might be considered the first to preach the message of what came to be the cultural storm known as the Reformation. They pressed the renegade theology of John Wycliffe, which taught that the priesthood was unnecessary as mediator between man and God, a teaching that upset the entire apparatus of the Church.

Wycliffe himself had been prebendary at Aust, in southern Gloucestershire. His disciple and fellow translator, John Purvey, had preached in Bristol, only twenty or so miles from where Tyndale grew up.

Linguistic Curiosity

Tyndale's native Gloucestershire was widely noted for its proverbs and local sayings. It is evident that he learned the local register* at an early age, that peculiar Gloucestershire sound and method, its rustic wisdom and generosity, its pithy verbal economy, the aesthetic that shaped his literary temperament. Small children particularly have an ear for language, a keen linguistic intuition that cools in the adult. It was this western countryside, this midland portion of England, that put its voice in William Tyndale.

The word *yarn* as it means "a tale" is a typical Gloucestershire effect—as is "spinning a yarn," "dyed in the wool," "unravel a mystery"—all metaphorical remnants of a thriving cloth industry. Tyndale's biblical phrases have that *homespun* Gloucestershire charm. "Consider the lilies how they grow: They labour not: They spin not," "the burden and the heat of the day," "It is easier for a camel to go through the eye of a needle . . ." All Tyndale. C. S. Lewis referred to this as "village homeliness,"[21] the voice we hear in the parables of Jesus.

> *Part of his genius as a translator was his gift for knowing how ordinary people used language at slightly heightened moments and translating at that level.*
>
> – DAVID DANIELL, *WILLIAM TYNDALE: A BIOGRAPHY*

Being raised around "the border of Wales" implies a close proximity to the Welsh language. Maybe the young Tyndale was enchanted by the strangeness of the Welsh tongue, by the music it made, a kind of jazz, the pleasant confusion and disorder it may have aroused in his struggle to understand it; or by the odd and lovely mechanic of its speech patterns, its verb-subject-object groove, the

---

* Linguistically, and in simple terms, a *register* is the particular sonic architecture of a given geographic locality, but it implies more than mere sound or dialect. It includes syntax, idiom, phrasing peculiarities, dynamics—however a typical dialect might be identified. Gloucestershire, with its natural lean toward pith and proverb, is the register that Tyndale applies in not only his translation of the Bible, but all his writings. He is identifiable.

carnival it made in the mouth, its mystifying orthography (spelling), its consonant heft.

The border that separated Wales from England may have been too irresistible for the precocious. Granted, this is wild speculation, I am aware, but we are still in the imaginative, forced to supply a memory his country lacks. However it happened, Tyndale became an exceptional linguist. It is not difficult to see where his fascination led him.

Considering this "about the border of Wales" condition of his early development, there is another observation we might make.

In Welsh, between words there exists a kind of warm citizenship, a highly relational element, a peace one word makes with its fellow. For example, the capital of Wales, *Cardiff*, has at least four different pronunciations, all of which depend on the word that precedes it in a sentence. If the sound made between the end of one word clashes or does not "marry well" with the beginning of the next, there is a medication built into the language.

In the words of one of her finest modern poets, Gwyneth Lewis, there exists within the Welsh language a whole system of mutations where two words "rub against each other and soften each other."[22] In the synapse, in that mutable seam where words meet, the sound actually changes, and for the sake of warmth and facility.

This personality distinction of the language makes Welsh flexible poetically, not to mention the transaction between words has a kind of romance in itself, submissive and aesthetically pleasing as great romances by nature must be. It is just a suggestion, but a mind as agile and as predatory as Tyndale's would not miss this linguistic curiosity. Add to that the pith and roundness of his proverbial Gloucestershire and we have the genesis of a gifted translator.

Tyndale translations like "Entreat me not to leave thee," or "Let not your hearts be troubled," or "In him we live, move, and have our being" have this agreeable community of words, a perfect union of compatible elements, a select brood, as if no other choice of words would do. They speak well together. And that is the entire point.

Shakespeare, who grew up not far from the border of Wales himself, understood the genius of the Welsh tongue. His occasional use was pure ornamentation. In *Henry IV, Part One,* a sad and doting Mortimer despairs, for "this is the deadly spite that angers me; my wife can speak no English, I no Welsh." He understands her tears, her kisses, her intimations of love, and returns them, but her speech is a part of her that remains unpossessed, out of reach. It is an impenetrable wall that makes desire more desirable.

> *I understand thy kisses and thou mine,*
> *And that's a feeling disputation:*
> *But I will never be a truant, love,*
> *Till I have learned thy language; for thy tongue*
> *Makes Welsh as sweet as ditties highly penn'd,*
> *Sung by a fair queen in a summer's bower,*
> *With ravishing division, to her lute.*[23]

Shakespeare's native Warwickshire is an immediate neighbor to Gloucestershire. The rivers Avon and Severn meet. Both are close to what might be the heart of England, a fitting Bethlehem for the nativity of her poets.

Refound

According to the register of Oxford University, Tyndale received his Bachelor of Arts on 4 July 1512, and Master of Arts in philosophy three years later, on 2 July 1515. This is the first official memory England has of him. Since the whole arts course took seven years, it is not unlikely that Tyndale first came to Oxford in 1508. He would have been fourteen, or no younger than thirteen. Entering university at such a young age was not uncommon in the sixteenth century.

Though the rule of Magdalen College (Oxford) allowed no one younger than twelve to enter into study, John Foxe placed Tyndale at Oxford before the age of twelve, attending the Magdalen grammar school as a *demie* (term used for a youth at Magdalen) in preparation for university.

Both Foxe and Mozley suggested that Tyndale always had a sense of calling. While this is appealing, and while it may well be true, it is just as likely that he may have discovered his love for Scripture and his love for language sometime after arriving at Oxford.

John Foxe used the word *addicted* when speaking of Tyndale and the Scripture in the same sentence. Foxe often played the Christian propagandist, but he just as often got it right.

> Brought up from a child in the University of Oxford, where he, by long continuance, increased as well in the knowledge of tongues, and other liberal arts, as especially in the knowledge of the Scriptures, whereunto his mind was singularly addicted; insomuch that he, lying then in Magdalen Hall, read privily to certain students and fellows of Magdalen College some parcel of divinity; instructing them in the knowledge and truth of the Scriptures. His manners and conversation being correspondent to the same, were such that all they that knew him reputed him to be a man of most virtuous disposition, and of life unspotted.[24]

At university, Tyndale would have studied as most young candidates studied. There were seven liberal arts, divided into what was classically known as the *Trivium* and the *Quadrivium*. These rather high-sounding names and the subjects they represented were the foundation of the *studia humanitatis*,[25] more popularly known as Renaissance humanism.

The *Trivium* consisted of logic, grammar, and rhetoric. The *Quadrivium* consisted of arithmetic, astronomy, music, and geometry. Collectively this course of study was known as the humanities. Within this press of subjects the university man was shaped.

Humanism was a powerful current in the evolution of thought. To move too swiftly by it or to consign it to the footnotes would be to deny its importance to our narrative. One twentieth-century writer characterized Renaissance humanism as "an enlightened revolt against barbarism."[26]

An intellectual force or spirit that began in Italy and migrated north, humanism reached back to what was finest among the Greeks and Romans, the past to enhance the present, to regain what was lost or forgotten in our deepest cultural awareness. Formally, it represented a return to classical modes of learning drawn from ancient Greek and Roman culture.

Humanist scholars sought diligently "to understand, translate, publish, and teach the texts of the past as a means of understanding and transforming their own present."[27] Humanism offered two major benefits to its followers: it fostered a belief that mastering the classics made one a more humane person, that is, a person able to more efficiently reflect on the moral and ethical problems of their own world. And the study of classical texts provided "the skills necessary for a future career as an ambassador, lawyer, or priest."[28] Skills learned through humanism were highly marketable, and the benefits were both individual and cultural.

Yet for all its power to move culture along toward the future, humanism became imperious in its command of the educational system. It wasn't until the mid-nineteenth century that the pegs began to loosen.

By the way, no one in the sixteenth century would have recognized the word *renaissance*. It wasn't until the nineteenth-century French historian Jules Michelet used the term that it became popular. It is a French word that means "rebirth," a useful word for Tyndale studies. For Michelet, the Renaissance was no less than "the discovery of the world and the discovery of man. The sixteenth century . . . went from Columbus to Copernicus, from Copernicus to Galileo, from the discovery of the earth to that of the heavens. Man refound himself."[29]

The Renaissance indeed began to define and give shape to the individual. As nineteenth-century Swiss academic Jacob Burckhardt observed, "the revival of classical antiquity, the discovery of the wider world, and the growing unease with organized religion meant 'man became a spiritual *individual*.'"[30]

There's Something in His Soul

Oxford University was known as the "Vineyard of the Lord," John Wycliffe wrote, "a place gladsome and fertile, suitable for a habitation of the gods." Tyndale was a serious student, but it is evident that he wasn't quite the fan of Oxford that Wycliffe had been. He thought the Oxford theologians "old barking curs . . . beating the pulpit with their fists for madness, and roaring out with open and foaming mouth."[31]

Oxford had also been the breeding ground for the Tyndale hostiles—Cardinal Wolsey, Thomas More, Cuthbert Tunstall, John Stokesley, and the arch-villain Henry Phillips. While this may or may not say anything, Cambridge, Oxford's younger and more rebellious sibling, was the home of the Tyndale friendly—Myles Coverdale, John Frith, John Rogers, and Thomas Cranmer.

In spite of the academic degrees he earned there, Tyndale was not an Oxford man.

The university system, like government, was linked to the Church, whose limbs stretched in most all directions. Students wore clerical gowns and spoke the Church Latin. At sixpence a year, rent was affordable and meals were about a penny a day. Students were housed two or three to a room, each room having study carrels, or "studyes" for individual reading. Each student had to provide "his own bedding, knives, spoons, candlesticks, a lantern, a pair of bellows and coffer for his books."[32]

The university was governed from inside, meaning that the chancellor held a court of his own, and had the power to deny a degree, expel, impose fines for infractions, and even excommunicate.

Magdalen (pronounced *maudlin*) in the early 1500s would have few students, perhaps no more than twenty or so. They rose at 5:00 a.m. for divine service, and the first lecture was at 6:00 a.m. They ate together in the commons (dining hall). A bell or a horn announced dinner at 10:00 or 11:00 a.m. and supper at 5:00 p.m. Before going to bed they chanted the *Salve Regina* or some antiphon to the Virgin together.[33]

On completing his degree requirements, the university student came away with, first, a very refined knowledge of Latin. Latin was the *lingua franca* (common language) of the academic community, as it was the sacred language of the Church.

Considered crude at best, English was not allowed except on holidays, in the privacy of your own room, or at feasts. Latin was the rule. Erasmus, the humanist scholar from Rotterdam, spent years in England, affected English spirituality and its thought life, and did not speak a word of English.

Second, the most important university subject outside Latin was logic. These two disciplines together armed the student for dispute, and disputation was the major emphasis of an academic degree program. The graduate was able to argue skillfully, and with the language skills to get it done. "Great store was set upon the ability to dispute; there were disputations in the university schools, and there were private and unofficial disputations, especially in the evenings, in the colleges and halls. A successful student would come out of it with much sharpness and mental agility, but little spiritual fire or reverence for truth. The course was an education in names rather than in things, a mental gymnastic rather than a cultural training."[34]

The liberal arts curriculum at Oxford, as broad as it was, and as closely bound to the Church as it was, offered no Bible study. Theology was offered only at the master's degree level, and even then it was a matter of disputation, of logic and wordcraft rather than meaning and spirituality. The central issue was how good an argument you could make. Even so, you were not allowed to argue until the Church was convinced that she was in no danger.

Instruction was both formal and artificial, dealing with "words and texts rather than spiritual realities."[35] It was an academic approach to God, indicative of a church that kept his identity somewhat of a riddle, and his voice mute to the general public. Tyndale was certain God could not be attained by intellect, reason, or logic. A student would not be allowed to preach, he said, until all traces of authentic spirituality were squeezed out of his voice. Tyndale was not shy toward the gatekeepers.

> In the universities they have ordained that no man shall look on the scripture, until he be noselled [trained, nurtured] in heathen learning eight or nine years, and armed with false principles, with which he is clean shut out of the understanding of the scripture: and at this first coming unto the university he is sworn that he shall not defame the university, whatsoever he seeth; and when he taketh first degree, he is sworn that he shall hold none opinion condemned by the church; but what such opinions be, that he shall not know; and then, when they

be admitted to study divinity, because the scripture is locked up with such false expositions and with false principles of natural philosophy, that they cannot enter in, they go about the outside, and dispute all their lives about words and vain opinions, pertaining as much unto the healing of a man's heel as the health of his soul: provided yet always, lest God give his singular grace unto any person, that none may preach except he be admitted of the bishops.[36]

Oxford gave him the tools he needed to move forward, but he asked nothing further of her. He had other things on his mind than following the usual career path of a university graduate. He did not want the priest's life, nor the academic's life. He did not want to strive for position in the court of Harry the King.

Tyndale wanted his own life, and though he may or may not have known what that was at the time, he knew what it wasn't.

Whether he was aware of any sense of calling or not, it is evident that something was at work in him, perhaps a kind of uneasiness. Or, as Shakespeare's Claudius says of the brooding Hamlet, "there's something in his soul."

2

Pandora's Jar

It has long been my cherished wish to cleanse the Lord's temple of barbarous ignorance, and to adorn it with treasures bought from afar, such as may kindle in generous hearts a warm love for the Scriptures.

— Desiderius Erasmus, *Enchiridion Militis Christiani*
(*Handbook of the Christian Soldier*)

NOT ALL TYNDALE BIOGRAPHERS ARE CONVINCED THAT HE WENT to Cambridge after leaving Oxford. However, there were things going on at Cambridge at the time that were of growing interest to him—opportunities for advanced study, a better Greek, a more daring flow of thought, people he may have been particularly drawn to—so let's assume for the moment that he did. Tyndale was obligated by his MA degree requirement to teach for a year at Oxford, so 1516 would have been the earliest he could have made his departure.

Greek at Cambridge had advanced significantly under the influence of Dutch humanist Desiderius Erasmus. And for anyone with appetite for the language, it would have been a difficult temptation to resist. Erasmus taught both Greek and theology at Cambridge from 1511 to 1514. Greek at Oxford had a slower start,[1] not to mention some opposition by conservative dons. And we have already witnessed Tyndale's aggravation with the university.

There were also revolutionary elements about Erasmus that may have been just as attractive to Tyndale. Whether the two of them ever met is doubtful, though not impossible.

Erasmus was a friend of Thomas More's. "I have not contended with Erasmus my derling [darling]," More wrote, "because I founde no such malicious entente with Erasmus my derling as I fynde with Tyndall. For hadde I founde with Erasmus my derling the shrewder entente and purpose that I fynde in Tyndall, Erasmus my derling should be no more my derling."[2]

Desiderius Erasmus (ca. 1467–1536) was the illegitimate son of a Dutch priest. He was born in the center of Europe (or the Europe of that time), in its bustling middle, situated at the mouth of the Rhine, in a country seated within immediate reach of "all the forces and influences, political, commercial, and religious, which were stirring in Europe of that time."[3]

Erasmus was big news. If not the greatest scholar of the age, he was certainly the most famous. This is no small tribute. He was considered prince of the humanists. It is little accident that he appeared in the twilight between the end of the medieval world and the beginning of an early modern one. No study of the Reformation or the Renaissance is complete without him.

A nomadic spirit, an insomniac, a writer of serious weight and volume (his productivity was immense, massive), a lover of language (except English perhaps), a lover of Scripture, a highly motivated educator, a geeky advocate of intellectual modernity, and a prophet of reform, he is much too wide to circumnavigate, to step quietly around. As one of the "chief agents in breaking the power of the medieval tradition,"[4] any effective study of the age must work through him.

Erasmus sought reform of the Roman Church, but from inside out.

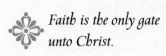

Faith is the only gate unto Christ.

– ERASMUS, *ENCHIRIDION*

He never sought to divide, overthrow, or even break from the Catholic faith. Though he privately thought of "conventional religion as a stew of superstitions,"[5] he was convinced that by scholarship, by a reacquaintance with ancient Greek language and thought, by a return to the Bible, by offering the Bible in the vernacular, and by a return to certain patterns of the early Christians it might effect an end to papal abuses and corrupt practices of the Roman Church. He thought the problem itself bigger than its particulars, that the abuses were more symptomatic. Change would require an altering of perception.

He sought to purify her from within.

Being illegitimate, born to a priest, to an officer of the Church who had taken a vow of celibacy, Erasmus was the child of a skewed morality, of a broken code. Later in life, his enemies would not let him forget this. An unfortunate condition of his birth, perhaps, but it is a part of a much larger script.

His Christian name is a Latinized form of his father's name, Gerard or Gierard, which means "to desire or long passionately."[6] That may explain dad.[7] The Latin *desiderius*, which Erasmus added himself, means "an ardent desire or wish; a longing, properly for a thing once possessed and now missed; a sense of loss."[8] But whatever his name may suggest, we are obligated to handle these elements as we might a promising metaphor, or an accidental stab of meaning, that is, with a kind of charmed indifference. Still, there is a certain justice in his intent to clean up.

Another Kind of Bird

It is not unreasonable to suggest that Erasmus prepared the way for reformation. "More than any other person," one modern observer noted, "Erasmus, through his publications and letters created the intellectual and spiritual milieu into which the Protestant Reformation was born."[9]

Though many elements came together to bring about the Reformation, it is not unfair to say that Erasmus gave the original nudge. A contemporary said, "Erasmus laid the egg that Luther hatched."[10] Erasmus, when at last flustered with the truculent monk, considering Martin Luther a creature of a different feather, responded to the barnyard metaphor by saying he "expected quite another kind of bird."[11]

Unlike Martin Luther, he thought persuasion a better tactic than brawling. And concerning translation of the Bible into the vernacular, it was Erasmus, not Luther, who gave Tyndale the nod.

> I totally dissent from those who are unwilling that the Sacred Scriptures, translated into the vulgar tongue, should be read by private individuals, as if Christ had taught such subtle doctrines that they can with difficulty be understood by a very few theologians, or as if the strength of the Christian religion lay in men's ignorance of it. The mysteries of kings it were perhaps better to conceal, but Christ wishes His mysteries to be published as widely as possible. I would wish even all women to read the Gospel and the Epistles of St. Paul.[12]

Erasmus is calling for the translation of the Bible into the vernacular, into all mother tongues. Christ should not be hidden. He should not be hoarded or disguised, counterfeited or left unheard. Though His mysteries are impenetrable, the way there should at least be intelligible, and not just to the select, but to all.

In the preface of his Greek New Testament he develops this thought, saying that the translations bring you "the speaking, healing, dying, rising Christ himself, and thus they render him so fully present that you would see less if you gazed upon him with your very eyes."

An English Scripture is one sentiment Thomas More did not share with his "derling." Erasmus continues with what amounts to a challenge.

> And I wish they were translated into all the languages of all people, that they might be read and known, not merely by the Scotch and the Irish, but even by the Turks and the Saracens. I wish that the husbandman may sing parts of them at his plough, that the weaver may warble them at his shuttle, that the traveler may with their narratives beguile the weariness of the way.[13]

Erasmus did not set out to be a religious reformer. At least not in the way the Protestant Reformation ultimately came into bloom. He was, rather, "the apostle of common sense and literary culture." His attitude was always more that of the scholar than of the ranting divine. "Still less had he any of the temper of the revolutionist."[14]

In 1500, Erasmus compiled and published a book of Greek and Latin adages, hundreds of old sayings, maxims, epigrams, and proverbs handed down from antiquity that he called, appropriately, *Adagia*. The *Adagia*, with its wide gaze, provided a glimpse into the mind of the ancients. Eight years later, the number of quotations had climbed from around 800 to 3,260. The final version at his death (1536) numbered 4,251.

Short pithy wonders like "In the land of the blind, the one-eyed man is king," or "Kings and fools are born, not made," "War is sweet to those who do not know it," and "Women—can't live with them, can't live without them." Phrases like "a necessary evil" are found in the *Adagia*, as is "squeeze water from a stone" and "let the cobbler stick to his last."

Erasmus is also credited with coining the phrase "Pandora's box." The actual container, however, is a large jar (*pothos*), and yet it is translated incorrectly as *pyxis*, a box. But whether it was a box or a jar, it was forever opened. And the effects are conspicuous.

Erasmus came to England armed with much more than brains and charm, and doubtless had a profound influence on Tyndale. For both Tyndale and Erasmus, love was the essence of the Christian life. Loving Christ and loving your neighbor was the sum of all true piety. This is, in part, what Erasmus referred to in his *Enchiridion* as "the philosophy of Christ."

Encomium Moriae (In Praise of Folly), an Erasmus best seller, was translated into a dozen languages. Forty editions were published in the author's lifetime. Besides its more disruptive elements, it echoed the twelfth-century monk Bernard of Clairvaux and the very Tyndale-like conviction that it is better to know God than to know about God, and that God must be first perceived as a God of love.

This daring little book was an outrage to the church hierarchy. Erasmus showed no mercy to the monk, to parish priests, inquisitors, cardinals, or popes. He referred to curative shrines, miracles, and "such like bugbears of superstition" as absurdities, good only for what "profitable trade"[15] they offered. He referred to "the cheat of pardons and indulgences." His satire was a razor's edge. And he got away with it. Anyone else would have been threatened with deadly censure.

If Erasmus was a brilliant, somewhat daring writer, he was also an entertaining one, working and producing "on the eve of events that would drive laughter from the world."[16]

In the Open Air for the First Time

In 1516, Erasmus published his Greek New Testament, his *Novum Instrumentum*. As might be expected, opposition was violent and disruptive. After all, the word *new* is always suspect, and this translation was the first challenge to the thousand-year dominance of Jerome's Latin Vulgate.

England was shaken to her foundation. There was suddenly the threat of riot in her thought life.

Henry Standish, a preacher of note, was so worked up, he fell on his knees before the king and cried out, rolling his eyes to heaven, that the works of Erasmus were about to destroy Christianity. One Erasmus sympathizer (possibly Thomas More) was standing by and asked the preacher about the highly revered St. Jerome and his translation of the Vulgate. *What about him?*

Standish replied that he did not object to the Vulgate because Jerome had translated the epistles of Paul from their original Hebrew. "Excuse me, Reverend Father," the sympathizer responded, "would you mind repeating that? I was not paying attention." (Which sounds like the impish More.) Standish raised his voice and repeated the folly. The queen made sure the king was listening.

A good example of how deep the ignorance was. And Standish was no fool.

For all its opposition, this New Testament was received with applause, and by cardinals, bishops, even a pope or two. In spite of his popularity among the dissenters, and in spite of his sharp wit, Rome ultimately felt that Erasmus could do them no real harm.

This new translation was no small event. It represented a better Greek, which liberated both Luther and Tyndale. The effect for Luther was essentially a new German, and Tyndale found in the Greek essentially a new English, which after almost five centuries still sounds modern.

Tyndale used this version to translate his English New Testament (1526), as did Martin Luther (1522). This same Greek New Testament was used by the King James translators almost a century after its introduction. It was eventually known as the *Textus Receptus* (the received text). For centuries to come, translators of all languages used this version of the Greek New Testament.

In the preface of his New Testament, Erasmus suggested an entirely new way to approach the Scripture, that is, no longer as a bystander or a spectator, but as an active participant.

> Let [the student] approach the text . . . with reverence; bearing in mind that his first and only aim and object should be that he may catch and be changed into the spirit of what he there learns. It is the food of the soul; and to be of use, must not rest only in the memory or lodge in the stomach, but must permeate the very depths of the heart and mind.[17]

Erasmus relied on a small number of late medieval manuscripts—a twelfth-century manuscript for the Gospels, and different twelfth-century manuscripts for the book of Acts and the Epistles. He used other available manuscripts to make corrections where necessary. For the Revelation of St. John he borrowed a manuscript from a German humanist friend—Johannes Reuchlin. Reuchlin's manuscript was hard to read in places, and portions were missing. Erasmus referred back to the Latin Vulgate to fill in the gaps.

Rushed somewhat by the printer, Johann Froben, and with a bid to have the first published version (*editio princep*), even Erasmus admitted the haste with which he assembled this first version. One contemporary writer noted that "Erasmus's editions (he made five, all based ultimately on the first rather hastily assembled one) became the standard form of the Greek text to be published by Western European printers for more than three hundred years."[18]

If Tyndale spent time at Cambridge, it would have been from 1516 until around 1521. It was during this time, on 31 October 1517, that Martin Luther nailed his *95 Theses*, a list of grievances, to the door of the Wittenburg Church. Luther had little clue that his hammer would make such a large noise. He thought of it as a local complaint. Instead, it created a viral marketing storm. In the fallout, at the emergence of the creature Reformation, much larger than Luther, he said simply that it wasn't his fault.

> Take me, for example. I opposed indulgences and all papists, but never by force. I simply taught, preached, wrote God's Word: otherwise I did nothing. And then, while I slept or drank Wittenberg beer with my Philip of Amsdorf the Word so greatly weakened the papacy that never a prince or emperor did such damage to it. I did nothing: the Word did it all. Had I wanted to start trouble . . . I could have started such a little game at Worms that even the emperor wouldn't have been safe. But what would it have been? A mug's game. I did nothing: I left it to the Word.[19]

Luther was referring, of course, to the Word of God, which Protestants began to use synonymously with the Bible. "The Word" was Luther's contribution to Christianese—pithy, condensed, this truncated title made it an even more direct, concrete, immovable reference, with a much more absolute authority. The Word. And authority was the central issue. The Church was to be validated by the Bible, Luther argued, not the Bible by the Church.

Thanks to the medium of print, Luther's texts began to spread widely and rapidly, infectiously. Between 1517 and 1520 he wrote more than thirty tracts, and three hundred thousand or more were printed and dispersed. The works of Martin Luther accounted for about a third of all German-language books sold between 1518 and 1525. By 1530, in the course of a little more than a decade, Luther had become the first best-selling author in the history of print.

Though Oxford was older, bigger, and had a better reputation, Cambridge was Luther-friendly and it would have been a logical step for Tyndale to take. David Daniell, convinced that Tyndale spent time at Cambridge, suggests that it is only by accident that his name doesn't appear on any record.[20]

> *The ecclesiastical orders had amassed to themselves, in the name of God, enormous riches and a great proportion of the land, and on this they claimed to be exempt from taxation. . . . Religion was divorced from the life of holiness. In a word, the church was rotten, sunk in sloth and selfishness, forgetful of its high calling, false to the trust which it had received of God.*
>
> – J. F. Mozley, *William Tyndale*

The times were wild, eager, and one event set off another. Some law of attraction worked among like-minded men. Erasmus didn't "just appear" in England, and Luther didn't wake up one day and invent the Protestant Reformation. Indignation and malcontent, like reform itself, was a gathering spirit, or storm.

There had been councils calling for reform long before Luther. But reform in the Church meant that the popes thought the cardinals needed reform, and the cardinals the bishops, and the bishops the popes, and so on. Reform was merely a medication, a salve of words to ease a troubled conscience. And as long as popes and priests were unwilling to give up their revenue streams, their privileges, and their monopolies, the attempts at reform went nowhere.

Erasmus was the premier humanist, the champion of the new learning, and he would eventually become best friends with Thomas More and meet Henry VIII, but he came to England initially to hear John Colet (1467–1519), who in 1497 offered a series of lectures at Oxford on St. Paul's Epistle to the Romans. Colet was advocating a return to the Scriptures as the central hub of life.

Of his meeting with Colet, Erasmus said, "Some kind providence brought me at that time to the same spot."[21]

Colet was something of a firebrand. Granted, his sermon was in Latin, but a dead language never preached so hot. (Had it been in English, Erasmus would not have understood a single word.) Later, in a convocation that met in 1511, one cardinal noted, "Colet's sermon, delivered on that occasion, is perhaps the most valuable contemporary account of the state of the Church in England."[22] Such an account revealed a very untidy state, at that.

> Taking for his text the words of St. Paul to the Romans—"Be not conformed to this world, but be ye transformed by the renewing of your mind, that ye may prove what is that good, and acceptable, and perfect will of God."—the learned and uncompromising Dean proceeded to speak boldly against "the fashion of secular and worldly living in clerks and priests." To the secularity of priests' lives Dean Colet attributed all the evils which had befallen the church, and he earnestly begged the English clergy to turn their minds to the reformation of abuses if they would desire to escape the dangers to religion which could be so plainly foreseen. There was no need for new laws, but those which existed should be put in force. Ordination should be given only to such as had led pure and holy lives, and the laws against clerics and monks occupying themselves in secular business should be put in force . . . bishops should first look to themselves. They should diligently look after the souls of those committed to them.[23]

There is somewhat of a divide among scholars concerning Colet and his real contribution. Some say it was Colet who inspired Erasmus to translate a Greek New Testament. Colet himself knew no Greek. After his lectures at Oxford, he attempted to learn the language, but abandoned the attempt because of its difficulty. He died knowing no Greek. Nor does Erasmus credit Colet with the inspiration, however he might have admired him. Still, the possibility exists. There is a kind of intersection where their paths meet, Erasmus with his refound Greek and Colet with his refound Scripture.

Some scholars imagine Colet as "one of the more obscure heralds of what eventually became the Reformation."[24] Others discount this as myth. But influence is often slippery. While it can be direct, it is just as often indirect, or oblique—an impulse, a mood, who knows what sets it off? Colet had "both a penetrating mind and a devout heart; in the popularity of the lectures might be seen the beginning of a movement in Oxford toward an emphasis on Scripture associated with the Christian life."[25] It is when smaller streams merge, creating flow and movement, that assigning influence, blame, or honor becomes difficult to detect.

Colet, Erasmus, Luther. These were the influencers, men of a generation older whom Tyndale watched closely.

Of Little Gnats Great Elephants

In the end, Erasmus failed to follow through, or at least that is how Luther and Tyndale interpreted his lack of commitment to the Reformation, his reluctance to go the distance. *Epicurean* is the word Luther used to describe Erasmus (or at least one of the more sanitized words he used). "His habits were expensive; he liked easy living, he saw no use in voluntary and unnecessary hardships. He went to plays, parties, and go where he would, the sparkle of his genius made him welcome."[26]

There is no real crime to speak of, but the "sparkle of his genius" began to arouse violent emotion in Luther. "I vehemently and from the very heart hate Erasmus," he said. As Luther sat at the table, just the mention of the Dutchman's name sent him into wild ranting. Luther thought Erasmus a man of words only, but no substance. This was an unfair judgment. It is difficult to fault Erasmus for his hesitation. From the beginning, his domain, his field of play, was that of the *idea*, the life of ideas, the evolution of thought, the liberation of mind and spirit. He never thought much of action. That was someone else's burden.

One critic referred to Erasmus as "a begging parasite, who had sense to discover the truth, and not enough to profess it."[27]

These excerpts from the following letters written by Erasmus to Luther at the beginning and at the end of their association are telling. The greeting is all that is necessary to note the dramatic change of climate between the two men.

Best greetings, most beloved brother in Christ. Your letter was most welcome to me, displaying a shrewd wit and breathing a Christian spirit. (Louvain, 30 May 1519)

To Martin Luther, greetings: Your letter has been delivered too late; but had it arrived in the best of time, it would not have moved me one whit . . . you have so tempered your pen that never have you written against anyone so frenziedly, nay, what is more abominable, so maliciously . . . (Basle, 11 April 1526)

Tyndale's animosity never plumbed so deep (but few could compete with such extremes, for there were no extremes like Luther's). Tyndale's objections to Erasmus are best echoed in this summation by Mozley, which states the condition accurately.

If apt and well-aimed words could have reformed the church, Erasmus would have reformed it. None saw the need more clearly than he . . . but his deeds were not correspondent with his words. He sat still, and let things take their course. He remained on friendly terms with popes, cardinals, bishops, kings, the very men who could have purged the church but refused to do so . . . When Luther comes to the front, Erasmus half-sympathizes, but he scents danger. He will not oppose him, for he fears he may be fighting against the spirit of God; he will not support him, for he has not the strength for martyrdom . . . The reformation advances, and he addresses to its leaders some excellent advice: but he does nothing himself.[28]

In his general preface to the Pentateuch, Tyndale mentioned Erasmus, and it is anything but flattery: "whose tongue maketh of little gnats great elephants and lifteth up above the stars whosoever giveth him a little exhibition."[29] Gnats and elephants were creatures of mockery Erasmus used in his own *In Praise of Folly*.

A Curious Step

There is no documentation, no date given, but sometime before leaving Cambridge Tyndale was ordained as priest. This could have taken place at Oxford. The traditional date is 1515. Though not every graduate was ordained, it was fairly common practice. Even years later, all but one of the King James translators were ordained. The following entry was discovered in the Hereford register:

> On June 10, 1514, the bishop held an ordination at Whitborne, at which "John Hychyns, Hereford diocese," was ordained acolyte; "William Hychyns, Hereford diocese," was ordained subdeacon "to the title of the priory of the blessed Mary of Overy in Southwark, Winchester diocese." Two days later (June 12) "William Hychyns, subdeacon," was granted letters dismissory for the other sacred orders.[30]

This may have been brothers John and William Tyndale ordained to minor orders, but again, it is another scrap of inconclusive detail.

For reasons known only to Tyndale, he left Cambridge and returned to his native county of Gloucestershire. That summer of 1522, he settled at Little Sodbury Manor, the home of Sir John Walsh, a wealthy Gloucestershire landowner and friend of Henry VIII. Lady Walsh, Anne Poyntz, was a Gloucestershire heiress. She was related to Thomas Poyntz, who would later become a friend to Tyndale in exile. Tyndale referred to her as a "stout and a wise woman." (By "stout" Tyndale meant resolute, as with a firm hand.)

Sir John had been crown steward for the Berkeley estate, as well as auditor and steward for Tewkesbury Abbey. Both of these positions he passed on to Edward Tyndale, William's enterprising older brother. Sir John had twice been high sheriff of Gloucestershire. As a young man, he had been at court with the eighteen-year-old Henry VIII, and served as his ceremonial champion at his coronation in 1509.

Henry and his new queen, Anne Boleyn, visited Little Sodbury Manor on 23 August 1535. Baby Elizabeth would have been almost two.

Little Sodbury Manor was a "rambling and friendly house of soft grey stone and mullioned windows that still stands in quiet splendour amid its lawns and ancient yews on a steep west-facing slope of the Cotswolds."[31] A view from the house reveals the tower of Chipping Sodbury Church, and the faint thread of the Severn in the distance.

The manor was about fifteen miles from Bristol, and within walking distance of Slimbridge and North Nibley, the two most promising contenders for Tyndale's boyhood home. Tyndale's room was on an upper floor at the back of the house, with heavy beams, typical of the age, and a window that looked out on a steep hill. Here he studied and slept.

Tyndale's return to Gloucestershire represents a curious step in his progress from eager student to translator-fugitive. Once settled at the Walshes', he became tutor—or so it is thought—to the Walsh children, two small boys, no older than six. This was doubtless a noble undertaking, and for the sake of room and board it may have been suitable payment. He may have been chaplain to the manor itself, or amanuensis (secretary) to Sir John.

No evidence exists to support any of these assumptions, but considering what he left behind, the vocation(s) he might have chosen, considering that culture was entertaining some grand mutiny in its heart, it is difficult not to read certain things into the moment.

The marketplace is abuzz with new voices, with the swift movement of ideas, thought, and shifting boundaries. And Tyndale retreats.

Not one to run with the herd, all we can say with any precision is that he is not afraid to walk away from the action. I cannot help but think he is in some state of suspended animation. He is aware of the prohibition against a vernacular Scripture, and yet all his training, the clear aim his scholarship has taken, all the deep movement of his convictions are nudging him forward to some end he is unsure of.

Maybe he needs time for some inner monologue, that is, to turn inward and consider his own council, his next move. Maybe he suspects, or even knows what his life's work is, but at the moment it seems larger than him. Or maybe he just needs some ignition to set it off.

Table Talk

I am one who, when love breathes in me, takes note,
and as it is dictated within, go setting it down.

—Dante Alighieri, *Purgatorio*

THE WALSH HOUSEHOLD WAS A PLEASANT PLACE, WITH A YOUNG spirit. It was a home with small boys, and all the bustle and animation that goes with it. And Tyndale had the warmth and possession about him to make a nice fit. The Walshes were a very kind, well-off, and hospitable couple. It is not difficult to imagine laughter and conversation, the soft magnetism of attraction.

Sir John and Lady Ann took to him readily. Tyndale had that kind of ease about him. He was approachable, accessible, personable. His translation of the Bible sometime later had these same character highlights. His approach to translation reveals a mediator able to speak at any level of culture. For all his great learning, attachments were not uncommon, and they seemed to happen with frequency.

This ease of acquisition and simple trust were weapons used against him at the end.

Occupied by a family of privilege, Little Sodbury Manor was host to the cream of the county, which, for the most part meant members of the clergy. (This smooth dairy product makes a sufficient metaphor. Skimming seemed to be part of the obligation to the collar.) The Walsh table was a place of conversation, for the exchange of ideas. And with the added presence of an opinionated young scholar fresh from the university, filled with new ideas and thoughts of a quite different God, it could not help but get animated, at times heated. Religion was the centerpiece, the recurring theme.

Having the endorsement of the Walsh household, young Tyndale was free to take part in any of the discussions at their table. If it is true that he tutored young boys all day, a little table talk with adults had to look somewhat inviting. But his opinions were very different from those of the usual guests.

The following excerpt from John Foxe's *Actes and Monuments* is an account by Richard Webb of Chipping Sodbury (told to Foxe around 1560). The report was corrupted with age even by the time it reached Foxe, and some of the details have been obscured (Tyndale having a degree from Cambridge and the name Welch instead of Walsh), but the tension between Tyndale and the "beneficed" men is evident.

> The said Master Tyndall being learned and which had been a student of divinity in Cambridge, and had therein taken degree of school, did many times therein show his mind and learning, wherein as those men and Tyndall did vary in opinions and judgments, then Master Tyndall would show them on the book the places, by open and manifest scripture, the which continued for a certain season, diverse and sundry times until in the continuance thereof those great beneficed doctors waxed weary and bare a secret grudge in their hearts against Master Tyndall. So upon a time some of those beneficed doctors, had master Welch and the Lady his wife, at a supper or banquet, there having among them talk at will . . . Master Tyndall thereunto made answer agreeable to the truth of God's word, and in reproving of their false opinions.[1]

Tyndale pressed his argument with persistence, logic, and precision. Not to mention command. He cited the necessary Scripture, and from memory, usually ending any debate (or at least halting it in its tracks, frustrating his opponent heatedly). The opposition became increasingly annoyed with the young upstart—by his manner, which was confident; by his intelligence, which was swift and scintillate; and by his method, which was well calibrated, steeled as it was with years of study and inward counsel.

Certain members of the clergy actually approached Sir John and Lady Walsh while dining out, and spoke to them about the dangerous opinions held by their young houseguest. Sir John sent for Tyndale shortly after and asked him about the charges. Tyndale opened the Scriptures and explained to Sir John reasons why the clergymen were in error, and why the word *dangerous* was misplaced.

Lady Walsh, however, reminded Tyndale who these men were. After all, they were the very cream. She even gave an inventory of how much each of them made per year, how much weight they carried, and how important they were to the community and to the Church. Her question was, essentially, why she and her husband should believe an impoverished, untried young tutor of small boys and sometimes preacher, against these older, successful, and learned men.

Tyndale made no immediate answer, but chose a quieter strategy.

Lady Walsh admired Erasmus, and Tyndale knew this. On her behalf, he translated *Enchiridion* from Latin into English, hoping that Sir John and Lady Walsh might be convinced, if not by his own words, then by the words of the revered Dutchman.

Enchiridion Militis Christiani (Handbook of the Christian Soldier) was not an obscure theological discourse, but a simple exploration of authentic Christian life, a life of love, beyond mere rites and ceremony, a life that relied heavily on the reading of Scripture.

Enchiridion was also an opportunity to take a few shots at the monastic life, those monks who, according to Erasmus, "live in idleness," who were "fed of other men's liberality, possessing that amongst themselves in common, which they never laboured or sweated for (yet

We shall be taking no very great risks if we assume that in the Enchiridion *we have a mirror reflecting very clearly the ideas which were shaping Tyndale's thoughts in the seclusion of the Walsh household.*

– C. H. WILLIAMS, WILLIAM TYNDALE

I speak nothing of them that be vicious)."[2]

Tyndale would later dismiss portions of the *Enchiridion*, but his translation of the work was enough to convince Lady Ann. She and Sir John began to see things as Tyndale had tried to explain them. The Walshes became converts of a sort, and from that moment on stood behind their young houseguest.

This was no small change and "it speaks well for the depth and simplicity of Tyndale's nature."[3] He was not only able to hold his own in these table debates, but he gained his master's support. "After they had read that book, those great prelates were no more so often called to the house, nor when they came, had the cheer nor countenance as they were wont to have, the which they did well perceive, and that it was by the means and incensing of Master Tyndale, and at the last came no more there."[4]

But if Tyndale made lasting friends with Sir John and Lady Walsh, and perhaps other notable families in the county, he made bitter enemies with the opposition. The clergy tired of him, and the "secret grudge" they entertained moved as swift gossip among their own kind.

Ignition

Tyndale was known to preach in nearby villages. His translation of the Bible would come to be known later as a "preacher's Bible"—for its orality, its effortless power, its aural splendor, and just for the deliciously forceful shape it took in the mouth.

All his great learning, all his great lyrical and rhetorical heft flushed forward on these afternoons before the Augustinian priory at St. Austin's, called St. Austin's Green in Bristol (now called College Green), an open-air pulpit of his day. He was known to preach there often, and in the pulpit at St. Adeline's chapel in Little Sodbury. (St. Adeline was the patron saint of weavers.)

He held nothing back in these sermons. He pounded away on current abuses of the clergy and certain conventions of the Church, and so on, using Scripture as the strong prop of each message. And again, the general public was unaccustomed to hearing sermons in English. Though the English Scriptures weren't totally unknown, they were known only by fragments and the odd memorable phrase—"Abraham's bosom," "the patience of Job," and so on.

We have no recorded sermons, but from his written works we can easily imagine the oratory. Tyndale's English was always about the spoken word. The following excerpt from one of his polemical writings will serve as good as any open field sermon. You can hear the alliteration, the drum beating in the background, the dread march beneath.

> *Therefore, that thou be not beguiled with falsehood of sophistical words, understand that the words which the scripture useth, in the worshipping and honouring of God, are these:*
>
> > *Love God,*
> > > *cleave to God,*
> > > > *dread, serve, bow, pray, and call on God,*
> > > > > *believe and trust in God, and such like . . .*[5]

For his efforts, and for his insufferable aplomb, he was summoned to the vicar general (chancellor) of the diocese, John Bell, at a gathering of the clergy in Gloucestershire. Well curdled due to the heat, Bell accused Tyndale of spreading seditious and heretical teaching with his endless sermon making. He intended nothing else but to silence him. Here we have the rare advantage of Tyndale's own words to describe the event:

> For when I was turmoiled in the country [that is, in or around Gloucestershire] where I was that I could no longer there dwell I this wise thought in myself, this I suffer because the priests of the country

be unlearned, as God knoweth there are a full ignorant sort which have seen no more Latin than that they read in their portesses and missals which yet many of them can scarcely read . . . and therefore (because they are thus unlearned, thought I) when they come together to the ale house, which is their preaching place, they affirm that my sayings are heresy. And besides that they add to of their own heads which I never spake, as the manner is to prolong the tale to short the time withal, and accused me secretly to the chancellor and other officers. And indeed, when I came before the chancellor, he threatened me grievously, and reviled me, and rated [berated] me as though I had been a dog, and laid to my charge whereof there could be none accuser brought forth, (as their manner is not to bring forth the accuser) and yet all the priests of the country were the same day there.[6]

Bell's rebuke was volume and heat only. For the time being, Tyndale seemed protected by a nonstick surface. He not only carried himself well and was respected by men of name and weight in the county, he also employed subtlety and craft to slip from the noose. Tyndale was released with no more than a sharp reprimand—no fine, no restrictions, no imposition to his freedom whatsoever—just a grumpy warning.

In the long passage above, there is the hint of flight, the faint suggestion of departure.

It was in this interlude of time that on one particularly volatile occasion, certain members of the clergy, already suspicious of the interloper at Little Sodbury Manor, were invited to the Walsh table. As might be expected, opposing sides being highly charged, things heated up.

Taking little notice of their number or their office, reputations, or pedigrees; arguing his case for Scripture, and for the authority of Scripture, the right for a vernacular Scripture, and so on, Tyndale caused a stir.

Fed up at last with his rant about the authority of the Scripture and of God's law, one of the guests said to Tyndale, "We were better to be without God's law than the Pope's." With one of the greatest comebacks of all time, Tyndale said:

I defy the Pope and all his laws, and if God spare my life ere many years, I will cause a boy that driveth the plow, shall know more of the scripture than thou dost.[7]

It has magnificent backbone. We cannot know for sure when the notion of translating the Bible into English began to press Tyndale, but this challenge rose from him with such clarity, it is not unlikely that the issue was long settled in his mind. He seems to have given Eramus's call for a vernacular Scripture a great deal of thought.

He is young. He is equipped. His blood is up. And in a single blast of defiance and epiphany, the English Bible is born.

It is a powerful moment for the young translator. "Tyndale's mission," Harvard professor Stephen Greenblatt observed, "is conceived in anger and rebellion and expressed with a considerable sense of self-importance."[8] Tyndale is certainly resolute. He does not seem to waver or shrink before the spirituality (clergy). And it is difficult to imagine taking on such a challenge without a powerful sense of self.

Whenever his decision was made, it was made thoroughly, completely. It owns him. His movements are all his own, driven, as he was, by a private conviction. There is no compromise in him or in his text. Unlike Luther, there are fewer hurdles in Tyndale—fewer complicated or blunt geometries to negotiate.

"Tyndale's is a life lived as a project,"[9] Greenblatt concluded. His commitment is final and all consuming. Tyndale becomes the ascetic, with all the monkish denials that art requires of its best.

A Kind of Tangle: London

The time had come for him to leave the comfort and sanctuary of his retreat at Little Sodbury Manor. Life would never be so warm and kind to him again. He would no longer be able to move about unguarded. All the leisure days were behind him. His idyllic Gloucestershire would become a force in his wordcraft—maintain a living presence in his voice—but he would see her no more.

Again, we have Tyndale's own account on what happened next. He is forced out. No longer to reflect or brood but to act. An English Scripture is at issue. It is the stone of offense. "A thousand books had they lever [rather] to be put forth against their abominable doings and doctrine, than that the scripture should come to light."[10] He accused the Church of "wresting" the knowledge of the Scripture into a kind of tangle—dark, twisted, and opaque—little resembling anything like itself or the truth it keeps. It was time to make an English translation.

> Because I had perceived by experience how that it was impossible to establish the lay people in any truth, except the scripture were plainly laid before their eyes in their mother tongue, that they might see the process, order, and meaning of the text: for else whatsoever truth is taught them, these enemies of all truth quench it again, partly with the smoke of their bottomless pit . . . That is, with apparent reasons of sophistry, and traditions of their own making, founded without ground of scripture, and partly in juggling with the text, expounding it in such a sense as is impossible to gather of the text, if thou see the process, order and meaning thereof.[11]

To alleviate any doubt, Tyndale decided to approach the bishop of London, to seek a position in his house under his sponsorship and protection, and there make an English translation. The bishop of London was Cuthbert Tunstall. He was an Oxford graduate, a friend to both Thomas More and Erasmus. Though Tunstall was "almost a saint to what one might call the Catholic humanists, almost an ogre to the pious reformed, he warrants neither label."[12]

In his *Utopia*, Thomas More wrote of Tunstall that he was "an excellent person . . . his learning and moral character . . . are too remarkable for me to describe adequately, and too well known to need describing at all." A curious tribute, in essence, More said nothing definite at all about Tunstall, and yet did so with such magniloquence.

Tunstall was a friend to Erasmus, which was reason enough for Tyndale to appeal to him in the first place. The bishop had assisted

Erasmus in the second edition of his Greek New Testament, and worked with him in Brussels, Ghent, and Bruges in 1516 and part of 1517. He lent Erasmus a Greek New Testament manuscript, helped with research, and even offered a suggestion or two. Tyndale would have been aware of this, and being aware, he assumed that Tunstall would be the first and most promising choice of patron. He was certainly powerful. Tunstall's response would have answers for Tyndale.

Tunstall was known to be considerate, a politically savvy man who was not interested in the extremes of either religious persuasion. He was praised for his eloquence and would even be mentioned on the title pages of the fourth and sixth editions of the Great Bible, published not long after Tyndale's death, and which would be predominantly and ironically Tyndale's translation.

In Tunstall's eight years as bishop of London, not one heretic was burned.

Tyndale would later call Tunstall a "ducking hypocrite born to dissemble," but for the present, surely this was a man with sufficient clarity of mind to see what the young translator's presence meant.

It was a reasonable choice on Tyndale's part to set his hopes on Tunstall. But to overlook the possibility that his own name and reputation may have already reached the bishop by means of the ecclesiastical grapevine, or to think Tunstall was about to overturn or step around the Constitutions of Oxford of 1408—that forbad anyone to translate, or even read, any part of a vernacular Bible without express permission from a bishop[13]—is evidence of either a naïveté or some uninformed optimism.

Tyndale's interview with Tunstall was sometime after 15 April 1523. Parliament was in session to raise money for the king, and Tunstall, enjoying a season of great favor, gave the opening sermon. He had also been given the position of Lord Keeper of the Privy Seal. He could not afford an indiscretion with a poor scholar, however noble his ambitions, or anything that might threaten his position in the eyes of the state.

Tyndale was granted audience with Tunstall through Sir John Walsh's friend Sir Harry Guilford. To show his mettle at translating, to prove he had the necessary skill, he translated an ancient Greek document for the bishop, an oration by Isocrates. Sir Harry delivered the translation to Tunstall in preparation for the meeting with Tyndale.

Isocrates (436–338 BCE) was a gifted writer who, among other things, wrote about the craft of writing. In the art of rhetoric he was an innovator. His was a name of weight among Greek-minded scholars. Tunstall would recognize the significance of the choice, and though the actual document Tyndale gave him has long disappeared, it would have been a sufficient indicator of Tyndale's skill in Greek, not to mention his insight as a critical thinker and rhetorician.

Ultimately it didn't matter what Tyndale had sent him, who introduced him, what affiliations Tyndale may have had, or who the bishop's best friends were. He was turned away. The following account is from Tyndale.

As I thought the Bishop of London came to my remembrance whom Erasmus praiseth exceedingly among others in his annotations on the new testament for his great learning. Then thought I, if I might come to this man's service, I were happy. And so I gat me to London, and, through the acquaintance of my master came Harry Gilford, the king's grace's controller, and brought him an oration of Isocrates which I had translated out of Greek into English, and desired him to speak unto my lord [Tunstall], and to go to him myself which I also did, and delivered my epistle to a servant of his own, one William Hebilthwayte, a man of mine old acquaintance. But God which knoweth what is within hypocrites, saw that I was beguiled, and that that counsel was not the next way unto my purpose. And therefore he gat me no favour in my lord's sight.

Whereupon my lord answered me, his house was full, he had more than he could well find, and advised me to seek in London, where he said I could not lack a service. And so in London I abode almost a year, and marked the course of the world, and heard our praters, I would say preachers how they boasted themselves and their high authority, and beheld the pomp of our prelates, and how busied they were as they yet are, to set peace and unity in the world (though it be not possible for them that walk in darkness to continue long in peace, for they cannot but either stumble or dash themselves at one thing or another that shall clean unquiet altogether) and saw things whereof I defer to speak at this time and understood at the last not only that there was no room in my lord of London's palace to translate the new testament, but also that there was no place to do it in all England, as experience doth now openly declare.[14]

By Tyndale's account, Tunstall's tone was civil, almost friendly. Yet Tyndale understood in his refusal that all other bishops or possible patrons would refuse as well under Tunstall's gaze. That same year, 1524, anticipating Tyndale, Tunstall gathered all London printers (there were only seven) and booksellers together and gave them a warning. They were not to print or sell heretical books. All new books had to be processed through a board of censors. Tunstall also issued the first license against imported books. No book was allowed entrance without the permission of the episcopate.

Tunstall had read Tyndale correctly. Here is a man with the right gifts and the right measure of desire, a man who possesses those dangerous qualities of precision and audacity, not to mention an innocence that has no consideration of Tunstall's obligations.

It has come to Tyndale slowly, advancing stage by stage. With his commitment to translate the Bible into English, he accepts the inevitable danger that will shadow every step. He will be on the run from the moment he leaves England.

We must accept the uncertainties, the ghost shapes we think we see. With a mind as comprehensive and an instinct for survival as alert as Tyndale's, he leaves little time or space for anyone to draw a target on his back, which includes our attempt at omniscient biography.

Man of the Cloth

After his meeting with Tunstall, Tyndale remained in London for a year under the roof of Humphrey Monmouth, a wealthy London cloth merchant. Monmouth swore under oath sometime later that he and

Tyndale met by chance, but this is unlikely. There was an entire network of Gloucestershire merchants trading in London at the time. It is not improbable that Tyndale had already begun the work of translation under Monmouth's roof.

Tyndale took a position at St. Dunstan's (Fleet Street) as a preacher. And we know how he spent his time. Monmouth recalled:

> I took him [Tyndale] into my house half a year; and there he lived like a good priest as methought. He studied most part of the day and night at his book; would eat nothing but sodden [saturated with liquid] meat by his good will, and drink nothing but small single beer. I never saw him wear linen [rich clothing].[15]

Not wearing linen could have been due to his financial standing, but it also implies a self-denial, a form of piety common to the medieval or early modern devotee. Tyndale never went so far as Thomas More or other penitents by whipping himself with a knotted rope or any other method of self-inflicted punishment. And the lack of linen may say nothing much at all other than Tyndale wore no linen. We might also detect an asceticism, the asceticism of the artist or holy man—in this case both—anticipating his flight, his lack of means, and the discipline to accomplish the task before him.

Humphrey Monmouth[16] was a member of a secret society called the Christian Brethren, an association of wealthy cloth merchants. They were also in the business of financing, smuggling, and peddling forbidden books and pamphlets. The Brethren financed Tyndale's work in the beginning and saw to it that his material was well dispersed. They had to move with caution, certainly, but because of their collective wealth and influence, they were "a caste which even the most powerful authorities dare not suppress."[17]

England commanded most of the world's cloth market, so this association with the Brethren was an advantage. To do what Tyndale was about to do with his life, he needed powerful friends. In time, Tyndale's translation and his other books were smuggled into England in bales of cloth.

The Time of My Departing Is at Hand

If Tyndale stayed for another year as he said, then his time of departure would have been late spring 1524. He continued to study, to preach, to weigh and consider.

By this time Luther's tracts were flooding the European market and England. Sometime between July 1520 and March 1521, Cardinal Wolsey had forbidden the importation and reading of Luther's books. We will explore the details of the many literary feuds in a later chapter, but Henry VIII wrote his *Assertio Septem Sacramentorum* (In Defense of the Seven Sacraments) in 1521. It won him acknowledgment from the pope and the title "defender of the faith," a title still held by English monarchs to this day.

Luther responded with an explosive attack on Henry. Henry, perhaps feeling outgunned, commissioned Thomas More to return fire, and More did so with *Responsio ad Lutherum* (Response to Luther) in 1523. The volume is now all the way up. The camps are bleating out hot threats one to the other, and many of the people are divided. The Reformation is on.

Luther's German New Testament was released in 1522. At that time, England had fewer printers than any European country. The first English printer, William Caxton (1422–1491), catered mainly to the rich who could afford books. Caxton's successors, Richard Pynson and Wynkyn de Worde were restricted in their movements. And printing a vernacular Bible, English or German, was against the law. A book like Luther's could not have been printed in England. England had neither the tools nor the stomach.

The logical move for Tyndale was Germany, in the general direction of reform. When we next hear of Tyndale he is in Cologne.

England had refused him. He would never see her again. Though his banishment was self-imposed, it was on the strength of her refusal, and therefore was no less banishment. Playing Pilate, she washed her hands of him. He was excommunicate from both her and her present handlers. And once he set sail, he no longer belonged to England. He belonged to all English. And there is a difference.

Language Is the Only Homeland

*Of all in this world who are deserving of compassion,
the most to be pitied are those who, languishing in exile,
never see their country again, save in dreams.*

—Dante Alighieri, *Convivio*

BETWEEN IMAGINATION AND FAITH THERE EXISTS A KIND OF twilight. That simply means in the divide between them, eyes are irrelevant. Sight comes by another method, by a deeper, more reliable sense. "We walk in faith and see not" (2 Corinthians 5:7 TNT). As Tyndale crosses the Narrow Seas to Germany and to the other side of his life, he is traveling somewhat blind into his future. He is alone, but life has prepared him to be alone. He has always been alone. And though exile cannot help but have some government over his thoughts, we may gather from what little we have seen of him that he is self-possessed, as a friend he is loyal, and attachments are not uncommon.

William Tyndale is a force of English refashioning, of English reimagining, a generative force of Englishness itself. An old world is dismantling, and that makes him a threat. Even he knows this. He hopes to remain hidden under the cover of obscurity. And for at least one long productive season this will work for him.

The way before him is not clear, and all he takes with him is the hope of his English translation. That is all the ambition he allows himself for the moment, all that he is burdened with.

> *For a controversialist who was recklessly brave in print, Tyndale had an extraordinary ability to fade into a background.*
>
> – BRIAN MOYNAHAN,
>   GOD'S BESTSELLER

We may imagine him already having translated much of the Scripture before leaving England. The quiet country retreat of Little Sodbury Manor, his upper room overlooking distant Wales and the Severn may have given it a start—or a garret in Monmouth's London home. An English Scripture is his only distraction at present, the only lash that drives him.

Arriving on the continent in 1524 and seeing his work on the press in Cologne only a year later may tell us as much. A printer would not begin the work unless it was complete.

There is a thrill beneath it all, a frisson, something you can almost feel, that shudders beneath the ice. A dark thrill certainly, and deadly, but it will do no harm to his art. The conditions actually liberate him and work in his favor.

Of course, he doesn't know he will never see England again or that in little more than a decade he will be dead. But every day he lives with that possibility. He is pew-fellow with death. He knows nothing. Everything he does now is by a faith that eclipses all of life, which overwhelms it and infuses his work. We will see the result in his writing. He lives by a fine nerve, one that heightens everything around him, that enhances life, and no artist can leave these things undone, or without expression.

What he sees, he sees clearly. What he hears, he articulates clearly, precisely, with an all-or-nothing kind of resolve. And England is never so sure to him as she is in his absence from her.

The act of letting go, of leaving home, of daring new landscapes and negotiating new tongues, drives his convictions even deeper. It is a desperate energy that moves him forward.

Stop the Presses

Mozley and others placed Tyndale first at Hamburg—and from there to Wittenberg, then back to Hamburg, and from there to Cologne. Hamburg was one of the three major trading ports in Europe, along with Cologne and Antwerp. Tyndale may possibly have completed his translation of the New Testament in Wittenberg. Thomas More, in his *A Dialogue Concerning Heresies*, said, "Tyndale, as soon as he gat him hence [left England], got him to Luther straight [Wittenberg]."

More got his information from a testimony given by Humphrey Monmouth in 1528. He continued, "Hychens was with Luther in Wittenberg . . . and the confederacy between Luther and him is a thing well known, and plainly confessed by such as have been taken and convicted here of heresy, coming from thence."[1]

Tyndale heard of More's report and denied it, saying, "When he [More] saith that Tyndall was confederate with Luther, that is not truth."[2] But this is only a denial of his confederacy with Luther, not that he was in Wittenberg.

William Roye, who Tyndale met on the continent, and who became his assistant, had matriculated at the University of Wittenberg. The register on 10 June 1525 reads *Gillelmus Roy ex Londino*. There is also a curious entry in the same university register on 27 May by the name of *Gillelmus Daltici ex Anglia*. It takes a bit of stretch, but the Latin is "William" and though the last name, Daltici, is riddling, Mozley suggested that it may have been a way to disguise his name: "By reversing the two syllables of *Tindal* you get *Daltin*."[3] The thought is that perhaps the careless, distracted, or uneven hand of the registrar could have easily written it *Daltici*. It may mean nothing at all, and it could be Tyndale playing the fiction writer with his name. This is just another entry in the growing reserve of Tyndale lore. A bit of elasticity comes with the territory.

But in spite of the mirage or the faint image we create in likely places, the first we actually hear of Tyndale on the continent, or have any reliable record, is in Cologne, at the print shop of Peter Quentell.

There are reasons why Cologne may have been a logical first stop. It was on the waterway of the Rhine and near the great book market at Frankfurt (today Frankfurt is still a great book market). Cologne was within close distance to ports and markets. It also had twice the number of printers than London.

Cologne—like all other continental cities—had its censors, its Catholic guard. The theologians at the University of Cologne were somewhat ahead of the rest of Europe. They understood the power of print to spread heresy. In 1475, the pope granted them a license to "punish the printers, publishers, and authors and readers of pernicious books."[4] This license was the first of its kind. But in the city, like most port cities where cultures fuse, mingle, and negotiate their goods and their cash, the tension between religious camps was an accepted part of life. It could not help but make the players wary, always moving about by naked instinct and caution.

But money was the only real negotiator, and money had no religious affiliation outside itself.

In Cologne, the above-mentioned William Roye accompanied Tyndale. Roye was a renegade Franciscan friar from the Observant house in Greenwich. He was not Tyndale's first choice, and though we do not know who Tyndale's first choice was (possibly Miles Coverdale, who joined Tyndale sometime later), Roye was a competent second.

The summer of 1525, Tyndale's New Testament began to slowly materialize in Quentell's shop. And though the restrictions weren't quite as inflexible in Europe as they may have been in England, a vernacular Scripture was against the law. The Church had eyes everywhere. Because of this, whatever instincts Tyndale may have had for wariness and caution were continually put to use.

Like most printers, Peter Quentell didn't seem to have any scruples when it came to that touchy problem of legality. Nor did he care about the content, spiritual or otherwise, nor which side of the argument you were on. Money was the deity of most printers. In 1522, Bishop John

Fisher, a friend of Thomas More's and Cuthbert Tunstall's, commissioned Quentell to print his *Assertionis Lutheranae Confutatio*, a diatribe against the growing Lutheran popularity. It is difficult to imagine Quentell caring one way or the other.

To a printer, especially in Europe at the time, the risk was worth taking because the pay was irresistible. Contraband was everywhere. The enterprising Quentell, himself a second-generation printer, was willing to do the work for Tyndale. All books were essentially self-published, and the printer was able to manage a percentage of the sales for himself. Martin Luther was making some printer, or actually a few printers, quite wealthy. His work was continuous and it was said to be lucrative enough to keep two presses going at the same time.

An author with a good record of sales could persuade a printer to print his books for nothing in advance.[5] Luther was in this small elite tribe. And Erasmus. The first four thousand copies of Luther's September Testament (his 1522 New Testament) sold out in ten weeks. Tyndale made such a no-cost-up-front deal with Quentell. He originally wanted six thousand copies, but only three thousand were printed. There was no contract. A contract would do neither of them any good. The entire transaction was illegal. Either way, Quentell expected a substantial return.

The cost of the undertaking is uncertain. One estimate set the cost at £125 for the entire run. Tyndale could live on £10 a year, so this sum was substantial. Luther's Bible sold in Germany for one *gulden*, the amount of money a farmer expected for a pig ready to slaughter.[6]

In this underground trade, Tyndale was still a novice. With tension as high and as present as it was, and with the number of eyes and ears about, there was little chance that this virgin enterprise could remain untouched. Hate and suspicion, cruelty and subterfuge were all of a much older order than this new flourish of translators and defectors.

At Cologne was an Englishman, a scholar by the name of John Dobneck, a "shallow and conceited man"[7] who went by the Latin name of Cochleaus. A prideful creature and a scathing enemy of the Reformation, he had been stung at least twice by an uprising of reformers in Frankfurt and Mainz; but now, settled in Cologne, he picked up the scent of Tyndale and Roye.

Church mouse and self-promotor that he was, Dobneck wrote about the incident in three separate accounts in 1533, 1538, and in 1549, the last being a history of Luther that included Dobneck's "valiant" deed against Tyndale.

By a trick of fortune, Dobneck had some business with Quentell at the same time Tyndale's Bible was being printed. As the story goes, following his suspicions, at the local tavern Dobneck acquainted himself with the printers from Quentell's shop. He encouraged them to drink, and when they were "in their cups"—that is, once they were well lubricated with alcohol—the printers did what Dobneck suspected they would do, what he encouraged them to do. They talked, and with little restraint. Dobneck recorded their words. (In the following narrative, Dobneck/Cochlaeus speaks of himself in the third person.)

> Having thus become more intimate and familiar with the Cologne printers, he [Dobneck] heard them sometimes boast confidently in their cups, that, whether the King and Cardinal [Wolsey] would or no, the whole of England would soon be Lutheran. He heard also that two Englishmen were lurking there, learned and skilled in languages and fluent . . . He invited therefore some of the printers to his own lodging, and when they were heated with wine, one of them in more private talk revealed to him the secret, by which England was to be brought over to the side of Luther.[8]

Dobneck coaxed the inebriate printers for more information and discovered that three thousand copies of Tyndale's New Testament were at the press and the work had progressed as far as the letter *K*.* Cochlaeus was not only alarmed, but pleased in himself. "Cochlaeus," he wrote of

---

* Using successive letters of the alphabet, or signatures, is a way printers keep track of their work. Tyndale's New Testament was printed in *quarto* (the size of a book when a page is folded to produce four panels which make eight pages of text front and back). There is so much to keep track of, particularly when pages are hanging on some line to dry. The use of signatures is an effective way of keeping track.

himself, "though inwardly astonished and horrified, disguised his feelings under a show of admiration."[9] He approached Hermann Rinck (a senator of Cologne, a knight, and friend to both the emperor and to Henry VIII) on the matter.

Rinck wasted little time and from the senate "obtained a prohibition on the printers against proceeding further with the work."[10] With this bill he also meant to impound Tyndale's entire inventory. Writing about it sometime later, Dobneck said, "The two English apostates [Tyndale and Roye], snatching away with them the quarto sheets printed, fled by ship, going up the Rhine to Worms."[11]

Both Rinck and Cochlaeus at once wrote letters to the king, to Cardinal Wolsey, and to the bishop of Rochester (John Fisher), warning them "to keep the strictest watch in all the ports of England, lest the most pernicious merchandise should be imported into the country."[12]

Pernicious was a popular word associated with biblical translation.

How Tyndale was alerted is unknown. He was convinced, however, that Roye boasted to the printers of their intentions, "throwing out defiance against king and cardinal, and pluming himself on a speedy triumph." In their own private conversation, Roye said enough to the canny Tyndale to make him suspicious. Roye was of a different moral stripe than Tyndale. Tyndale was driven by an obligation that someone of Roye's character would never understand.

Roye, as might be expected, had a loose tongue, with or without the alcohol.

Tyndale had no tolerance for behavior that would endanger the enterprise, if not their lives. He was already learning the advantages of obscurity, and with the help of individuals like Roye and Dobneck, his education was hastened along. It was not possible for Tyndale and Roye to share the same vision, and Tyndale was not one to suffer folly.

Years later, long after Tyndale and Roye had parted company, Roye returned fire on Dobneck in a book of rhymes.

> *Cochlaye, A little praty foolish poad;*
> *But although his stature was small,*

> *Yet men say he lacketh no gall,*
> *More venomous than any toad.*[13]

Cochlaeus saw himself as Mordecai to Henry VIII's Ahasuerus, the watchman at the gate to his sovereign (chapter 2 of the book of Esther). Henry saw no such thing, and paid the little man no real mind.

Who Is So Blind?

All that was left of this initial work at Cologne was the book of Matthew (up to chapter 22) and the prologue. It was fresh. Its language was familiar, and there was nothing dead about it. Long buried by time, and with all the mystery surrounding its existence, this "Cologne fragment," as it was called, was rediscovered by a London bookseller in 1834 bound in another book. It is now in the British Museum.

There is no title page, and therefore it has no date or place of origin (printer), but it has marks that identify it with Cologne. It contains the signatures from *A* to *K* as Cochlaeus described. The fragment also contains a woodcut of St. Matthew dipping his pen into an ink pot being held by an angel.

The *Prologue to the 1526 New Testament* is an important document in our pursuit of Tyndale. It is not only his inaugural work, it is also the first Protestant tract to be circulated in England. This is Tyndale's debut, the first course. And appetite was waiting in England when it arrived.

The *Prologue* was the beginning, but a beginning that was both penetrating and attractive. Its idea of divine citizenship, as in all of Tyndale's writing, is democratic, egalitarian. There is no longer a gatekeeper. No riddling Sphinx counterfeited as a virgin mother. There is no toll to pay,

> ❋ *If "simple men" to use Wycliffe's phrase, can read and understand the Bible then they may take its lessons to heart; the Bible might then become an agent of social revolution.*
>
> – Peter Ackroyd, *Albion: The Origins of the English Imagination*

and no toll keepers. There is equality in the ranks. Indeed, there is no rank, no distinction. King and commoner, rich and poor, have an equal share in the kingdom of heaven, a kingdom that is indifferent to wealth, position, title, pedigree.

Because of the explosive nature of such a proposal, we add anarchy to the list of state objections against Tyndale. And though he wore the title of master, Tyndale was ever the student. He was still learning. He was always "at his book." As we will see, he had a talent for expounding a text or an opinion. Unlike the 1526 New Testament, Tyndale's 1534 revision included a prologue to almost every book of the Bible, and an introduction to the entire work itself. Still, it is safe to assume that he did not start out to be anything other than a Bible translator.

Tyndale has been described as a polemicist, a propagandist, a political reformer, a moralist, a theologian, an enemy of the Church, and yet his first thoughts are those of the translator, the laborer-craftsman. His first complaint is about the Word of God being sealed shut. "They have taken away the key of knowledge and beggared the people," he said. Translation is primal cause for Tyndale.

> I have here translated, brethren and sisters most dear and tenderly beloved in Christ, the new Testament for your spiritual edifying, consolation, and solace: Exhorting instantly and beseeching those that are better seen in the tongues than I, and that have higher gifts of grace to interpret the sense of scripture and meaning of the spirit than I, to consider and ponder my labor, and that with the spirit of meekness. And if they perceive in any places that I have not attained the very sense of the tongue, or meaning of the scripture, or have not given the right English word, that they put to their hands to amend it, remembering that so is their duty to do. For we have not received the gifts of God for ourselves only, or for to hide them, but for to bestow them unto the honoring of God and Christ, and edifying of the congregation, which is the body of Christ.[14]

This is not the voice of hostility. The warmth is evident. The humility is evident. He applies his text with meekness and sincerity. He is not shouting. He does not command nor does he plead. He reasons. He appeals.

Tyndale allows room for his text to evolve, to grow within him, and to achieve a greater bloom beyond him. The King James translators often modified Tyndale's text—sometimes for the better, and sometimes not. Just as often they copied his translation word for word. The point is, in the excerpt above, Tyndale has given them permission to do so.

Tyndale has liberated the future and made allowances for those evolutionary states that he knows will succeed him—I Corinthians 13:1 is an example of such a change.

> WILLIAM TYNDALE NEW TESTAMENT: Though I speak with the tongues of men and angels, and yet had no love, I were even as sounding brass: or as a tinkling cymbal.
> KING JAMES 1611: Though I speake with the tongues of men & angels, and haue not charity, I am become as sounding brasse or a tinkling cymbal.

Editorially, the King James translators made a subtle improvement, particularly to a modern ear. "I-am be-come as-sound ing-brasse" has a powerful beat. But I am lost on the substitution of *charity* for *love*. Here, Tyndale has given the English-speaking world something truly revolutionary, and for the very first time.

The Greek word αγαπε (*agapē*), the same word found in I John 4:8 and 4:16 that reads "God is love." This, too, is revolutionary. The Latin Vulgate refuses God this kind of warmth and immediacy (*Deus caritas est*).

Even Wycliffe, by some sense of obligation to the Latin text, translated accordingly, "God is charity." While translation is admittedly a compromising art, Tyndale challenged a perception of God and a revered translation (Vulgate) that was more than eleven centuries old.

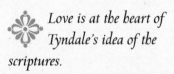

Love is at the heart of Tyndale's idea of the scriptures.

– DAVID NORTON, *A HISTORY OF THE ENGLISH BIBLE AS LITERATURE*

All modern translations follow Tyndale. Even the New King James Bible makes the switch to *love,* as does the New American Bible and the Jerusalem Bible (both, oddly, Catholic Bibles). Only the King James Version and Duoay-Rheims retain the word *charity.**

We must remember, also, that Tyndale's target audience has long been under a different influence. They are not yet a *people of the book.* The Bible is not yet the central voice. Scripture is but a secondary authority. To the general believer, the Scripture is still remote, inaccessible. The Church alone is the higher authority.

Tyndale challenged that perception.

Though unremarkable perhaps to a modern reader for its calm and reasonable voice, the Church thought Tyndale's *Prologue to the 1526 Cologne New Testament* so dangerous "that it could only be countered by the most vicious burnings, of books and men and women."[15] Tyndale gave us the reason for his trouble, why he bothered with a translation in the first place. Continuing the *Prologue,* Tyndale shaped this explanation in the form of a question:

> Who is so blind to ask why light should be showed to them that walk in darkness, where they cannot but stumble, and where to stumble is the danger of eternal damnation, or so despiteful that he would envy any man (I speak not his brother) so necessary a thing, or so bedlam mad to affirm that good is the natural cause of evil, and darkness to proceed out of light, and that lying should be grounded in truth and verity, and not rather clean contrary, that light destroyeth darkness and very reproveth all manner of lying.[16]

Tyndale framed his question in the mildest language possible. In the body of the *Prologue* he used Bible phrases such as "spirit of meekness," "gift of God," and "walk in darkness," which the Church interpreted

---

* Duoay-Rheims is an English translation of the Latin Vulgate. The Vulgate is the Bible translated by Jerome in the fifth century. It was the Bible of Thomas More and the Catholic Church.

as heresy by stealth. (Each of these phrases is a Tyndale innovation and appears in his New Testament.)[17]

Within the *Prologue* were artifacts, certain audible remnants of Martin Luther, and yet Tyndale, affirming his own ground, reached somewhat beyond the German. While we need hardly doubt Tyndale's admiration for Luther, and that Luther provided a place to start—the great shout that set the game afoot—to suggest heavy reliance or that Tyndale merely Englished Luther, as some historians have implied, is to misstate the case altogether. Tyndale was not the English Luther, nor was he entirely Lutheran.

The Worm of Conscience

Tyndale and Roye fled from Cologne with what documents they could carry. In the 1988 film *God's Outlaw*, the sight is a rather pitiful one, the two men narrowly escaping the authorities with bundles of paper and odd books in their arms, Roye taking the last bite of his sausage, bundling his food with his papers. Such a sight may be less exaggerated than we might think. We do not know. And Tyndale is a quick study. For whatever haste and alarm, and for whatever was lost in the scramble, he will regather quickly, and learn. He will not make the same mistake again. Not to mention that his days with Roye are numbered.

From Cologne, Tyndale and Roye took a boat upriver to the more Luther-friendly Worms. Here, Tyndale may have thought Roye's loquacity would do less harm.

Worms was the site, in 1521, where Luther faced an imperial Diet (formal legislative assembly), and made his famous stand. Patrick Collinson, in *The Reformation: A History*, presented the image clearly with a face-to-face David and Goliath moment between the Middle Ages and the Reformation.

> April 18, at six o'clock in the evening, in a crowded and stiflingly hot room in which only the emperor was allowed to sit, Luther made a dignified but uncompromising speech in both Latin and German, which drew from the master of ceremonies the rebuke that he was obligated to believe without question. The Middle Ages had spoken. Now the

Reformation retorted, not with the famous "Here I stand," which is probably apocryphal, but with these no less memorable words: "Unless I am proved wrong by the testimony of Scriptures or by evident reason, I am bound in conscience and held fast to the Word of God . . . therefore I cannot and will not retract anything, for it is neither safe nor salutary to act against one's conscience. God help me. Amen."[18]

By 1525, Worms was still aglow with a kind of defiant light. The Holy Roman Emperor, Charles V, in the fallout of Luther's stand, made the following declaration:

> For this reason we forbid anyone from this time forward to dare, either by words or by deeds, to receive, defend, sustain, or favor the said Martin Luther. On the contrary, we want him to be apprehended and punished as a notorious heretic, as he deserves, to be brought personally before us, or to be securely guarded until those who have captured him inform us, whereupon we will order the appropriate manner of proceeding against the said Luther. Those who will help in his capture will be rewarded generously for their good work.[19]

Worms was, appropriately, the birthplace of William Tyndale's first complete New Testament. The first Bibles of the Reformation, both German and English, Luther's and Tyndale's, were printed here.

If you will indulge a slight diversion, long before Shakespeare used the little creature in his *Richard III* (Margaret's curse to the usurper king, "the worm of conscience still begnaw thy soul"), Tyndale coined the phrase himself. And though "the worm of conscience" has nothing whatsoever to do with the German city, it is interesting nonetheless because of the sting that Tyndale's literature would give his native England.

His Bible, his prologues, his scriptural exegesis, his heated blasts against the abuses of the Roman Church, and England's captivity to it, would prove to be a "worm of conscience" to the national soul, that is, her spiritual center. Tyndale was the *goad*, the *prick* against which England would kick its troubled conscience.[20]

First Love

The date of printing is late 1525 or early 1526. The accepted year is 1526. The currents moved swiftly too. Copies of Tyndale's New Testament were selling in the streets of London shortly after—Coleman Street and Hosier (or Honey Lane; there is a record of a "Master Garrett, Curate of All Hallows in Honey Lane London" by February 1526).

For the first time, England has a New Testament in its own English, translated from the original Greek. Into the stream of language and thought comes a fresh offering, wave after wave of new text, of stunning new shapes and linguistic forms. The great partition was brought down, and this new Bible would say different things to people about the God they only thought they knew.

Imagine reading the Christmas story for the first time, or having it read to you in your own language, a story you vaguely knew something about, and now there are images and movement, and in a language you recognize as your own. The nuance, the subtle patterns and shifts, where it weeps, where it exults, where it groans, where it questions, where it commands.

If the following text sounds familiar to our ears, it was startlingly new to theirs. The original spelling allows us a chance to read over someone's shoulder, the way it came to them.

And Mary sayde. My soule magnifieth the Lorde. And my sprete [spirit] reioyseth in god my saviour For he hath loked on the povre [poor] degre of his honde mayde. Beholde now from hence forth shall all generacions call me blessed. For he that is myghty hath done to me great thinges and holye is his name . . .

And she brought forth her fyrst begotten sonne and wrapped him in swadlynge cloothes and layed him in a manger because ther was no roume for them in the ynne. And ther were in the same region shepherdes abydinge in the felde and watching their flocke by nyght. And loo: the angell of ye [the] lorde stode harde by them and the brightnes of ye lorde shone rounde aboute them and they were soare afrayed. But the angell sayd vnto them: Be not afrayed. For beholde I bringe you tydinges of greate ioye yt shal come to all ye people: for vnto you is borne this daye in the cite [city] of David a saveoure which is Christ ye [the] lorde. And take this for a signe: ye shall fynde ye [the] chylde swadled and layed in a manger. (William Tyndale New Testament 1526, excerpt from Luke 2)

Into the fluid rush and bubble of English life there is a new presence—fire-new phrases, easily accessible, memorable, buoyant, and more than anything, familiar. Each one seasoned with a folky Gloucestershire charm. Tyndale, for the first time in English history, gives God room to be God, and gives the Englishman room to imagine God in ways that have been denied him—and with a new English that fuses glory and simplicity.

Within each of the following lives a splendor unknown to the English language until Tyndale liberated it.

I am the light of the world

Rise, take up thy bed, and walk

So then faith cometh by hearing

For the just shall live by faith

No room for them in the inn

Let this cup pass from me

Take, eat, this is my body

Blessed are the poor in spirit

Father glorify thy name

God is love

Christ in you the hope of glory

From glory to glory

A thief in the night

Psalms, hymns, and spiritual songs

Work out your own salvation with fear and trembling

I am not ashamed of the Gospel

A man after God's own heart

Death, where is thy sting?

The glory of the Lord

I am the vine, and ye are the branches

Be strong in the Lord, and in the power of his might

Tyndale's English gave the Englishman a new way to speak to God directly, without mediation, and in a language he understood. God was suddenly closer. This change in perception would demand a new way to worship.

It would take time for culture to change around this new order—a lot of anger and misunderstanding; a lot of misdirected passion, treachery, burning flesh; and a lot of deaths (including Tyndale's), but the cornerstone was laid, that "good foundation against the time to come."[21]

Author and Finisher

*Tyndale's English became the model for biblical English and
he is indeed the father of English biblical translation.*

— David Norton, *History of the English Bible as Literature*

It is not an exaggeration to say Tyndale's 1526 New
Testament was a phenomenon. It was "the finest English prose yet written, and it defined what was yet to come."[1] In his book on the English
imagination, *Albion*, Peter Ackroyd said that the effect of Tyndale's New
Testament was "immediate and profound . . . to impart the scriptures
in English, apparently plain and simple English at that, was to create an
entirely new religious world."[2] "God had found a voice," one modern historian noted, "and the voice was English."[3]

It was the common Greek (*koine*) materialized as common English,
and in such a way that elevated both. And Tyndale's name was not even
on it. He had his reasons, and they were not just tactical.

Peter Schoeffer printed Tyndale's 1526 New Testament; some
sources say six thousand copies, others say three thousand, which is more
likely. No accurate figure can be determined. Out of whatever number

was printed, only three copies have survived. One is at the Baptist College, Bristol, and another is in the library of St. Paul's Cathedral, near the site where Wolsey had made his bookish fires. A third was discovered in Stuttgart, Germany, and after a few changes of hands, found its current home in the Wurttembergische Landesbibliothek (Wurttemburg State Library) in 1935.

Instead of continuing what he had brought with him from Cologne (the *Prologue* and the book of Matthew), Tyndale sold what inventory he had and chose instead to print a smaller book with no glosses (explanations, liner notes). The Cologne fragment was printed in *quarto*. The Worms New Testament was printed in *octavo*, which simply means that a single page was equivalent to one-eighth of a single large sheet. It measured roughly 6 3/4" by 4 1/4" (170 mm x 108 mm). It was small, and practical in its smallness.

This little brick of paper could easily be tucked in a gown or a sleeve (pockets were not in fashion just yet). Stealth was the wiser fashion for an outlawed book. Concealment was part of the charm of having one.

It was not printed on vellum, that is, sheepskin shaven and treated. Though it was in vogue, vellum was also expensive, and a book as dense as Tyndale's with the numbers he printed could doom an entire flock. Something cheaper and more practical was needed.

White linen rag, discarded and tossed, was necessary for quality paper. It was cut up in small pieces and left to soak and ferment in a cellar. It was processed at mills, usually where a lot of clean water was accessible—a brook, a stream, a river.

The *octavo* brought down costs because it used less paper. By leaving out the prologues and prefaces of the abandoned Cologne edition, which Tyndale did, cost was diminished even more. The type itself, the size and face, was the same as that of the *quarto*.

Less than six months after his arrival in Worms, Tyndale's New Testament was finished. It was shorter in length than Luther's, due to the economy of English over the German, and after abandoning the glosses. An epistle to the reader was included, but placed in the back of the book. But what about style? or Tyndale the craftsman?

Wordcraft

To introduce William Tyndale, the craftsman-priest-translator, the writer-artist-holy-man that he was, I love what Pat Conroy has to say to the critics of novelist Thomas Wolfe (1900–1938). My own devotion to Wolfe mimics Conroy's, but his color and verve are too good to pass up. "'He's not writing, idiots,' I wanted to scream at them all. 'Thomas Wolfe's not writing. Don't you see? Don't you understand? He's praying . . . He's praying.'"[4]

Descriptive text aside (which I omitted), with its plow-hardy effervescence, it provides a suitable introduction. Tyndale is up to much more than the mere task of writing or finding equivalents from one language to another. By a passion that was "never purely academic,"[5] we might say Tyndale's wordcraft is, indeed, a form of prayer. The result is a transcendent text.

> *We speak of the man or woman in the work; we might better speak of the work in the person. And yet we scarcely know how to discuss the influence of a work upon its author, or of a mind upon itself.*
>
> – HAROLD BLOOM, *GENIUS: A MOSAIC OF ONE HUNDRED EXEMPLARY CREATIVE MINDS*

Benson Bobrick described Tyndale's 1526 New Testament as a *tour de force*. The "rhythmical beauty of his prose, skillful use of synonyms for freshness, variety, and point, and 'magical simplicity of phrase,'"[6] made its presence known in all future versions. And this is not mere hyperbole. Compare the following translations of Matthew 5:3–8.

TYNDALE NEW TESTAMENT 1526 (SPELLING MODERNIZED):
Blessed are the poor in spirit:
for theirs is the kingdom of heaven.
Blessed are they that mourn: for they shall be comforted.
Blessed are the meek: for they shall inheret the earth.
Blessed are they which hunger and thirst for righteousness:
for they shall be filled.
Blessed are the mercifull: for they shall obtain mercy.
Blessed are the pure in heart, for they shall see God.

KING JAMES BIBLE 1611:

Blessed are the poore in spirit: for theirs is the kingdom of heauen.
Blessed are they that mourne: for they shall be comforted.
Blessed are the meeke: for they shall inherit the earth.
Blessed are they which doe hunger and thirst after righteousnesse:
for they shall be filled.
Blessed are the mercifull: for they shall obtain mercie.
Blessed are the pure in heart: for they shall see God.

NEW AMERICAN STANDARD 1960:

Blessed are the poor in spirit, for theirs is the kingdom of heaven.
Blessed are those who mourn, for they shall be comforted.
Blessed are the gentle, for they shall inherit the earth.
Blessed are those who hunger and thirst for righteousness,
for they shall be satisfied.
Blessed are the merciful, for they shall receive mercy.
Blessed are the pure in heart, for they shall see God.

NEW INTERNATIONAL VERSION 1973:

Blessed are the poor in spirit, for theirs is the kingdom of heaven.
Blessed are those who mourn, for they will be comforted.
Blessed are the meek, for they will inherit the earth.
Blessed are those who hunger and thirst for righteousness,
for they will be filled.
Blessed are the merciful, for they will be shown mercy.
Blessed are the pure in heart, for they will see God.

CHRISTIAN STANDARD BIBLE 1999:

Blessed are the poor in spirit, because the kingdom of heaven is theirs.
Blessed are those who mourn, because they will be comforted.
Blessed are the gentle, because they will inherit the earth.

Blessed are those who hunger and thirst for righteousness,
because they will be filled.
Blessed are the merciful, because they will be shown mercy.
Blessed are the pure in heart, because they will see God.

Other than a minor alteration, *will* for *shall*, *gentle* for *meek*, *satisfied* for *filled*, *receive* or *will be shown* for *obtain*, and the occasional transposition of a word, there is no significant change. It remains the voice of William Tyndale, though the divide between Tyndale and the Christian Standard Bible is almost five hundred years. And again, the laurel granted to the King James Bible, the high honor it has enjoyed in its four hundred years, rightly belongs to William Tyndale.

Tyndale worked without a model. He had the Greek, but he had no English predecessor, no one to emulate or "counterfeit," as he put it, no fixed register or sonic architecture in which to shape his text other than what the originals suggested and that which his own linguistic heritage and gifts provided.

> *Tyndale did not simply translate the Bible. In the sense of restoring its sweep and drama, he recreated it.*
>
> – BRIAN MOYNAHAN,
> GOD'S BESTSELLER

Tyndale would have certainly been acquainted with the Wycliffe Bible, but its dependence on a dead language (Latin) and its odd linguistic geometries were enough to keep Tyndale at a distance. Wycliffe Bibles were both scarce and outlaw, and the distance between Middle English and Tyndale's early modern English was significant.

Admittedly, Tyndale was on his own.

What we must keep in mind is that this is the opening pitch, the first printing of the New Testament in English. Tyndale's 1534 revision, in spite of its numerous changes, does not alter the beauty of the original as much as it simply finishes it. The 1526 version of Matthew 5:9 reads:

Blessed are the maintainers of the peace:
for they shall be called the children of God.

The revised version of 1534 makes the following single alteration to the selection above.

> *Blessed are the peacemakers:*
> *for they shall be called the children of God.*

The change is minimal: *peacemakers* replaces *maintainers of the peace*. One word replaces three. Three syllables replace six. This is a Tyndale fundamental. Economy. Simplicity. Elevation. Favoring the Saxon form over the Latin or the French (*maintainers* has a French ancestry). The meaning is unaltered. Only the music has changed—the step. Not to mention that it loses its passivity and its weakness, if not its pretension. Once Tyndale found his voice, he committed to it.

The Heresy of Explanation

William Tyndale had a great ear. The fascination that drove him, that drove his craft and his book, was an aural fascination. And yet beyond these conspicuous elements, there is no suitable explanation. Tyndale simply knew it when he heard it. The rest he left alone. That same fascination lives in the text.

Mentioned earlier, perhaps the most fundamental element of Tyndale's art is his orality. His text possesses a kind of practical beauty, an accessible magnificence. It speaks well. It also sings well. Listening to Andrea Bocelli sing *The Lord's Prayer* might end any argument to the contrary.

Because of its musicality, its lyrical grandeur, because of the beat it keeps, the hidden march, Tyndale's translation is easy to memorize. "O our father, which art in heaven, hallowed be thy name . . . In the beginning was the word and the word was with God and the word was God . . ." Each of these phrases has a beat. Each lives by a kind of musical step.

The following is an example of a thoroughly modern translation (The Message, 2002) of Matthew 5:3–8.

You're blessed when you're at the end of your rope.
With less of you there is more of God and his rule.
You're blessed when you feel you've lost what is most dear to you.
Only then can you be embraced by the One most dear to you.
You're blessed when you're content with just who you are—
no more, no less.
That's the moment you find yourselves proud owners of everything
that can't be bought.
You're blessed when you've worked up a good appetite for God.
He's food and drink in the best meal you'll ever eat.
You're blessed when you care. At the moment of being "carefull,"
you find yourselves cared for.
You're blessed when you get your inside world—your mind and heart—
put right. Then you can see God in the outside world.

Representing a more modern appetite, *The Message* is a clear departure from Tyndale. It no longer depends on his identifiable register. The translation is upbeat. It is optimistic. It is sincere. And it is certainly readable. These are admirable qualities. But rhapsody has been exchanged for explanation (paraphrasis). *What it means is . . .*

The background music has changed. The weight has changed. It has stepped out of the soft amber light into a fluorescent one, harsh and unsympathetic. Ultimately, it reflects an age of information.

We can cite another comparison from Matthew 6:11. For Tyndale's "Give us this day our daily bread," *The Message* prays, "Keep us alive with three square meals." The only similarity is the eight count. "Give me the information," it says, "I have no time to sing." Perhaps it is impossible not to read judgment in my words. That is not my intent. The comparisons simply help sharpen our image of Tyndale.

Indeed, Tyndale gave permission for future translations to evolve beyond him, according to the needs of the plowpeople of their own age. He understood the English language enough to do so.

The New Century Version (1991) departs from Tyndale as well. It, too, strives to explain.

Those people who know they have great spiritual needs are happy,
because the kingdom of heaven belongs to them.
Those who are sad now are happy, because God will comfort them.
Those who are humble are happy, because the earth will belong to them.
Those who want to do right more than anything else are happy,
because God will fully satisfy them.
Those who show mercy to others are happy,
because God will show mercy to them.
Those who are pure in their thinking are happy, because they will be with God.

In spite of current appetites, not everything can be, will be, or even should be explained. At least this is how Tyndale understood it. "Our darkness," he wrote, "cannot perceive his light." He added, "Let us therefore give diligence rather to do the will of God, than to search his secrets which are not profitable for us to know."[7]

Paraphrasing Tyndale, God is not obligated to tell us everything. He is not obligated to our need to know. He is not tidy. The mystery is a mystery for a reason. It remains necessary. The distance was written into the original transmission. He was not, nor is not, explaining anything, though the modern translator has redefined his obligation to the text. Robert Alter referred to the phenomenon as the "heresy of explanation."

The unacknowledged heresy underlying most modern English versions of the Bible is the use of translation as a vehicle for explaining the Bible instead of representing it in another language, and in the most egregious instances this amounts to explaining away the Bible.[8]

Translation and interpretation are not the same thing, and that is Alter's point.[9]

Before exploring Tyndale as craftsman, in defense of *The Message* and translations like it, though it is a paraphrase of the original texts, it is nonetheless a vernacular Scripture, that is, it aims at a newer pitch of language, a newer audience. It comes, therefore, with Tyndale's nod of assent.

Tyndalian

Renowned literary critic and author Harold Bloom said that William Tyndale is the "only true rival of Shakespeare, Chaucer, and Walt Whitman as the richest author in the English language." Only Shakespeare's prose "is capable of surviving comparison with Tyndale's."[10] This is no small tribute, nor is it an isolated one. In his book, *Renaissance Self-Fashioning*, Stephen Greenblatt wrote, "Our sense of supreme eloquence in English is still largely derived from Tyndale—attempts at sublimity in our language tend to be imitations, most often unconscious and frequently inept, of the style of the English Bible—and he [Tyndale] seems to have accomplished this remarkable achievement by transforming his whole self into that voice."[11]

There are certain identifiable stylistic elements that make a text Tyndalian, of which simplicity and rhapsody, precision and audacity are among the first. An accounting of these elements and others like them will give us a closer look at how Tyndale processed each word, how he negotiated meaning and thought, and the rule he applied to the text.

Tyndale fascinates and instructs at multiple levels. Before considering his style, we can begin by looking at his actual practice, those good habits he cultivated that made him the craftsman he came to be—those things he considered important as a writer.

The first of these might just be desire, that is, the level of commitment one is willing to invest, into both the craft of writing and to a specific text. What distance is a writer willing to go? What sacrifices is he willing to make? Is that extra mile really worth the trouble or is it just a cliche? How many polishes must a text endure before it is liberated of all excesses and all impurities, before we can say it is truly *finished*?

To desire we might add tenacity. Tyndale never gave up, against all adversity, all outrages against him.

Tyndale revised his work continually. The word he chose for Hebrews 12:2 was *finisher*, ΤΕΛΕΙΟΤΈ (*teleiotes*), which Wycliffe translated as *perfecter*. The clarity Tyndale sought would hardly leave him alone until it was spun out of him, until it was quiet. "Give us this day our daily bread" is as complete as a thread of text can be complete. There is no further need of revision. And it never seems to age.

The infinite is liberated through the finite, that is, through the absolute completeness of a line.

Because a particular line of text can meddle with our senses so deeply, I think too often we look toward our finer literary craftsmen as if words just poured out of them with little or no effort. This is just not so, then or now. Tyndale "cut and shaped and polished and reworked and grabbed every help there was."[12] The fact that he made thousands of revisions to his 1526 New Testament is evidence of an editorial slavishness, and a dedication to the twin elements clarity and splendor.

Against each word, each phrase, each construction, as it flowered into another sentence, another paragraph of text, he set an intense rigor, to which he heaped all his dedication, conviction, and great love.

We must remember, too, that William Tyndale was the first to witness these lines as they materialized before him. The one compensation for all his trouble. It gives pause to consider being the first to behold, or even more the first to introduce, "For thine is the kingdom and the power, and the glory forever" into so weary an English conscience.

The Scripture first had its effect on the translator himself.

To wed the homespun with the eloquent takes mastery of the craft, a lot of work, seasoned with the high command of genius. Even so, for Tyndale it was not an aesthetic consideration. Being literary was not the first thing on his mind. As C. S. Lewis noted, "Souls were at stake."[13] Tyndale reaches at times "a piercing quality."

Because of Tyndale's fine ear, we have all been tuned sufficiently.

Unlike other forms of literature, the Bible is one of those rare books that an individual is apt to read again and again—discuss, memorize, and treasure. The continual habit of the

> *Tyndale's translation appealed to its adherents because it made more readily intelligible the mystical holy word. It reformed, or refashioned Scripture in the image of man.*
>
> – DAVID GINSBERG, *PLOUGHBOYS VERSUS PRELATES*

71

Word, empowered by a persuasive aesthetic, instructs the appetite. Tyndale is the ghost among our thoughts.

Another very important consideration of Tyndale's might be what Stephen King calls the IR, that is, the Ideal Reader. Tyndale's first and only thoughts were of the plowboy. His whole adventure began with the plowboy in mind. It was the trigger that set him off. Indeed, Tyndale risked everything for his IR. His first commitment was to his faith, of course, but he championed the vernacular Scripture at an unimaginable cost.

Every writer has his or her plowboy. Whoever aspires to the craft has such a creature to consider. "Even the most inward-looking work imagines a reader."[14] And once discovered, the next step is to cultivate that reader, to direct your best thought toward them and in a language they understand. Only then can you dare to lead, instruct, and enchant. Shakespeare had a specific audience. Walt Whitman and Dante Alighieri imagined their perfect reader and shaped their songs accordingly. Speaking to his own tribe, to craftsmen like himself, John Updike wrote:

> Our task as we sit (or stand or lie) is to rise above the setting, with its comforts and distractions, into a relationship with our ideal reader, who wishes from us nothing but the fruit of our best instincts, most honest inklings, and firmest persuasions.[15]

Without a firm understanding of who your audience is—how they think—there exists a kind of blindness, lethal to any text, however promising that text might be. Addressing a specific audience imposes limits, certainly, but far from restricting the writer, it liberates him. He knows where the restraints are and his language is free to find its best voice within those restraints.

Whether you write books, or aspire to write books, or if your text is limited to a smaller field of play, anyone writing today can benefit from exposure to Tyndale's craft. Spiritual considerations aside, the elements of Tyndale's writing style are as indispensable as they are timeless.

C. S. Lewis referred to William Tyndale as "the best prose writer of his age,"[16] and yet Tyndale never set out to establish an English prose style. Even so, his influence in the works of those generations immediately beyond him is indisputable. He is rightfully dubbed "a remarkable artist."[17]

> Tyndale's artistic example had a seminal influence. In the homiletic or controversial work of Latimer, Bradford, Hooper, Becon, Jewel, and Whitgift the literary historian can find a studied plainness in diction, syntax, and appeal or an equally artful richness in rhythm and evangelical similitude that echo Tyndale insistently. What became, for seventeenth-century Reformers, an identifiable "plain style" or a "rhetoric of the spirit" appears in a compelling if nascent form throughout the pioneering prose of a remarkable artist, William Tyndale.[18]

The argument once existed in Tyndale scholarship concerning his use—or rather the lack of use—of conscious literary effects. One school would argue that he did not intentionally use such effects but sought rather a plainness and perspicuity outside the use of literary devices. The other school, however, with a much better argument, defines Tyndale as he is: a craftsman, an artist who knew how to draw the best out of the tools he was given.

He used the rhetorical device to compose his thoughts however he saw fit. And he was good at it. To get the results he wanted from his text "he used most of the resources of the rhetorician . . . to achieve it."[19] At this time in English history, the written form of the English language was in its nativity, taking its first steps. Tyndale was in position to father it forward.

The Art of Art

Considering elements of style, the closest parallel among the large figures of American letters may be the nineteenth-century poet Walt Whitman (1819–1892). He and Tyndale share certain stylistic features, and that makes him useful to our inquiry. To both Tyndale and Whitman, simplicity was the first order of style, and yet a simplicity that was both sage and penetrating—an informed simplicity. In the prologue of his 1855 version of *Leaves of Grass* Whitman wrote:

> The art of art, the glory of expression and the sunshine of the light of letters is simplicity. Nothing is better than simplicity . . . nothing can make up for the lack of definiteness. To carry on the heave of impulse and pierce intellectual depths and give all subjects their articulations are powers neither common nor very uncommon. But to speak in literature with the perfect rectitude and insouciance of the movements of animals and the unimpeachableness of the sentiment of trees in the woods and grass by the roadside is the flawless triumph of art. If you have looked on him who has achieved it you have looked on one of the masters of the artists of all nations and times.[20]

Here—and quite innocently—though the translator is nowhere in his thoughts, Whitman captures Tyndale. And not surprisingly, of all things that affected his craft, it was the King James Bible that most influenced Whitman.* Its breadth, its eloquence, its use of cadence and the monosyllable, its general music, its preference of the Anglo-Saxon word over the Latinate, and most particularly its use of anaphora (repeating a phrase at the beginning of successive lines: *"a time* to kill, and *a time* to heal, *a time* to break down, and *a time* to build up"), and polysyndeton (the use of several conjunctions in succession: "shall tribulation, *or* distress, *or* persecution, *or* famine, *or* nakedness, *or* peril, *or* sword").

Considering this influence upon the American poet, it is not an exaggeration to say it was Tyndale's presence in the King James text that did the influencing.

Both Tyndale and Whitman wrote in the vernacular. Whitman

---

* Whitman also said that had it not been for Italian Opera he could not have written *Leaves of Grass*. (*Voices and Visions*, Annenberg Media, 1988)

created a truly American poetry, with the butcher boy in mind, the streetcar conductor, and the workman at the docks. Whitman loved the use of the colloquial, with its casual charm. "So long!" was a phrase Whitman loved. Tyndale introduced many such phrases into English, like "full swing," "eat, drink, and be merry," "the twinkling of an eye," and countless others already noted.

Both Whitman and Tyndale refused to add ornamentation or any unnecessary weight or flourish that might exclude the general reader. In his introduction to the 1855 *Leaves of Grass*, Whitman said, "I will not have in my writing any elegance or effect or originality to hang in the way between me and the rest like curtains. I will have nothing hang in the way, not the richest curtains. What I tell I tell for precisely what it is."

> *It is the plainness of Tyndale that startles and that made the Word of God seem so raw and fresh to his readers.*
>
> – BRIAN MOYNAHAN, *GOD'S BESTSELLER*

Beauty, Whitman urged, lives in simplicity. There is an immense generosity in both Whitman and Tyndale. "You shall stand by me," the poet says, "and look in the mirror with me."[21]

Another element of Tyndale's craft, which is a perfect complement to the first, and its closest sibling, was his desire to make sense. Sense and simplicity were the governing principles of his craft.

Translation, with all its compromise and approximation, can be slippery. Often a biblical translator will render a word with what they hope is a philological equivalent and yet because it is Scripture, because faith and belief are the argument, it is often translated in some hope that God will give the reader understanding that is not apparent in the translation itself. Ecclesiastes 11:1 provides a useful example. "Lay thy bread upon wet faces," from the Bishop's Bible (1568), was replaced by the familiar and sensible, "Cast thy bread upon the waters" of the King James translation (1611).

The hope was that because a word was divinely inspired, God might supply the necessary revelation. It didn't have to make sense. Tyndale thought otherwise.

> ❀ *Translation, like politics, is an art of compromise; inevitable compromise between the resources of From-ish and those of To-ish. When the unique riches of From-ish—all the accidents of its associations and accidence—have been exploited to the full by a poet of genius, the compromise must be all the greater.*
>
> – Brian Boyd, from the introduction to *Verses and Visions*, by Vladimir Nabokov

While he certainly believed in being led by the Holy Spirit, he avoided obscurity at all costs. In other words, it was better to be plain and approximate than perfect and obscure.

Tyndale avoided repetition wherever possible, particularly if the offending word or phrase was close at hand—as in the same chapter. Mark 2:15 begins, *"And it came to pass,* as Jesus sat at meat in his house . . ."* In verse 23, Tyndale translated the same Greek word γινομαι *ginomai* (ghin'-om-ahee) as *"And it chanced* that he went through the corn fields . . ."* In other locations he used *"And it fortuned"* or *"And it happened."* The King James translators used *"And it came to pass"* in both verses, and used the same construction throughout. Where would the Christmas story be without Tyndale's "And it came to pass"?

Tyndale bordered on excess concerning these variations, all for a cleaner sound.

Another stylistic charm of Tyndale's, perhaps my personal favorite, is his use of the coordinating conjunction at the beginning of a sentence—*and, but, yet, nor,* and so on.

How Sweet the Sound

Tyndale was certainly an original. But his originality was not bred of some stubborn artistic neediness. His psychology did not make those kinds of demands. His motive was higher than that. It was important to him that the work maintain a linguistic purity. As the artist must, Tyndale created his own conventions, discovered his own rule.

In the following excerpt from *The Parable of the Wicked Mammon*, all of the elements mentioned above work agreeably together.

And be the sinner never so weak, never so feeble and frail, sin he never so oft and so grievous, yet so long as this lust, desire, and mourning to be delivered remaineth in him, God seeth not his sins, reckoneth them not, for his truth's sake, and love to Christ. He is not a sinner in the sight of God that would be no sinner. He that would be delivered hath his heart loose already. His heart sinneth not, but mourneth, repenteth, and consenteth unto the law and will of God, and justifieth God; that is, beareth record that God which made the law is righteous and just.[22]

And be the sinner never so weak, never so feeble and frail. It could be a lyric from one of the great hymn writers of the past—Fanny Crosby, William Bradbury, even Charles Wesley—gifted craftsmen in their own right who owed Tyndale a debt

> *Style is not merely a constellation of aesthetic properties but is the vehicle of a particular vision of reality.*
>
> — ROBERT ALTER, *PEN OF IRON*

for their art. His presence is felt in hymns like "He Hideth My Soul In the Cleft of the Rock," "Savior, Like a Shepherd Lead Us," and "Christ The Lord Is Risen Today." The most beloved lyric of all time, "I once was lost but now am found, was blind but now I see," begins in Tyndale.[23]

And if the sample above has the familiar sound of Scripture, it is not an illusion, nor is it a mimic. It is the assertion of genius, the voice of the gifted at the height of his powers.

Farewell, Unhappy, Hopeless, Blasphemous Rome

Dort, wo man Bücher verbrennt, verbrennt man
am Ende auch Menschen. (Where they have burned
books, they will end in burning human beings.)

—Heinrich Heine, *Almansor* (1821)

IN THE FALLOUT OF THIS DAZZLING NEW PIECE OF ENGLISH
history and because of the heavy trafficking of Tyndale New Testaments,
Cardinal Wolsey called a meeting of bishops in 1526. No record exists
today of the proceedings, but Henry VIII, never at a loss for a royal
opinion, said:

> With deliberate advice of the Cardinal and other reverend fathers of
> the spirituality determined the said corrupt and untrue translations
> to be burned with further sharp correction & punishment against the
> keepers and readers of the same.[1]

The king complained about "certain prefaces and other pestilent glosses in the margins." At this time in his life, Henry VIII was still under the spell of Cardinal Wolsey. The fuss was loud. You could hear the swish of clerical robes in the bustle.

Cuthbert Tunstall, Tyndale's old acquaintance, sent out a proclamation on 23 October 1526. Tyndale bashing officially became vogue. An odd English pride made him the English Luther, though he was no such thing. Luther provided the brute force that opened the door perhaps, but Tyndale was eventually perceived more dangerous in England than the German. Hate and pride are sibling passions. Tyndale was English, and, as the "trayterous" often are, the most hated man in England (at least by the Catholic zealotry).

Burning books was the answer.

The language of this document offers an example of the immediate impact of Tyndale's New Testament. "Many children of iniquity, maintainers of Luther's sect, blinded through extreme wickedness and wandering from the way of truth and the catholic faith, craftily have translated the New Testament into our English tongue, intermeddling therewith many heretical articles and erroneous opinions." Tyndale was the hairball they were desperately hoping to cough up.

"Corrupt . . . untrue . . . extreme wickedness . . . wandering from the way of truth," and these descriptions were just the opening act. Whole new adjectives had to be imagined. A continuous stream of invective flooded the marketplace from the moment the new Bible was smuggled into the country and began to find its way around. They were brought in either nested among other books being unloaded at the docks, or in bales of cloth.

Outlaw that it was, Tyndale's Bible and all reformer literature called into being whole illegal industries—smuggling, printing, pamphleteering. And the cast it gave off was attractive, as defiance often is.

Cuthbert Tunstall accused Tyndale of having "profaned the hitherto undefiled majesty of holy scripture with cunning perversities and heretical depravity."[2] He used words like *pestiferous* (carrying infectious disease) and phrases like *pernicious poison* to describe the new Bible. He threatened anyone in possession of the book or anyone caught reading it with excommunication and a charge of heresy.

No Holocaust Could Be More Pleasing to God

Within days of this October declaration, Tunstall preached at Paul's Cross in London and a bonfire was lit to consume all the apostate text, most particularly Tyndale's New Testament. In his sermon Tunstall referred to the new Bible as *doctrinam peregrinam*, that is, alien (strange) doctrine. Engaging the usual hyperbole, he claimed that Tyndale had made two thousand or more errors.

Responding to Tunstall's accusation, in his introduction to the Penateuch, Tyndale wrote that his accusers "have yet now so narrowly looked on my translation, that there is not one *i* therein if it lack a tittle over his head, but they have noted it, and number it unto the ignorant people for an heresy."[3]

Tyndale was actually shocked at the report of the burning of the New Testament—as if some new line of depravity had been crossed. It appears that he never recovered from the injury. It is from this point that Tyndale began to vent his own hostility toward the Church. As we have already witnessed, he had little use for Tunstall anyway, but in *The Practice of Prelates* he dismisses all doubt.

> And as for the bishoprick of Durham, to say the very truth, he [Cardinal Wolsey] could not of good congruity but reward his old chaplain [Cuthbert Tunstall], and one of the chief of all his secretaries withal, still Saturn [gloomy, louring, grim], that so seldom speaketh, but walketh up and down all day musing and imagining mischief, a ducking hypocrite, made to dissemble: which, for what service done in Christ's gospel came he to the bishoprick of London; or what such service did he therein? He burnt the New Testament, calling it Doctrinam peregrinam, "strange learning."[4]

Cardinal Lorenzo Campeggio, cardinal protector of England, in a letter to Cardinal Wolsey dated 21 November 1526, delighted at the burning of "the sacred codex of the bible, perverted in the vernacular tongue, and brought into the realm by perfidious followers of the abominable Lutheran sect . . . no holocaust could be more pleasing to God."[5]

Book burning was not necessarily new. In a time when learning was in a state of acceleration and florescence, it was the Church's way of implying much more than their annoyance with any particularly aggravating text or author. In June 1520, a bull from Pope Leo X (*Exsurge domine*) ordered that the books of Martin Luther were to be burned all over Europe. It also stipulated that Luther was under threat of excommunication. Flames went up in Cologne and Louvain, and, of course, Rome.

Just before the bull was issued, Luther sent the pope his latest book, *Freedom of a Christian*. Accompanying the book was a letter addressed to the pope himself. With his usual pluck, Luther left very little to mystery. We might remember that his monastic life started with a bolt of lightning. Much more than mere ignition, it left an imprint, like the cleavage in a young oak, that became part of his identity as a monk-scholar-revolutionary-communicator.

The letter started out nicely enough. "I freely vow, that I have, to my knowledge, spoken only good and honorable words concerning you whenever I have thought of you." But once the introductions were over, all the courtesies acknowledged, the mood changed.

> I have truly despised your see, the Roman Curia, which . . . neither you nor anyone else can deny is more corrupt than any Babylon or Sodom ever was . . . Farewell, unhappy, hopeless, blasphemous Rome.[6]

In retaliation to the pope's decree, at nine o'clock in the morning on 10 December 1520, a bonfire was lit just outside the gate of Wittenberg. Books of canon law, various decretals (papal documents), and books by Johann Eck and other enemies of Luther's were tossed into the flames. Luther stepped up and, before an audience of townspeople and university students, tossed a copy of Leo's papal bull into the fire. His papers of excommunication went into the flames next.

Wolsey responded to all the smoke by setting a prohibition against the importation, sale, or translation of anything by Martin Luther. The pope commended Wolsey's efforts, but suggested that burning was more efficient. "A general bonfire would be more satisfactory," he said. It is more visible, tactile, more consuming, and finite.

Knowing the height from which he eventually fell, I suspect that fire made Wolsey nervous.

In spite of Tunstall's sermonizing and all the rant, it was still the Word of God he consigned to the flames. And the response the bishop got was not the response he wanted or had imagined. It was an odd sight to many, a shameful act. With his usual clarity, in a letter to John Frith, Tyndale summarized well:

> I guessed long ago that God would send a dazing into the head of the spirituality, to catch themselves in their own subtlety: and I trust it is come to pass. And now methinketh I smell a counsel to be taken, little for the profits in time to come. But you must understand that it is not of a pure heart, and for love of the truth; but to avenge themselves, and to eat the whore's flesh, and to suck the marrow of her bones.[7]

According to Sir Thomas More, if heresy was a symphony, William Tyndale was the "bass and tenor whereupon [others] would sing the treble with much false descant."[8] "It is enough," More wrote, "for good Christian men to abhor and burn up his [Tyndale's] books, and the likers of them with them."[9]

A Heap of New Testaments

There is a wonderful story surrounding Tyndale's 1526 New Testament in Edward Halle's Chronicles (1542). And while there is always the possibility it could be factual—for there are factual elements woven into the tale—it is more likely a fable, well spun certainly, but more of a convenient yarn. John Foxe repeated the tale in his *Actes and Monuments*.

Augustus Packington, a London mercer (cloth merchant) was in Antwerp at the same time that Cuthbert Tunstall happened to be there. According to Halle, Packington "greatly favoured" Tyndale but to the bishop he put on another face and "utterly shewed himself to the contrary."[10] Duplicity was part of the script. Everybody had to play.

Packington had discovered that part of Tunstall's business in Antwerp was to find and destroy Tyndale's work. Halle continued, "Here is to be remembered, that at this present time, William Tyndale had newly translated and imprinted the New Testament in English, and the Bishop of London, not pleased with the translation thereof, debated with himself, how he might compass and devise to destroy that false and erroneous translation, (as he said)."[11]

Packington said to the bishop, "My Lord, if it be your pleasure, I can in this matter do more, I dare say, than most of the merchants of England that are here; for I know Dutchmen and strangers that have bought them of Tyndale, and have them here to sell; so that if it be our lordship's pleasure to pay for them, (for otherwise I cannot come by them, but I must disperse money for them) I will then assure you to have every book of them, that is imprinted and is here unsold."

Tunstall, "thinking that he had God by the toe," after a quick thought, replied, "Gentle Mister Packington, do your diligence and get them, and with all my heart I will pay for them, whatsoever they cost you; for the books are erroneous and naught [meaningless], and I intend surely to destroy them all, and to burn them at Paul's Cross."

Packington then went to Tyndale and said, "William, I know thou art a poor man, and has a heap of New Testaments and books by thee, for the which thou has both endangered thy friends and beggared thyself; and I have gotten thee a merchant, which with ready money shall dispatch thee of all that thou hast, if you think it so profitable for yourself."

"Who is the merchant?"

"The Bishop of London."

"O, that is because he will burn them," the translator assured him.

"Yea, marry," quoth Packington (Halle's dialogue attribution).

"I am the gladder," said Tyndale, "for these two benefits shall come thereof: I shall get money of him for these books, to bring myself out of debt, and the whole world will cry out upon the burning of God's word. And the overplus of the money, that shall remain to me, shall make me more studious to correct the said New Testament, and so newly to imprint the same once again; and I trust the second will much better like you than ever did the first."

Halle concluded with a merry note: "And so forward went the bargain: the bishop had the books, Packington had the thanks, and Tyndale had the money."[12]

It is a very tidy narrative. It is also highly unlikely. For Tyndale to pay the heavy price he paid, to live in exile and poverty by choice and for the sake of his calling, and that he would agree to sell his Bibles knowing they will burn is too much to ask.

In Halle, Packington is not finished with the bishop just yet.

Afterward when more New Testaments were imprinted, they came thick and threefold into England, the bishop of London hearing that still there were so many New Testaments abroad, sent for Augustus Packington and said unto him, "Sir how cometh this, that there are so many New Testaments abroad, and you promised and assured me, that you had bought all?" Then said Packington, "I promise you I bought all that then was to be had: but I perceive they have made more since, and it will never be better, as long as they have the letters and stamps [actual print elements], therefore it were best for your lordship to "buy the stamps too, and then are you sure." The bishop smiled at him and said, "Well Packington, well." And so ended this matter.[13]

In spite of my doubts, the above story does reference Tyndale's condition as perceived and documented by Packington (via Halle), that he has "endangered his friends and beggared himself." Tyndale is not only exiled from England and from his past life, he lives in exile from all the usual conventions of life. He has forfeited anything "normal." He is not the common citizen of the world.

Tyndale has one thing on his mind and lives in the margins of life that, for him, are sufficient, and safer. He cares about nothing but his translation and about his continuing studies, his precious Greek and Hebrew. This image Packington gives us provides an adequate appraisal of the dedication and discipline Tyndale's art and spiritual life demand of him.

Tyndale is deeply convinced, enough to live *other* than the rest of the world.

The Lion in Defense of the Lamb

William Tyndale has been referred to as the first Puritan. Some go so far as to refer to him as the "father of the Puritans." It is not difficult to come to this conclusion, until you consider the severity of the times, and the severity of Tyndale's opposition, how big and how loud the growl he inspired, how deep the claim the Church made on the soul of everyone, how long its reach and how intricate the weave.

Severity had to be met with severity, and severity always has the appearance of Puritanism. C. S. Lewis said, "Nearly every association which now clings to the word *puritan* has to be eliminated when we are talking of the early Protestants. Whatever they were, they were not sour, gloomy, or severe; nor did their enemies bring any such charge against them."[14]

By the reaction to his new English translation of the Bible, Tyndale was forced into a kind of metamorphosis, a change he was somewhat reluctant to make, in spite of how well he played the game. And he played it well. The best writers often do their finest work with a little clench of the teeth, or by closing a fist around their pen.

The somewhat naïve translator became Tyndale the vociferous, Tyndale the vindicator, Tyndale the forerunner, the uncompromising Baptist, playing Elijah to their Jezebel, the "voice of a cryar in the wilderness,"[15] as his own gospels declared, the lion in the defense of the lamb.

John Foxe introduced Tyndale as "God's mattock to shake the inward roots and foundation of the pope's proud prelacy."[16] Tyndale had little choice. The action flushed him to the surface. He had the right gifts and training, the mature art of the comeback. His immediate response was not shy or retreating in any way. Reacting to the critics he wrote,

> But our malicious and wily hypocrites, which are so stubborn and hard-hearted in their wicked abominations . . .
>
> And as for my translation, in which they affirm unto the lay-people (as I have heard say) to be I wot [know] not how many thousand heresies, so that it cannot be mended or correct; they have yet taken so great pain to examine it, and to compare it unto that they would fain have it, and to their own imaginations and juggling terms, and to have somewhat to rail at, and under that cloak to blaspheme the truth; that they might with as little labour (as I suppose) have translated the most part of the bible.
>
> . . . Finally, in this they be all agreed, to drive you from the knowledge of the scripture, and that ye shall not have the text thereof in the mother-tongue, and to keep the world still in darkness, to the intent they might sit in the consciences of the people, through vain superstition and false doctrine, to satisfy their filthy lusts, their proud ambition, and unsatiable covetousness, and to exalt their own honour above king and emperor, yea, and above God himself.[17]

The Million-Footed Manhattan

Tyndale did not seek some remote, hidden, out-of-the-way retreat in which to work, but rather the bustle of some "million-footed Manhattan," as Walt Whitman might have described Antwerp. After the publication of the 1526 New Testament, Tyndale remained at Worms for a year or longer, perhaps managing the sale of his Bibles. From Worms he resettled in Antwerp. When he arrived is not known, and we use the word *settled* or *resettled* with a bit of optimism.

Though he continued to move about, from this point in our story Antwerp was Tyndale's base. The word *home* misleads.

In Antwerp he continually revised his New Testament. He also published *The Parable of the Wicked Mammon* (1528), *The Obedience of a Christian Man* (1528), *The Practice of Prelates* (1530), *Tyndale's Answer to Sir Thomas More's Dialogue* (1530), *Pentateuch* (1530), the *Book of Jonah* (1531), and the Old Testament books of Joshua through 2 Chronicles (1531).

Tyndale's desk is more of a metaphor. It moves with him.

Hermann Rinck, friend of the king's and confidant to Wolsey, who almost bagged Tyndale in Cologne, has not given up. Tyndale is a prize. If I have cast the translator as the fox, I must also cast him as the owl—vigilant, alert, wise, and poised for flight. He traveled often to Germany, mainly for the Hebrew and to remain out of Wolsey's reach, and then More's.

But in spite of his continuous movement, it would be a mistake to assume Tyndale was friendless and without a network of associates. With notoriety comes celebrity, and as much as he wanted to remain unnoticed, it was highly improbable that he did. Tyndale biographer C. H. Williams wrote, "Far from being a lonely figure he was the most determined and authoritative English interpreter of the new religious thought emanating from Luther, and was acknowledged by this group of English refugees as their most powerful representative."[18]

Antwerp was known as "the metropolis." Its population at the time of Tyndale's arrival was double that of London's. It hummed with enterprise and with the traffic of alien feet. Antwerp was polyglot, both in tongue and thought, custom and manners. By the beginning of the fifteenth century, it was surpassing Venice as the commercial capital of Europe.

Antwerp printers did not know English that well, nor did they have much respect for it. But again, coin overruled conscience.

They exercised the more modern ideal that commerce held more dominion than the Church, and that heretic cash was just as viable as the pope's. Coin was coin. Printing was a highly profitable enterprise, and therefore it was irresistible. The presses were occupied with reformer literature as well as Church literature, and often in the same house at the same time. It was all quite outside the law, but there was so much of it, regulation was complicated.

With its safety-in-numbers appeal, Antwerp was ideal for a heretic-translator in need of a place to live and go about unnoticed. There was no Church and no university, so there was no authority to breathe down anyone's neck. At least ten printers in Antwerp printed heretical material not only in English, but also in French, Dutch, and Spanish. Other printed literatures included Italian, Latin, Greek, and Hebrew. More English-language books were printed in Antwerp than in London.

> *Christ's blood-shedding hath bound us to love one another with all our might and to do the utmost of our power one to another.*
>
> – WILLIAM TYNDALE, *THE OBEDIENCE OF A CHRISTIAN MAN*

Officials in Antwerp considered religious intolerance bad for business. Antwerp, as Brian Moynahan described it, was a phenomenon, "a Catholic city that was a centre of Lutheran, and then Anabaptist and Calvinist propaganda."[19]

Perhaps the greatest of all European ports, Antwerp had a number of English merchants, many of whom were reform minded. Tyndale lived at the English House, a mansion the city magistrates had given the English merchants decades earlier to encourage trade. What might loosely be called an embassy, the English House stood "in its own alleyway in a block of streets"[20] adjacent to restaurants and lace shops, just north of the Grote Market (the great market square).

There is a science to running—knowing when to move, when to plant, when to play dead, when to look like a tree, at what depth to engage with others. Of all these items listed, Tyndale was master, with exception of the last. He had a blind side.

Pastime

Tyndale worked five days a week—writing, translating. The remaining two days, Saturdays and Mondays, Tyndale called his "days of pastime."

On these days he exercised the priesthood inside him, his obligation to Christ. Mondays he visited English men and women who had fled to Antwerp, and those who were sick and diseased, whom he "did liberally comfort and relieve." Saturdays he went about town, looking for old people and for struggling families, looking into "every corner and hole" for those whom he could help, who might be "also plentifully relieved."[21]

Tyndale, living in poverty himself, gave "the most part" of what he had to the poor. The English merchants in Antwerp eventually gave him a stipend—a small but sufficient one—the first secure income he had since leaving Little Sodbury. Sundays he read to the merchants "some one parcel of scripture." He read for at least an hour after dinner. It was said (in Foxe) that he read so "fruitfully, sweetly, and gently" that he brought "heavenly comfort" to his audience.

The remainder of the week, his attention was given "wholly to his book."[22]

Shipwrecked

When Tyndale left England there was no Hebrew at either Oxford or Cambridge.[23] The University of Wittenberg had a professor of Hebrew, but reliable teachers of Hebrew could also be found at Hamburg, Worms, and Marburg. It is certain that Tyndale spent time with a rabbi(s) learning the language of the Old Testament.

According to the Tyndale legendary, in 1529 he left Antwerp on a ship bound for Hamburg. He had the Old Testament translation on his mind and it made sense to work near the Hebrew teachers. Hamburg would offer a quieter place to work. And movement was always safer. But the ship was caught up in a winter gale and wrecked on the Dutch coast. In the disaster, Tyndale lost all his books and any manuscripts he had, including any work on the Old Testamtent.

Tyndale biographers are divided on this story. As sensational as the story is, Tyndale never mentioned it. Foxe has the only account of any such shipwreck. It is a great story, but is it more Tyndale mythology? The argument for the historian and biographer is often over scraps of evidence that just as often misdirect. Propaganda was common on both sides of the religious argument. Foxe, therefore, must be approached with caution when seeking a particular line of inquiry.

> For at what time Tyndale had translated the Fifth Book of Moses, called Deuteronomy, minding to print the same at Hamburgh, he sailed thitherward; where by the way, upon the coast of Holland, he suffered shipwreck, by which he lost all his books, writings, and copies, and so was compelled to begin all again anew, to his hinderance, and doubling of his labours.[24]

To Tyndale's own index of sufferings we must add the lonely state of banishment. Self-imposed or not, Tyndale is uncountried. For the translator-artist, for the ascetic-writer-creator whose work is hardly separated from his life, a thorough study of Tyndale is not possible without considering the effects of exile.

It Was England to Him

The proof of a poet is that his country absorbs
him as affectionately as he has absorbed it.

—Walt Whitman, *introduction to Leaves of Grass* (1855)

BRITISH POET AND EXPATRIATE W. H. AUDEN (1907–1973) SAID
that to understand your own country you need to live in at least two others. American novelist Thomas Wolfe (1900–1938), whose titles include
Look Homeward, Angel and *You Can't Go Home Again*, both suggesting a kind
of exile, had a similar thought.

> I had found out during all these years of wandering that the way
> to discover one's own country was to leave it; that the way to find
> America was to find it in one's heart, one's mind, one's memory, and
> one's spirit, and in a foreign land. So it had been with me. Around me
> day by day in all these months and years and voyages to Europe I had
> seen the million forms and shapes and patterns of an alien life. My life
> had been enriched and quickened immeasurably by contemplating and
> experiencing them, and always when I saw them I had the profit of a

vast, fertile, inestimable comparison. All of my powers of memory and experience were constantly brought to bear as I compared the life of which I was a part, the country from which I came, with this new and alien life in which I lived and wandered as a stranger.[1]

In this appraisal of his homelessness and its effect on him as an artist, Wolfe provides a context, a way we might approach Tyndale the exile, the expatriate. A transition of this magnitude cannot help but have a psychological effect on the artist, and therefore on his art. Absence is a powerful muse.

This passage is taken from a lecture Wolfe gave at the University of Colorado Writer's Conference in 1935. He is speaking to writers, to those who negotiate thought and speech, who interpret their world at the level of art—or at least those who desire to—who wish to live by means of the word. And while it is always wise to use caution when applying any generalization among artists (for the artist is exile no matter where he lives), there is no reason not to accept Wolfe's observation as it applies to the literary.

What it suggests is that Tyndale's sense of English became acute in his retreat from it. A kind of homesickness infused all he wrote.

To be exile is one thing, but to be exile under threat of death is quite another. But far from having any power to diminish or cripple, the danger enhances. It makes glory more glorious, magnificence more magnificent. The severity and asceticism of art are stepped up by degrees. All the primal instincts are flushed forward. They are scintillate, alert, and on call. The nerve beneath it all remains taut, tuned to a musical pitch. Ask the veteran warrior about duty, and the wearing of his senses in sustained combat. William Tyndale is alive in ways that were not possible under fairer conditions. Exile and death are a particular boon to his art.

Reimagination: The Wound of Fortune

Due to a complicated political coup in 1301, which included a pope (Boniface VIII) and a divided city, Dante Alighieri (1265–1321) was forced at sword-point to leave his native Florence and warned not to return except on pain of death (burning at the stake). Leaving behind a wife and children, he never saw his beloved city again.

This shock, this violent disruption of a life, was the making of Dante.

In time, he came to regard his life up to this moment as a kind of false start. Despair, yes. A cry for help, doubtless—and disorientation. But without this bitter expulsion from his "city on the lovely Arno's shore,"[2] his name would not have the dimensions as we have come to recognize it. Instead of thinking of his banishment as a monstrous injustice, he began to see it as Exodus, "which all Christians metaphorically or not face during their lives."[3]

> Since it was the pleasure of the citizens of the most beautiful and famous daughter of Rome, Florence, to cast me out of her sweet bosom—where I was born and bred up to the pinnacle of my life, and where, with her good will, I desire with all my heart to rest my weary mind and to complete the span of time that is given to me—I have traveled like a stranger, almost like a beggar, through virtually all the regions to which this tongue of ours extends, displaying against my will the wound of fortune for which the wounded one is often unjustly accustomed to be held accountable. Truly I have been a ship without sail or rudder, brought to different ports, inlets, and shores by the dry wind that painful poverty blows.[4]

Stranger, beggar, wound of fortune, rudderless. Literary critic Harold Bloom observed, "A nature that powerful and that given to celebration and self-celebration is also capable of enormous anguish. Without that *The Commedia* [The Divine Comedy] could not have been written. So, in a sense, exile, was a fortunate fall for Dante."[5]

A banished Dante helps explain Tyndale.

Dante scholar Giusseppe Mazzota said that for the exile "the very idea of identity and sense of who you are is literally destroyed, undone. He [Dante] could no longer be defined as being a Florentine. Now he can take a universal standpoint . . . Exile is the key to his extraordinary universal vision."[6] No longer a citizen of a flag-bearing, walled, and isolated geographical point, the exile is citizen of the bigger world.

Exile opened Dante up, that is, inspired a greater bloom. It called up something aboriginal, a savage purity of intellect akin to what we know as genius. Vladimir Nabokov (1899–1977), himself an artist in exile, wrote, "There is no such thing as real life for an author of genius: he must create it himself and then create the consequences."[7] Tyndale was certainly forced into this kind of reimagining. He had little choice. Like Dante, he was shaped by fortune.[8]

Transcending Exile: Sing or Go Silent

Tyndale would never see England again, and though we can only speculate, it is not unreasonable to suggest that his imagination was alive with her. Being away from her, she was ever more present to him. Her voice rose in sharp relief against the voices around him, and it could not help but be elevated in his thoughts, reawakened and reimagined as it was.

The translation was first in his thoughts. It was England to him.

Our inquiry in this chapter aims at the effects of exile as processed by the artist, with the assumption that only by his art is he able to transcend it. Being away from home enhances the sense of home, allowing it to expand in the artist's conscience. If his art is literary, then language itself becomes his homeland.

Czeslaw Milosz—1980 Nobel Prize winner in literature—himself a Lithuanian-born American transplant, noted that when living among a foreign people, after a while the writer is able to sense his native tongue in a whole new way. Milosz said that it does not diminish the native linguistic capacity but, on the contrary, "new aspects and tonalities of the native tongue are discovered, for they stand out against the background of the language spoken in a new milieu."[9]

Like William Tyndale, Thomas Wolfe had a fine ear for music, and knew how to coax it forward, particularly when applied to the commonplace, to the ordinary and misprized among people and things. Wolfe was never better than he was when writing about his native Asheville,

North Carolina, though he wrote about it while in Paris, London, and New York. Sifting Tyndale through the art of Thomas Wolfe allows us to imagine the translator's emotional posture and its imprint upon his translation.

> I think I may say that I discovered America during these years abroad out of my very need for her. I found her because I had left her. The huge gain of this discovery seemed to come directly from my sense of loss. I had been to Europe five times now; each time I had come with longing, delight, with maddening eagerness to return, and each time how, where, and in what way I did not know, I had felt the bitter ache of homelessness, a desperate need and longing for America, an over-whelming desire to return.
>
> Now during that summer in Paris, I think I felt this great home-sickness more than ever before, and I really believe that from this emotion, this constant and almost intolerable effort of memory and desire, this thing that would not let me rest, this memory of home that could not be appeased, that would not stop or vanish even when I slept—from this huge and hopeless memory of home, I say, I think the material and the structure of the books I now began to write were derived.[10]

Through flight and distance Wolfe found his voice as an act of redis-covery. It is not difficult, considering our gentle translator, to imagine him discovering his own England by that same sense of loss. In a 1998 article from the Modern Language Association, Maeera Schreiber said there are two choices when confronted with the sense of loss and distance suffered in exile.

> Exile, as a mark and consequence of a profound severing of the relation-ship between God and the people of Israel, makes for a collective crisis in aesthetic production. One solution to the catastrophe is, of course, to go silent—to hang up one's lyre and acknowledge that forced home-lessness dooms the possibility of song, which depends on and affirms

a link to the divine principle that bestows meaning on the community. The alternative is to turn a liability into an asset; the question is also the answer. God's absence or perilous distance makes for a condition of chronic loss that becomes the subject of binding song.[11]

Sing or go silent. Transcending exile will ask one or the other.

The following excerpt is a response to what Tyndale discovered was Henry VIII's displeasure with him (specifically, his book *Practice of Prelates*). The details are not important for the moment, but here, in Tyndale's own words, we get an impression of what he suffered. Note the movement of his passion, the cadence it makes, the plaintive *if*, the gentle roll of its music.

> If for my pains therein taken, if for my poverty, if for mine exile out of my natural country and bitter absence from my friends, if for my hunger, my thirst, my cold, the great danger wherewith I am everywhere encompassed, and finally, if for innumerable other hard and sharp fightings which I endure, not yet feeling their asperity by reason I hoped with my labors to do honour to God, true service to my prince, and pleasure to his commons; how is it that his Grace, this considering, may either by himself think, or by the persuasions of others be brought to think, that in this doing I should not show a pure mind, a true and incorrupt zeal and affection to his Grace?[12]

Here, Tyndale has identified the conditions by which he translated the Bible and his other works, that is, in a state of poverty, exile and bitter absence, hunger, thirst, cold, danger, and in hard and sharp fightings.

Notice in the above passage the subtle identification with the Scriptures, that is, by sound—the beat, the sublime music. It could be Paul to the Romans. It is evident even here that Tyndale was saturated with Scripture. It is asylum. And faced with the challenge to sing or be silent, we know how he chose.

Who shall separate us from the love of God? shall tribulation? or anguish? or persecution? or hunger? or nakedness? or peril? or sword? As it is written: For thy sake are we killed all day long and are counted as sheep appointed to be slain. Nevertheless in all these things we overcome strongly through his help that loved us.
(Romans 8:35 TNT)

Part of any translator's task is to determine as closely as possible the right sense of a word, to find an equivalent that best conveys a thought as it migrates from one language to another, and to do so while mimicking both intensity and weight. While this is no small task for any translator, I am not sure there could be a more adequate broker for the complex emotional stresses of this passage in Romans than Tyndale.

No one could negotiate the apostle's thought quite like one whose life was so strikingly similar to his own. Much more than a mere exercise of the mind, it presents a kind of linguistic empathy. There is, indeed, a certain cooperation between Tyndale and Paul in all that Greek.

The Greek word Tyndale rendered as *tribulation* (θλιψις *thlipsis*) might also mean "affliction, trouble, anguish, persecution." The literal meaning is "a pressing, pressing together, pressure"[13] and "oppression, affliction, tribulation, distress, straits" (metaphorical). These are conditions Tyndale understood.

Something lives in Tyndale's Paul beyond mere equivalents of language. They were both hunted men. Both were uncountried, unkinged, and by choice. Neither of them suffered fools. Each had their John Mark, their William Roye, and perhaps others. They were both literary men, well educated above their fellows. Both had the gift of expression, the ability to draw from the quick of life. Both were called, appointed of God to carry out a specific work. Both were completely surrendered to their task and to the life it demanded of them. Each of them lived and worked against a hostile spirituality. They both perceived and processed their lives accordingly. And forgive the crude parallel, but both the apostle Paul and William Tyndale were arrested, condemned, and executed by Romans. In *The Parable of the Wicked Mammon* Tyndale wrote,

If Paul were now alive, and would defend his own learning, he should
be tried through fire; not through the fire of the judgment of Scripture,
(for that light men now utterly refuse) but by the Pope's law, and with
fire of fagots.[14]

Could we have the same Bible without these conditions? Perhaps.

In spite of the menace that surrounded Tyndale and whatever medication there may have been for him in the original manuscripts, whatever
comfort or identification with any author or authors, and in spite of whatever imaginative sympathies that might have existed between Tyndale and
Paul, none of the words of the original Greek were exaggerated or altered
in any way. Tyndale made that clear to us. In a letter written a few years
before his death he said,

I call God to record, against the day we shall appear before our Lord
Jesus to give a reckoning of our doings, that I never altered one syllable of God's word against my conscience, nor would do this day, if
all that is in the earth, whether it be honour, pleasure, or riches, might
be given me.[15]

His exile and its deep effects would distill into all he did. It could not
be helped. The translation of the English Bible was sifted through this
deadly and yet penetrating aesthetic. His life could be required of him
any moment. He understood this. It was a condition of life that Tyndale
accepted, and he crafted an English masterpiece from it.

It wasn't fear. Death merely provided another muse.

Tyndale maintained a powerful identification with his English
translation, a word by word intimacy, not unlike Walt Whitman and
his one book, *Leaves of Grass*, which was continuously sharpened under
the poet's editorial gaze.* Whitman, like Wolfe, had much to add on
Tyndale's behalf.

---

* Whitman continually edited his book from its first release in 1855 until his death in 1892,
a span of thirty-seven years.

The greatest poet hardly knows pettiness or triviality. If he breathes into any thing that was before thought small it dilates with the grandeur and life of the universe. He is a seer . . . he is an individual . . . he is complete in himself . . . the others are as good as he, only he sees it and they do not.[16]

If Tyndale's soul troubled at the distance between himself and his old life, the medication lived in the work before him. England lived in his words. Both in the Scripture and in the English he fashioned it with lived his past, his present, and his future, all bound together. As Czeslaw Milosz wrote, "Language is the only homeland."

The Banished Prince

Exile has been an integral part of Judeo-Christian theology from its inception. The story of Adam and Eve in the garden of Eden (Genesis 2) is ultimately one of expulsion and banishment, and with such consequence that cherubim were placed at the Eastern gate with a flaming sword to assure the unfortunate couple would not attempt a return.[17]

This state of exile is the deepest memory in man. Beneath the surface of the Scripture, in its quiet heart, is the call to come home.

According to Christian theology, Christ willingly left his abode in heaven to take on the nature of a man. And though this exile was self-imposed, Christ—or as Paul (through Tyndale) called him, "the last Adam"[18]—was himself a banished prince. His presence on earth stood counter to the systems of this world, and not just spiritually, but culturally and politically. So much so that both secular and ecclesiastic authorities demanded his silence and his life.

With a few obvious exceptions, Tyndale's condition was not unlike that of his Master. Church and state had a peculiar bond and worked together toward his demise and the demise of countless others. To condemn a man to death, the Church had to surrender the heretic over to the state for execution, very Pilate-like. According to one of its own rules, the Church itself could not shed blood (*Ecclesia non novit sanguinem*). The hypocrisy was profound.

The Christian life begins with a kind of exile, a separating out. Saying, as speaking to the world, *I am no longer a part of you.*

> *Wherefore come out of among them, and separate yourselves [saith the Lord].* (2 Corinthians 6:17 TNT 1526)

> *See that ye love not the world, neither the things that are in the world. If any man love the world, the love of the Father is not in him.* (I John 2:15 TNT 1526)

For the translator of an English Scripture to do his work as an outcast, as one banished from his homeland, only empowered the text before him. All the elements rally. We hear Wolfe once again:

> It was familiar to me as my mother's face, and yet it would seem to me now that I had never really known it; that I had just discovered it; that I had never found a name for it, a tongue to give it utterance . . . my life would ache with the whole memory of it; the desire to see it again; somehow to find a word for it; a language that would tell its shape, its color, the way we have all known and felt and seen it.[19]

Moses wrote the five books of the Pentateuch as a banished prince (almost literally, being raised as he was in the house of an Egyptian princess), a volume of five books that could have been written no other way. Moses was born into exile, set adrift as a baby in a foreign land.

In time, he became leader of a people in exodus, in search of a home. It empowered his own text, as he put something of himself into the work. The nation of Israel wandered in the desert forty years. They were homeless, complaining. The groan was long and deep and all their songs reflect the pilgrimage, the homesickness. They were strangers in a strange land, and yet, like the ark of the covenant that bore the presence of God before them, they had a sense of home that they carried within them.

Adam, Moses, Hagar, Jacob, Daniel, Isaiah, Jonah—all exile. The theme is inescapable. It lives in both testaments, old and new. A Patmos was necessary for John to write the Revelation. Tyndale's own banishment was, in image and substance, essentially that of Israel—the heart in exodus, in pilgrimage, in struggle, aching for home.

The Breath, the Blood, the Substance of Our Lives

Exile is a deep fixture in the Jews. Coming to English from the Greek, *diaspora* means "to disperse, to scatter." The *Oxford English Dictionary* defines it with some formality as "the Dispersion; i.e. (among the Hellenistic Jews) the whole body of Jews living dispersed among the Gentiles after the Captivity (John vii. 35); (among the early Jewish Christians) the body of Jewish Christians outside of Palestine (Jas. i. I, I Pet. i. I)."

For the Jew and the Christian, diaspora is an inevitable part of the inheritance. It is not unlike an imprinting, written in the code of faith at the deepest, most cellular level. The awareness may be faint, its movement subtle and unnoticed perhaps, but it is always present nonetheless. Earth becomes the strange land; the believer becomes the stranger who treads upon it. This condition lives gloriously in the music.

> *By the rivers of Babylon, there we sat down, yea, we wept, when we remembered Zion. We hanged our harps upon the willows in the midst thereof. For there they that carried us away captive required of us a song; and they that wasted us required of us mirth, saying, Sing us one of the songs of Zion. How shall we sing the LORD's song in a strange land? If I forget thee, O Jerusalem, let my right hand forget her cunning. If I do not remember thee, let my tongue cleave to the roof of my mouth; if I prefer not Jerusalem above my chief joy.* (Psalms 137:1–6 KJV)

David, son of Jesse, before he ever ruled in Israel, found himself outcast, alone, abandoned, despised, hounded by Saul from his homeland with the threat of death all around him, aware the entire time that from his boyhood he was anointed king by the prophet Samuel. David was once celebrated in Saul's army. "Saul has slain his thousand, and David his ten thousand" (I Samuel 18 TNT). Saul rewarded him with the gift of his daughter Michal.

But Saul tired of the songs. David fell prey to Saul's bitterness. He became the hunted, Saul the hunter. The prince became a toad in one jealous shot of a spear.

In Psalm 22 we hear the outcast David cry out, "My God, my God, why hast thou forsaken me?"[20] For all his anointing, the bright aura of election that rested upon him, David suffered greatly and he suffered alone.

His particular kingship of Israel,[21] a name that implies struggle, could hardly be shaped any other way. All his Goliaths and all his Sauls were necessary. And David was known as the sweet singer of Israel, her true king. To understand this is to understand the nature of the lyric itself, that mystical expressive afterglow—the inward life suddenly emancipated by an ecstasy that flows upward, forward, as from a deep gulf. David's joy was ever as large and imprudent and unrestrained and electric and shameless and weeping as his sorrows.

Abandonment, sifted through the psalmist's art, gave us our songs and taught us how to praise, how to complain or lament, how to reckon our groans. Did his injury give his words a higher life? Did they "sound" him, as in the plundering of some depth? The psalms are answer enough.

And what David wrote is not the kind of text you just sit down one day and write. There is a life within it, a peculiar moving of his soul, the life of alienation, of brokenness, of humility, and ultimately, the voice of praise and exultation, of triumph and crazy love.

His transgression with Bathsheba, for instance, stealing her from her husband Uriah as he did, having the poor unsuspecting guy murdered, being, as David was, blind with lust and power, provides another example. When the prophet Nathan confronted him, David was stricken, sick at heart. Psalm 51 is the result. David turned his sorrow into a powerful lyric.

> *Have mercy upon me, O God, according to thy lovingkindness:*
> *according unto the multitude of thy tender mercies blot out my*
> > *transgressions.*
> *Wash me throughly from mine iniquity, and cleanse me from my sin.*
> *For I acknowledge my transgressions: and my sin is ever before me.*

Against thee, thee only, have I sinned, and done this evil in thy sight: that
thou mightest be justified when thou speakest, and be clear when thou
judgest. (Psalms 51:1–4 KJV)

David is no one's angel. He is the most human of kings. In Tyndale's translation David is, according to God, a "man after mine own heart."[22] Not one to argue with God once he is found out, and knowing God the way he does, he pleads not to be driven away or banished from God's presence. The pain of separation is too much for him—the thought of being excommunicated, out of communion with God. He is overcome. He has suffered his own Egypt, his own Exodus. And after a few verses, it is no longer about the girl. It is an issue between him and his God. It begins to materialize out of his desperation. "Cast me not away from thy presence; and take not thy Holy Spirit from me" (v. 11).

His complaint registers in his songs. You can hear it, and again the point is made that without the injury, he would not have sung with the beauty that he did. David's words are alive. He has too thoroughly lived them. He transcends his grief with his art.

The following stanza of Wolfe's lecture gives us a glimpse of how vocation and calling awaken in the artist's imagination.

These and a million other things which all of us have known, which all of us remember, which are the breath, the blood, the substance of our lives, but now come back to me in a blazing imagery, in a torrential flood tide of aching and intolerable memory, and suddenly I understood clearly for the first time in my life that I had no language for them, no words to give them utterance, no tongue to tell their shape, dimension, tone, and special quality, and all the meaning and emotion that they have for us. And when I saw and understood this thing, I saw that I must find a language for myself, find for myself the tongue to utter what I knew but could not say. And from the day and moment of that discovery, the line and purpose of my life was shaped. The end toward which every energy of my life and talent would be henceforth directed was in such a way as this defined.[23]

Can we interpret or translate Tyndale through a reading of Thomas Wolfe or King David, through the exiled John on Patmos, through Whitman's poet, or Dante's pilgrim of eternity? I am convinced that we can. When the artist is finally aware of his or her vocation, when the conditions are right, the work has taken shape already. It is alive within them. In a certain way, it is ready when they are. All that is left is expression.

The Mother of All Good Works

*A poet's work is to name the unnameable, to point
at frauds, to take sides, start arguments, shape
the world and stop it from going to sleep.*

— Salman Rushdie,
    The Satanic Verses (1988)

THOMAS MORE DESCRIBED IT AS "A VERY TREASURY AND WELL-spring of wickedness—*mammona iniquitatis.*" Once it was in their hands, the archbishop of Canterbury, William Warham, called a council of his fellow divines to examine this new book by Tyndale, which they found teeming with heresy. Wolsey instructed the ambassador of the Low Countries to demand the extradition of Tyndale, Roye, and whoever else they could get their hands on who might be guilty of such pollution.

Tyndale once again played the fox to a very slow, lumbering, and yet ubiquitous brood of hounds. The date of the first printing of *Wicked Mammon* was 5 May 1528. Once it was released, an intense persecution broke out in England. The following is an excerpt from *A Public Instrument by the Bishops, for the Abolishing of the Scripture, and Other Books to be Read in English* issued by William Warham, archbishop of Canterbury.

> We signify unto you all, and let you well to wit and know by these presents, that the king, our sovereign lord, hearing of many books in the English tongue, containing many detestable errors, and damnable opinions, printed in the parts beyond the seas, to be brought into divers towns, and sundry parts of this realm of England, and sown abroad in the same, to the great decay of our faith catholic, and perilous corruption of his people, unless speedy remedy were briefly provided.[1]

From 1528, with the printing of *The Parable of the Wicked Mammon*, all of Tyndale's books were printed in Antwerp. The colophon (the printer's identifying marks) on *Wicked Mammon* was "Hans Luft of Marburg." It was a fictitious name, as most colophons were among those who printed contraband literature. Hans Luft was the name of an actual printer in Wittenberg who printed many of Luther's works, but the Antwerp Hans Luft (John Air) was "borrowed" to evade arrest.

For many years Hans Luft was thought to be an alias for Johannes Hellenius van Hoochstraten (cited by Mozley, Moynahan, Williams, and others), and that Hoochstraten was Tyndale's publisher. Recent discoveries, however, have determined that it was not Hoochstraten but an Antwerp printer named Martin (Marten) de Keyser.

De Keyser was the main printer of Protestant, or "Lutheran," literature in Antwerp. His credits with Tyndale include *The Parable of the Wicked Mammon*, *The Obedience of a Christian Man*, *The Practice of Prelates*, *Answer to Thomas More's Dialogue*, the 1530 *Pentateuch*, and the 1534 revised New Testament. De Keyser also printed works by Tyndale's friends, Myles Coverdale, John Frith, and William Roye.

Rede Me and Be Nott Wrothe

The Parable of the Wicked Mammon is the first of Tyndale's works that has his name on the title page. Above the preface it reads "William Tyndale, otherwise called Hychins to the reader." In the body of the preface, he tells us why he will now use his name and why he omitted it on the 1526 New Testament.

> The cause why I set my name before this little treatise and have not rather done it in the new testament is that then I followed the counsel of Christ which exhorteth men (Matt. vi.) to do their good deeds secretly and to be content with the conscience of well doing, and that God seeth us, and patiently to abide the reward of the last day, which Christ hath purchased for us and now would I fain have done like wise but am compelled to do otherwise.[2]

For anyone else, such an explanation might be suspect—the righteous puff that is part of the idiom. Not Tyndale. He actually meant it. He also found it necessary. The use of his name on *Wicked Mammon* and all succeeding works, which will include future printings of his Bible translation, is tactical, precautionary.

After completing the Bible at Worms, Tyndale's assistant, William Roye, abandoned him and went to Strasburg and found his way into the confidence of a fellow English exile, another renegade friar like himself, Jerome Barlow. Tyndale knew Barlow and tried to warn him about Roye.

Roye and Barlow produced a scathing little book of rhyme called *Rede Me and Be Nott Wrothe* that attempted to be polemic and cartoonish at the same time. The little book, which was also called *The Burying of the Mass*, attacked the Tudor Catholic establishment and the papacy. It satirized the Catholic Mass as the spring of clerical wealth and power, and placed Wolsey in the center as the chief abuser. "O miserable monster, most malicious, Father of perversity, patron of Hell . . . to thee I speak / O Caitiff cardinal so cruel / Causeless charging by thy cursed commandment to brenne [burn] God's word the holy testament," and so on. A cartoon of the round man prologues the book.

Burning Tyndale's Bible had incited new fury against the cardinal.

But *Rede Me* does all this while trying to laugh at the same time, which was an embarrassment for Tyndale. It was also the kind of poetry that

Tyndale despised. He was accused by some of writing it himself, which only added to his annoyance with Roye and the distance he chose to put between them. The title was part of a rhyme."Rede me and be nott wrothe, For I saye no thynge but trothe." The issue was the burning of the Word.

Without making you suffer more rhyme, it just didn't work. C. S. Lewis noted that the world could "get on better without it." Tyndale shared the sentiment.

Not one to suffer fools, and in order to distance himself from the indiscreet Roye, Tyndale chose to use his own name on *Wicked Mammon* as a precaution against the unfortunate taint of association. This sounds harsh, but Roye, for all the help he was to Tyndale in the beginning, proved insincere and unruly, and the confusion he generated was apparently enough for Tyndale to make the dissolution between himself and Roye public. The integrity of the translation was at stake.

Tyndale's vexation with Roye covers a third or more of the preface. Some, including Thomas More at first, thought Tyndale had written *Rede Me*, so Tyndale felt it necessary to disclaim Roye and his book.

> While I abode, a faithful companion, which now hath taken another voyage upon him, to preach Christ where, I suppose, he was never yet preached, (God, which put in his heart thither to go, send his Spirit with him, comfort him, and bring his purpose to good effect,) one William Roye, a man somewhat crafty, when he cometh unto new acquaintance, and before he be thorough known, and namely, when all is spent, came unto me and offered his help. As long as he had no money somewhat I could rule him; but as soon as he had gotten him money, he became like himself again. Nevertheless, I suffered all things till that was ended, which I could not do alone without one, both to write, and to help compare the texts together. When that was ended, I took my leave, and bade him farewell for our two lives; and, as men say, a day longer.[3]

Roye's recklessness was detrimental to everything Tyndale was doing. He was not capable of investing his whole heart into it, nor was he capable of the dedication Tyndale required of himself. He felt strongly that Roye's disposition toward folly devalued "the only currency God has."[4] Tyndale continued:

> Which Jerome, with all diligence, I warned of Roye's boldness, and exhorted him to beware of him, and to walk quietly, and with all patience and long-suffering, according as we have Christ and his apostles for an ensample [example], which thing he also promised me. Nevertheless, when he was come to Argentine, William Roye (whose tongue is able to make fools stark mad, but also to deceive the wisest, that is at the first sight and acquaintance,) gat him to him, and set him a work to make rhymes, while he himself translated a dialogue out of Latin into English, in whose Prologue he promiseth more a great deal than I fear he will ever pay.[5]

Not finished with Roye just yet, Tyndale spoke his mind once again on the use of poetry. Tyndale's aggravation with Roye was only exacerbated by Roye's rhyming business. While Tyndale was anything but apoetical, he had little tolerance or mercy with rhymers. Note that until the Elizabethan age, poetry was considered "light," because of its lesser themes and its singsong disposition. That doesn't make the poetry less valuable, but it is not yet the age of Shakespeare, Donne, or Spenser.

> It becometh not then the Lord's servant to use railing rhymes, but God's Word, which is the right weapon to slay sin, vice and all iniquity. The Scripture of God is good to teach and to improve. (2 Timothy iii and 2 Thessalonians ii) Paul speaking of Antichrist, saith, "Whom the Lord shall destroy with the Spirit, or breath of his mouth," that is, with the word of God. And (2 Corinthians x) "The weapons of our war are not carnal things, (saith he) but mighty in God to cast down strong holds," and so forth; that is, to destroy high buildings of false doctrine. The word of God is that day whereof Paul speaketh, (1 Corinthians iii) which shall declare all things, and that fire which shall try every man's work, and consume false doctrine: with that sword ought men sharply to fight, and not to rail with foolish rhymes.[6]

The preface goes silent at last on Roye's name, and Tyndale turned his aggravation with Roye into a lesson on spiritual warfare and the deception of the devil, how good and evil "go always together, one cannot be known without the other." Antichrist is not "an outward thing" but a spiritual thing, he says, but his nature is that "when he is overcome with the word of God to go out of play for a season, and to disguise himself, and then to come in again with a new name and new raiment."

But before saying our own goodbyes to Roye, we have his words about Tyndale. Printed in 1527 in his apropos titled *Brief Dialogue Between a Christian Father and His Stubborn Son*, he wrote, "It is not unknown to you all . . . how that this last year, the new testament of our saviour, was delivered unto you, through the faithful and diligent study of one of our nation . . . named William Hitchyns, unto whom I was . . . as help fellow, and partaker of his labours."[7]

Roye almost seems harmless. He is obviously intelligent or he would have been little help to Tyndale. He simply does not understand the gravity of the situation. He does not see the noose around Tyndale's neck. Roye is not the threat Tyndale is. He is not a bad man, just the wrong man.

I Did My Duty, and So Do I Now

In *The Parable of the Wicked Mammon* we begin to see Tyndale at full throttle. He is not bound to a libretto, to an old manuscript, to any prescribed form. He is not negotiating an ancient tongue. His only obligation is to be true to his own conscience and to the counsel of Scripture. And he performs brilliantly.

In humility and in his desire for correctness, Tyndale once again, as he did in his "Epistle to the Reader" in the 1526 New Testament, gave his *Wicked Mammon* room to evolve.

Some man will ask, peradventure, Why I take the labour to make this work, inasmuch as they will burn it, seeing they burnt the gospel? I answer, In burning the New Testament they did none other thing than that I looked for, no more shall they do if they burn me also, if it be God's will it shall be so. Nevertheless, in translating the New Testament I did my duty, and so do I now, and will do as much more as God hath ordained me to do. And as I offered that to all men to correct it, whosoever could, even so I do this. Whosoever, therefore, readeth this, compare it unto the Scripture. If God's word bear record unto it, and thou feelest in thine heart that it is so, be of good comfort, and give God thanks. If God's word condemn it, then hold it accursed, and so do all other doctrines: as Paul counselleth his Galatians:— Believe not every spirit suddenly, but judge them by the word of God, which is the trial of all doctrine, and lasteth for ever. Amen.

Wicked Mammon was a countermeasure directed against the church's insistence on works. According to Tyndale and the reformers, the church had "corrupted the pure word of God" and had taken away the key of knowledge, keeping the faithful in darkness and mute obscurity. It opens with an abstract that sets a tone and penetrates to the central nerve of the text.

That faith, the mother of all good works, justifieth us, before we can bring forth any good work: as the husband marrieth his wife before he can have any lawful children by her. Furthermore, as the husband marrieth not his wife that she should continue unfruitful as before, and as she was in the state of virginity, (wherein it was impossible for her to bear fruit) but contrariwise to make her fruitful; even so faith justifieth us not, that is to say, marrieth us not to God, that we should continue unfruitful as before, but that she should put the seed of his Holy Spirit in us, (as St. John in his Epistle calleth it) and to make us fruitful. For, saith Paul, (Eph. ii) By grace are ye made safe through faith, and that not of yourselves: for it is the gift of God, and cometh not of the works, lest any man should boast himself. For we are his workmanship, created in Christ Jesus unto good works, which God hath ordained that we should walk in them. Amen.[8]

One of the first things you notice when reading Tyndale, is that in spite of the liberty he exercises, whether he is quoting the Scripture as he does often, or is simply speaking his mind, the sound is familiar and consistent. (*Thees* and *thous*, the *—eth* and *—st* endings were modes of speech in Tyndale's England.) With anyone else this would amount to imitation or affectation, but not in the translator himself. It is not as if Tyndale is *trying* to sound like Scripture. Scripture sounds like Tyndale. English Scripture, or at least the music it makes, originates in him.

> *Get thee to God's word, and thereby try all doctrine, and against that receive nothing.*
>
> – WILLIAM TYNDALE, *PARABLE OF THE WICKED MAMMON*

Both *Wicked Mammon* and *Obedience* share the same register as Tyndale's translations, essentially the sound I encountered when I first read the King James Bible years ago, though I had not been formally introduced to William Tyndale.

When Tyndale inserts Scripture in his nontranslation text, the transition is seamless, almost unnoticed at times. And his quotes are not always exact, which indicates he is speaking from memory, that he is so immersed in the Scripture it flows from him in natural procession, with facility and grace. Any imprecision is forgivable.

Works Are Servant to Faith

In my copy of *The Parable of the Wicked Mammon*, which amounts to a book of about eighty-six pages, there are but few references to the parable itself (Luke 16:1–9). Exegesis is not the point. Tyndale examines the motive behind the Church's emphasis on works, and this theme provides a subtext throughout, but the greater argument Tyndale makes here and elsewhere is that the Christian is under another rule, another governing dynamic altogether. "Love seeketh not her own profit (I Corinthians 13), but maketh a man forget himself, and to turn his profit to another man, as Christ sought not himself, or his own profit, but ours."[9]

The tone of *Wicked Mammon* is more gracious and instructive than it is biting and satirical. I found it to have a warm heart. Orthodox belief relies on a harmony between faith and works, without which neither is complete nor effective. It is upon this harmony that Tyndale muses.

> For God giveth no man his grace that he should let it lay still and do no good withal, but that he should increase it and multiply it with lending it to others, and with open declaring of it with the outward works, provoke and draw others to God.[10]

As his own marginal note says, "God's grace is to be exercised in us."[11]

The word *mammon* is Aramaic. It signifies "riches or temporal goods, and namely, all superfluity, and all that is above necessity, and that which is required unto our necessary uses, wherewith a man may help another without undoing or hurting himself."[12] "Wicked" implies its unrighteous use. "Riches are called evil," Tyndale wrote, "because evil men bestow them amiss and misuse them."[13] To have wealth is not criminal, but to have excess (superfluity) and not tend to your neighbor's need is.

Misleading title aside, the real theme of *Wicked Mammon* is justification by faith, which Tyndale argues well. The defense is mounted from the *Epistle of Paul to the Romans*. The following are perhaps the vanguard Scriptures, as translated in the 1526 Tyndale New Testament (original spelling).

> *For I am nott a shamed of the gospel of Christ because it is the power of God vnto salvacion to all that beleve namly to the iewe and also to the gentyle. For by it the right-ewesness [righteousness] which commeth of God is opened from faythe to faythe. As it is written: The iust shall live by fayth [The just shall live by faith].* (Romans 1:7)

> *We suppose therfore that a man is justified by fayth with out the dedes of the lawe.* (Romans 3:28)

> *Be cause therefore thatt we are iustifyed by fayth we are at peace with god thorowe oure lorde Jesus Christ.* (Romans 5:1)

The Epistle of Paul to the Romans was the epicenter of Reformist thought. Both Luther and Tyndale considered it the chief work of the New

Testament. Tyndale referred to it as the "most pure evangelion," a word that makes its first appearance in Tyndale.[14] It simply means "glad tidings" or gospel. In his *Prologue to the Epistle of Paul to the Romans*, Tyndale encouraged the reader not just to be familiar with this epistle, but to commit it to memory.

> Forasmuch as this epistle is the principal and most excellent part of the new testament and most pure evangelion, that is to say glad tidings, and that we call gospel, and also is a light and a way unto the whole scripture, I think it meet that every christian man not only know it, by rote and without the book, but also exercise himself therein evermore continually, as with the daily bread of the soul. No man verily can read it too oft, or study it too well; for the more it is studied, the easier it is; the more it is chewed, the pleasanter it is; and the more groundly it is searched, the preciouser things are found in it, so great treasure of spiritual things lieth hid therein.[15]

Daily bread of the soul. Tyndale thought of Romans as a bright light. Through an understanding of this epistle, the believer is better prepared to process all Scripture. Romans is both lamp and door.

Tyndale insists that works are of value, but that works are servant to faith. One declares the other in a living unity. In the earlier pages of *Wicked Mammon*, he describes a necessary condition of the heart that must preface all good works—Tyndale's "precious thing."

> There must first be in the heart of a man before he do any good works, a greater and more precious thing than all the good works in the world . . . That precious thing which must be in the heart, ere a man can work any good work, is the word of God, which in the gospel preacheth, profereth, and bringeth unto all that repent and believe, the favour of God in Christ. Whosoever heareth the word and believeth it, the same is thereby righteous, and thereby is given him the Spirit of God, which leadeth him unto all that is the will of God, and is loosed from the captivity and bondage of the devil, and his heart is free to love God, and hath lust [desire] to do the will of God. Therefore it is called the word of life, the

word of grace, the word of health, the word of redemption, the word of forgiveness, and the word of peace; he that heareth it not, or believeth it not, can by no means be made righteous before God.[16]

As hot as it preached, *Wicked Mammon* was considered heretical. It was also popular. The appetite, like the passion it aroused, was quick and consuming.

Tyndale wrote that good works are "the fruits of the Spirit (Galatians 5)," and before all works there must be first a "righteousness within the heart, the mother of all works, and from which they spring."[17] Good works and faith are known together. They are inseparable. "Thou canst never know or be sure of thy faith but by thy works, if works follow not."

In another place he said, "For where right faith is, there bringeth she forth good works; if there follow not good works, it is (no doubt) but a dream and an opinion or feigned faith."[18] Faith, therefore, is known by its fruit. We will know "the inward faith and love by the outward deeds. Deeds are the fruits of love, and love is the fruit of faith."[19]

Martin Luther described the Epistle of James as "a right strawy epistle without any evangelical sense." He felt that it stood counter to the writings of Paul and the other books of the New Testament with its implied insistence that works justify.

> *Ye see then how that of deeds a man is justified, and not of faith only . . . For as the body without the spirit is dead, even so faith without deeds is dead.* (James 2 TNT)

If the Epistle to the Romans was the high point of the New Testament, surely James was the lowest. Though Luther eventually rethought the option, he argued that this epistle of straw should be omitted from the New Testament canon altogether.

Tyndale did not share this sentiment with Luther.

In his *Prologue to the Epistle of James and Judas* (Jude), Tyndale wrote, "Faith which hath no good deeds following is a false faith, and none of that faith justifieth or receiveth forgiveness of sins."[20] Likewise, in *Wicked Mammon* he said that if works do not follow faith "it is a sure and an evident sign that there is no faith in the heart, but a dead imagination and dream which they falsely call faith."[21]

Again, it is the harmony, the active participation between faith and works that justifies the believer.

A Present Paradise

Tyndale's idea of eternity is consistent with his belief in the living Word. Heaven is not simply a remote paradise reserved for the righteous. For Tyndale, eternal life begins the very moment a person embraces the life of faith. "We are in eternal life already," he wrote, "and feel already in our hearts the sweetness thereof, and are overcome with the kindness of God and Christ and therefore love the will of God, and of love are ready to work freely."[22]

Heaven is a shared event. Each believer is Christ to his neighbor.[23] This rule of engagement implies a heaven that is not only close (or *nigh*), but interactive, palpable. Eden (צרן *Eden*) means "pleasure." Paradise (παραδεισό *paradeisos*) means essentially "an enclosed park." Eternity is to be enjoyed not in some distant otherworld, but here and now. Christ is the reality of a present paradise.

For Thine Is the Kingdom

The mere act of translation implies an intimacy with the Word of God, and Tyndale pursued the Word with tenacity, both as a translator and as a man of faith. His mind was thoroughly awash with the Scripture. "Seek the word of God in all things," he wrote, "and without the word of God do nothing, though it appear never so glorious. Whatsoever is done without the word of God count idolatry."[24]

To pursue God's Word is to pursue God, to join oneself intimately with God, which is the summit of the spiritual life.

God worketh with his word, and in his word. And as his word is preached, faith rooteth herself in the hearts of the elect, and as faith entereth, and the word of God is believed, the power of God looseth the heart from the captivity and bondage under sin, and knitteth and coupleth him to God, and to the will of God; altereth him, changeth him clean, fashioneth, and forgeth him anew, giveth him power to love, and to do that which before was impossible for him either to love or do, and turneth him into a new nature, so that he loveth that which he before hated, and hateth that which he before loved; and is clean altered, and changed, and contrary disposed; and is knit and coupled fast to God's will, and naturally bringeth forth good works, that is to say, that which God commandeth to do, and not things of his own imagination.[25]

The true mirror will respond to the one who looks into it. To know God is to ultimately know oneself, to throw off counterfeits. Once God and man are knit together, once the law of God is "written and graved in his heart," words like *obedience* and *submission* hardly apply. God does not have to formally command anything. His command lives in his Word, and rightly governs the heart in a man.

"He that hath God's Spirit understandeth it," Tyndale wrote. "He feeleth that good works are nothing but fruits of love, compassion, mercifulness, and of a tenderness of heart which a Christian hath to his neighbor, and that love springeth of that love which he hath to God."[26] A believer's love for God is confessed in his love for his neighbor. "How much I love the commandment [to love my neighbor], so much I love God."[27]

> *The life of a Christian man is inward between him and God, and properly is the consent of the spirit to the will of God and to the honour of God. And God's honour is the final end of all good works.*
>
> — WILLIAM TYNDALE, *THE PARABLE OF THE WICKED MAMMON*

It is within this paradigm that faith and works meet, agree, and consent one with the other, where they find their true measure and their rightful place in the order of God. He that "worketh of pure love, without seeking of reward, worketh truly."[28] Works declare love.

Love makes all things common. "Every man is [the] other's debtor, and every man is bound to minister to his neighbor, and to supply his neighbor's lack of that wherewith God hath endowed him."[29]

Love Me, Love My Dog

One curiously long paragraph in *Wicked Mammon* stood out among the others. I am partial to the canine for a book load of reasons, but I particularly love the following quote for its love-me-love-my-dog charm. Here Tyndale joins lightness and gravity, and he does so effectively. He makes a lovely argument and, like Shakespeare, throws in a dog for general appeal.

> He that loveth not my dog loveth not me. Not that a man should love my dog first, but if a man loved me, the love wherewith he loved me would compel him to love my dog, though my dog deserved it not, yea, though the dog had done him a displeasure, yet if he loved me, the same love would refrain him from revenging himself, and cause him to refer the vengeance unto me . . . If I loved God purely, nothing that my neighbour could do were able to make me either hate him, either to take vengeance on him myself, seeing that God hath commanded me to love him, and to remit all vengeance unto him.[30]

Is it metaphor? Is it life as art, the mirror held up to nature? In the throes of composition, or in negotiating his English thought with the Greek one, does the gypsy translator look down occasionally from his writing table at the stray collected at his feet? Is it medication enough for the long hours of solitude? Does it have a name? *Sir Thomas* perhaps? *Harry?* or *Martin?* Be assured, Tyndale has that levity in him.

While there is no documentation that says Tyndale had a dog, there are none that deny it either. He mentions "my dog" four times, and with a finesse deserving of the species. For the point he makes, he chose his creature wisely.

Oddly enough, the *Oxford English Dictionary* credits Bernard of Clairvaux (1090–1153), with the first usage of the phrase "Love me, love my dog," (*qui me amat, amat et canem meum*). This is both unexpected and fortunate. To hear it echo in Tyndale is a personal delight.

Saint Bernard (as the Catholic knows him) was a frail and yet driven little monk who loved God with such severity he would often forget to eat. When he was older, his taste buds were so ruined he could hardly tell if he was drinking lamp oil or water. But here is another man of genius, a man of incandescent spirit and wit, another literary, like Tyndale, whose art flowed from his faith. And that distinction alone makes Bernard useful to our inquiry.

Bernard and Tyndale shared an uncommon resolve, both as men of God, and as writers, artists. Desire within each of these men was formidable. Like Bernard, Tyndale's art was bound to his spiritual life. The one empowered the other. Like Tyndale, Bernard could be a difficult piece of work. He rattled kingdoms down in his time. But he was well acquainted with and wrote profusely about a God of love. "The reason for loving God is God himself," he wrote, "and the measure of love due to him is immeasurable love."[31] For Bernard, the reward is in the loving itself. In this, he anticipates the English translator.

Like Tyndale, Bernard was also lyrical. From him flowed a powerful hymnody. "O Sacred Head Now Wounded" and "Jesus, the Very Thought of Thee" are examples of Bernard's craft.

Tyndale's next installment was even more impactive, and it came with a bright heat, a lovely hand, a timeless wordcraft, a deep probing eye, and, at last, the favor of a future queen.

A Book for Me and All Kings to Read

*I loved her not a little, for the love which I judged
her to bear towards God and his gospel.*

— Thomas Cranmer, *in a letter to Henry VIII about Anne Boleyn*

TO THE CATHOLIC CHURCH SHE WAS YOKO ONO, THE INTERLOPER, the harpy sent to turn the prince's head and break up the band. Eustace Chapuys, the chatty imperial ambassador, when he wasn't calling her "the concubine," he and others (many others) were calling her "the whore." Some claimed Anne Boleyn was a witch, that among other things, the extra digit, the sixth finger seemed to say so.*

But she held the gaze of the king, and the rest just didn't really matter.

---

* While such rumors were exaggerated, especially by her enemies, one of Anne's attendants, Anne Gainsford, admitted that there was a rudimentary sixth nail "upon the side of her nail upon one of her fingers, which yet was so small, by the report of those that have seen her, [and] which was usually hidden." (Alison Weir, *Henry VIII: The King and His Court*, 258)

Anne Boleyn's legend seemed to glow with an intense, feverish, brilliant, but tragic light. She was not the paragon of beauty, though some contemporary observers described her as "very beautiful," and with "an excellent figure," "young and good looking." One priest said the king's mistress, Bessie Blount, was "more beautiful." Anne was not the current fashion. She was by no means the delicate little creature, with the "peaches and cream complexion and fluttering eyes."[1]

The Venetian diplomat Francesco Sanuto described her, saying, "Madame Anne is not one of the handsomest women in the world; she is of middling stature, swarthy complexion, long neck, wide mouth, bosom not much raised, and in fact has nothing but the English king's great appetite and her eyes, which are black and beautiful."[2] She was witty, feisty, ambitious, and confident. In spite of the descriptions favorable or unfavorable, she had what might be called sex appeal.

For the poet Thomas Wyatt, Anne was the true lady of his imagination. He wept at her death, watching, as he was, from his own prison cell in the Tower. In many ways Anne Boleyn was exceptional, beyond her own times.

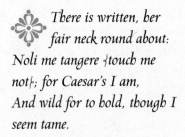

There is written, her fair neck round about:
Noli me tangere {touch me not}; for Caesar's I am,
And wild for to hold, though I seem tame.

– SIR THOMAS WYATT (1503–1542),
"WHOSO LIST TO HUNT"

She was a friend to the English Reformation, a prime mover. She was certainly a prime mover of Henry. She was the captain's captain. Spiritually, between Henry and Anne, she was the experimenter, untangled and unbound from the old religion. According to Joanna Denny, "Anne Boleyn was the catalyst for the Reformation, the initiator of the Protestant religion in England."[3] Whether or not this assertion is completely accurate, Anne was at the center of the king's little problem.

Henry was conflicted with an obsessive desire for a male heir (whom Catherine did not give him), with the nagging thought that he had sinned by marrying his dead brother's wife (against the injunction in Leviticus that came with a curse of childlessness), and with the rage of his own ardor inspired by Anne Boleyn. Out of this confliction, England eventually broke with Rome, the first large step toward religious autonomy.

Assigning parenthood to any historical movement is always a spurious practice (the father of this, the mother of that). In spite of our need to assign credit (or blame), it tends to be a confused genetic, if not unknown. Still, for Henry VIII and his break with Rome, Anne Boleyn played an essential part. It doesn't seem to happen without her.

To compress this history, Henry Tudor, second son of Henry VII, became Prince of Wales (the immediate heir to the English throne) at the death of his older brother, Arthur, who had married Catherine of Aragon only months before he died. Henry had been designated for a life in the Church.

At the death of Henry VII in 1509, the seventeen-year-old became King Henry VIII. Before he became the monster of his latter years, he was tall, attractive, well built. He had reddish-gold hair, and was feverishly ambitious. He was incredibly popular and showed genuine promise in his earlier years.

Bluff Hal was everything his father was not. This was both good and bad. His father had been very wise with money—frugal—almost miserly by the end of his reign. H7 left his son a handsome fortune; H8 was a money hose. H7 was hesitant to go to war; H8 couldn't seem to find one quick enough. All the restraints upon him as a prince were now relaxed, which made him somewhat reckless, or too daring as a young king. No lack of ego, he wanted to prove his greatness to the world. And he did achieve the fame he wanted, but not exactly as he might have first imagined.

By an agreement his father had made with the king of Spain a few years earlier, the young prince took his brother's widow, Catherine of Aragon, as his queen. Catherine was six years older than Henry. She was the daughter of Ferdinand and Isabella, the financiers of Columbus the year after Henry was born. The next twenty years of married life for Henry and Catherine sped along peacefully.

Then Anne Boleyn came along.

According to Henry's own words, he was "struck with the dart of love." Their relationship began around 1526. Henry's motto that year was

Declare je nos (Declare I dare not). Anne was twenty. Henry was thirty-five. The neglected Catherine was an aging forty-one.

The dart-wounded young king quite literally turned over an entire world for Anne. A master tactician as her daughter would prove to be (the future Elizabeth I), Anne maddened Henry with her refusals, with her carrot-stick playfulness. She not only refused him sexually, she would not consent to be his mistress as acknowledged at court. (Her sister Mary had been mistress to Henry at one time, and discarded.)

It would seem that sex, or the lack of it, moved the Reformation forward in England.

Her eyes dark, impenetrable, her wit scintillate, her spirit unbroken— truly a young woman with sizzle and appeal, whatever the perception—Anne Boleyn held power in England. Not to mention that Queen Catherine, already much shorter and much older than Anne, was much rounder as well.

All this was for a season only. Once Henry's ardor cooled, as we might say, even Anne knew she was in real danger.

For whatever the reasons, by breaking away from the Roman Church and declaring himself head of the Church of England, Henry VIII set a powerful precedent, with daring that was unheard of at the time, even for spoiled boy-kings.

> *Whoever could help in its execution would do a meritorious work since it would prove . . . a remedy for the heretical doctrines and practices of the Concubine {Anne Boleyn}—the principal cause of the spread of Lutheranism in this country.*
>
> – Eustace Chapuys, imperial ambassador, letter to his master, Charles V, the Holy Roman Emperor, concerning the assassination of Anne Boleyn

Henry's break with Rome had layers and layers of meaning, some more conspicuous than others, some latent. And there were certainly more elements in the break than lust or the desire for a male heir, but these were the initiators.

The divorce of Henry Tudor and Catherine of Aragon is a secondary event; but the divorce of England and the popedom is a primary event, one of the great watersheds of history, a creative act (so to speak) which still exercises a profound influence over the destinies of mankind . . . it was only by emancipating themselves from this priestly dictatorship that modern nations could advance safely in the pathos of liberty, order, and greatness.[4]

Anne Boleyn supported the trafficking of Tyndale's New Testament into England. In 1534, when she was queen and the English New Testament was still an outlaw Bible, she not only had a copy, she kept it on a lectern in her chamber for her ladies to read. Her copy was printed on vellum with gold leaf on the edges. It was hand colored with woodcut illuminations with the words *Anna, Regina Anglia* (Anne, Queen of England) engraved on them.

She also had a copy of Tyndale's *The Obedience of a Christian Man*, a book that was precious to her.

You Kiss by the Book

There are two accounts of how *Obedience* came into the possession of the king. Both include Anne. The details overlap, which usually suggests there is only one story. After so many centuries there remains a bright youthfulness about it—as the presence of something playful and innocent in a world of monsters—something out of *Othello*, perhaps.

Anne loaned her copy of *Obedience* to one of her attendants, a young woman named Anne Gainford. Ms. Gainford had a suitor, a boyfriend, a young man named George Zouche. Seeing his beloved rapt in the book as she was (and, I suppose, not so rapt in him), George playfully tore it out of her hands and would not let her have it back in spite of her protests (carrot and stick was a popular pastime in Henry's court).

George started reading the book and became rather taken with it himself. Imagine, book in one hand, and fending off his lovely Anne with the other, ignoring her little cries, her tearful protests, his eyes never leaving the page.

The dean of the Chapel Royal, Richard Sampson, happened to see

George reading the book during a service and demanded it from him. Reformer literature was forbidden, particularly anything by William Tyndale. And *Obedience* was, according to Thomas More, a "holy book of disobedience whereby we were taught to disobey Christ's holy catholic church."[5]

The good dean took the book directly to Cardinal Wolsey, and Wolsey took it directly to the king. The idea might have been to win points with his master while undermining Anne Boleyn. But Wolsey had not been able to secure a divorce for Henry, so his influence had weakened significantly.

When Ms. Boleyn asked Ms. Gainford for the book, the panicked young maid fell on her knees and confessed all that had happened. Anne did not get angry with the couple, nor was she sorry that it happened. "But, well," she said, "it shall be the dearest book that ever the dean or cardinal took away."[6]

Ever aware of her own influence with Henry, the future queen went to the king and on her knees asked for his help on the matter. Shortly after, the king gave her the book. She then requested with feeling that he read it for himself. (She had marked passages with her nail that she thought would be of particular interest to him.) Henry read the book, and delighted in it. So much so that he said, "This is a book for me and all kings to read."[7] Unintentionally on the part of its author, the book appealed to the most royal vanity of Henry VIII.

> God hath made the king in every realm judge over all, and over him there is no judge. He that judgeth the king judgeth God and he that layeth hands on the king layeth hands on God, and he that resisteth the king resisteth God and damneth God's law and ordinance.[8]

In another version of the story above, *Obedience* is not named. It says simply that the book deals with "controversies concerning religion, and specially of the authority of the pope and his clergy, and of their doings against kings and states."[9] In spite of Henry's endorsement, the book remained outside the law. Still, *The Obedience of a Christian Man* was one of two books commonly found on offenders (the other being Tyndale's New Testament).

It Is Forbidden Thee in Pain of Life

The Obedience of a Christian Man was released 2 October 1528, five months after *Wicked Mammon*. Next to the Scripture, it is Tyndale's most important work. He acquired a taste for this kind of writing with *Wicked Mammon*. While they share similar themes, *Obedience* is a more seasoned work, with a more polished fire. Print was the one place Tyndale did not have to hide or conceal himself. With the translation, there was always a measure of restraint. Tyndale could exercise his linguistic prowess, certainly, but only within the limits of the original manuscript.

Obedience, however, is a pulpit.

It was a dangerous book, both to write and to read. Tyndale makes this clear from the first few sentences of the preface. "Let it not make thee despair neither yet discourage thee O reader, that it is forbidden thee in pain of life and goods or that it is made breaking of the King's peace or treason unto His Highness to read the word of thy soul's health."[10] He has no illusions about the penalty of his chosen profession. But *Obedience*, as *Wicked Mammon* and the translation, is a matter of his own obedience, his obligation to a higher throne.

Death followed this book around as aggressively as it followed its author.

True to its title, it indexes and expands on the duty (obedience) of the believer. Throughout, Tyndale argues the supremacy of the Scripture over the Church, the supremacy of the king over the state, and other specific types of obedience we will name.

Every page of the book is alive with Scripture. Here again Tyndale fuses the Word of God so agreeably with his own words that it is difficult to know where one ends and the other begins.

Popeholiness

Obedience is divided in three sections: a preface he calls "William Tyndale otherwise called William Hychins' unto the reader," precedes a prologue. The main body of the book is divided into smaller sections, with subtitles like "The obedience of all degrees proved by God's word and first of children unto their elders," "The obedience of wives unto their husbands," "The obedience of servants unto their masters," and one that got the attention of Henry VIII, "The obedience of subjects unto kings, princes and rulers."

Tyndale briefly explores (the following are section titles): "The office of a father and how he should rule," "The office of a husband and how he ought to rule," "The office of a master and how he ought to rule," "The duty of landlords," and "The duty of kings and of the judges and officers."

There are also sections on "Prayer," "Understanding the scripture," "Against the Pope's power," the "Sacraments" (which for Tyndale there are only two, baptism and the Lord's Supper). He offers his opinion on confession, penance, absolution, wedlock, contrition, confirmation, miracles, and worshipping and praying to the saints.

To the pope—that "Satan and Antichrist"—Tyndale gives no quarter whatsoever. He mimics Thomas More in repetition and harshness, for he hardly lets up in a few hundred pages.

He wrote, for instance, that if St. Paul had only preached about certain abuses and left circumcision and other essentials of the Jewish faith alone, he might have lived a bit longer. In the same way, if Tyndale and the other reformers had merely preached about corruption, lechery, and extortion, and left the essentials alone (sacraments), they, too, might have fared better.

> But touch the scab of hyprocrisy or popeholiness and go about to utter their false doctrine wherewith they reign as gods in the heart and consciences of men and rob them, not of lands, goods and authority only, but also of the testament of God and salvation that is in Christ: then helpeth thee neither God's word, nor yet if thou didst miracles, but that thou art, not an heretic only and hast the devil within thee, but also a breaker of the King's peace and a traitor.[11]

At the end of the preface to the reader, Tyndale wrote, "Finally that this threatening and forbidding the lay people to read the Scripture is not for love of your souls (which they care for as the fox doth for the geese) is evident and clearer than the sun."

Tyndale insisted that the Church would rather the believer read Robin Hood, Hercules, or Hector than read the Scriptures in their own tongue "with a thousand histories and fables of love and wantonness and of ribaldry as filthy as the heart can think, to corrupt the minds of you withal, clean contrary to the doctrine of Christ and of his apostles."

But it is to the king that *Obedience* gives its greatest courtesy, its lowest bow. Tyndale's enemies have accused him of sedition, saying that the presence of a vernacular Bible is a source of insurrection. Tyndale turns this accusation back on his accusers. To his enemies he replies that kings are "dupes and puppets" of the pope.

> Let kings defend their subjects from the wrongs of other nations, but pick no quarrels for every trifle, no let not our most holy father make them no more drunk with vain names, with caps of maintenance like baubles, as it were popetry for children, to beggar their realms and to murder their people, for defending of our holy father's tyranny.[12]

Kings have been given power for good. Like the Old Testament judges, they are to execute the commandments of God. "For the law is God's and not the king's. The king is but a servant to execute the law of God and not to rule after his own imagination."

This may have proved more pill than Henry had throat to swallow, but he was pleased with the little book nonetheless. Again, Anne Boleyn may have tuned Henry for the occasion.

Prudential Bargaining

In *Wicked Mammon*, Tyndale exposed the church's "mistaken reliance" on works, suggesting that such wholesale misdirection encourages superstition, which obscures true spirituality, making itself equal to it. He also implied a kind of spiritual commercialism, the bargaining of salvation central to medieval Christianity, an incentive faith based on the principles of accounting. It was the life of faith in a man reduced to measurable, exchangeable goods that outraged the reformers.

Purgatory was the medieval cash cow. One of Martin Luther's complaints, which mirrored Tyndale's, was shaped in the form of a question. "Why doesn't the pope empty purgatory for the sake of holy love and of the dire need of the souls that are there?" Luther thought indulgences a shameful ransom, the wretched suspension of a soul in torment, particularly for the sake of "miserable money with which to build a church."[13] Tyndale would agree. As C. S. Lewis explained:

> Heaven, hell, and purgatory had been too long and too vividly presented. If in the resulting religion, with its fasts, pilgrimages, penances, and treasuries of "merits," Tyndale could see nothing but a system of prudential bargaining, I will not say that he was right: but he was not grossly, nor inexplicably wrong. From all this spiritual commercialism—this system in which the natural and economic man could be as natural and economic about religion as about anything else—he had found freedom in his doctrine of faith. Here at last a man could do something without a business motive.[14]

In *Obedience* Tyndale wrote rather scathingly, "Through covetousness with feigned words shall they [the clergy] make merchandise of you." He accuses them of taking away the Scripture and with it "faith, hope, peace, unity, love and concord." It doesn't end there. The "pattering of their prayers increaseth daily. Their service, as they call it, waxeth longer and longer and the labour of their lips greater, new saints, new feasts and new holy days . . . But they take away first God's word with faith, hope, peace, unity, love and concord then house and land, rent and fee, tower and town, goods and cattle, and the very meat out of men's mouths."

According to the *OED*, *purgatory* is "a condition or place of spiritual cleansing and purification; a place or state where the souls of those who die in a state of grace undergo such punishment as is still due to forgiven sins, and expiate their unforgiven venial [pardonable] sins." According to Tyndale, it was an invention of a greedy spirituality. "But thou must suffer for every sin seven years in purgatory, which is as hot as hell, except thou buy it out of the pope."[15]

> Covetousness is the conclusion: for covetousness and ambition that is to say, lucre and desire of honour is the final end of all false prophets and of all false teachers. Look upon the Pope's false doctrine, what is the end thereof and what seek they thereby? Wherefore serveth Purgatory but to purge thy purse and to poll thee and rob both thee and they heirs of house and lands and of all thou hast, that they may be in honour. Serveth not their pardons for the same purpose? Whereto pertaineth praying to the saints but to offer unto their bellies?
>
> Wherefor serveth confession, but to sit in thy conscience and to make thee fear and tremble at whatsoever they dream and that thou worship them as Gods . . . And of their false expounding of Scripture and drawing it contrary unto the example of Christ and the Apostles and holy prophets unto their damnable covetousness and filthy ambition take an example.[16]

As we might conclude, Tyndale's cut, like his aggravation, is getting sharper with each round. His next installment, triggered by Thomas More, is pure stiletto. Even so, the lyricism in *Obedience* was much more pronounced, particularly as the text began to pray.

> I serve thee not because thou art my master or my king; for hope of reward or fear of pain, but for the love of Christ. For the children of faith are under no law but are free. The spirit of Christ hath written the lively law of love in their hearts which driveth them to work of their own accord freely and willingly, for the great love's sake only which they see in Christ, and therefore need they no law to compel them. Christ is all in all things to them that believe, and the cause of all love.[17]

As his passion rises, so does the music it makes. As the heat around him accelerates, so does the occasional aria. His rhapsody is in season.

The Soft Warm Middle

Tyndale wrote of the behavior of children to their parents, but the formula applies to every relationship. Whatever the dynamic between individuals, Christ is the center. Christ is the currency of exchange, particularly when there are no words. He is the rule of community. It is to Christ that we speak, and act, and serve in the other person, that we obey or disobey.

> Understand also that whatsoever thou doest unto them (beit good or bad) [that is, to parents, but also to wives or husbands, to your neighbor, to servant or master] thou doest unto God. When thou pleasest them thou pleasest God: when thou displeasest them thou displeasest God: when they are angry with thee, God is angry with thee, neither is it possible for thee to come unto the favour of God again (no though all the angels of heaven pray for thee) until you have submitted thyself unto thy father and mother again.[18]

While expounding themes he began in *Wicked Mammon*, the lesson is so raw and immediate, so new to the English ear and to English spirituality, that Tyndale's occasional repetition is a forgivable offense.

It is not difficult to detect Tyndale's theology. Again, he says my neighbor *is* myself. My neighbor *is* Christ to me. To seek Christ is to seek Christ *in* and *through* my neighbor. To know and to love God is to know and to love God *in* and *through* my neighbor. To love my neighbor is to love that which God loves. In loving my neighbor I am loving God, I am living in the obedience of God, the order he has established from the beginning.

For all that is admittedly unattractive about *Obedience*, with its sudden pugilistic tone (against the pope particularly), its harsh offensive, the book nonetheless has a strong immovable interior. "God is

> ❀ *Thou must love Christ above all things.*
>
> – WILLIAM TYNDALE, *THE OBEDIENCE OF A CHRISTIAN MAN*

love." This is how Tyndale knows him, how he translates him, how he processes and metabolizes his thought. And this is what gives *Obedience* its soft warm middle, in spite of its prickly outer skin.

With only a few rare exceptions, the medieval and early modern Christian knew no such God. A God of love was strategically unprofitable.

It is Tyndale who made the introductions.

Tyndale's New Testament introduced a warm, generous, loving God, a meddling God, a God truly interested in the affairs of everyday life, a God who cared for the neglected, those consigned to the margins. Majesty at home with the plowboy and the shipwright; high royalty breaking bread at the table of the fishwife and the egg vendor.

> *No clergyman besides Tyndale saw fit to give the layman his due, to impress upon him his personal relation to Scripture, i.e., that it was indeed for his hands and eyes to hold and to interpret. . . . Tyndale did more than just offer a look into the scripture, he showed the possibility of a personal relationship with it.*
>
> – DAVID GINSBERG, *PLOUGHBOYS VERSUS PRELATES*

With Tyndale's New Testament came the subtle message that the Church had long deserted the layman. The Church, by "alienating the common man from the Bible, has, according to Tyndale, alienated itself from man."[19]

It is interesting to note that one long-standing image of the Savior was usurped by a newer and more attractive one. Jesus was no longer the agonized, bleeding, silent, suspended, crucified figure, but a personal, communicative God; a divine, benevolent monarch; a most indifferent God who cared nothing for the usual social conventions—wealth, family name, or how big one's house is. This representation of Christ was counter to the Roman image that inspired judgment and torment.

One modern historian noted that "the affective devotion of the English has been free of lachrymose [tearful, weeping] or penitential excesses," that even the English prayer books "consistently invoke the incarnation rather than the Passion."[20]

Continuing his "every man is Christ to another" theme from *Wicked Mammon*, the following text from *Obedience* is an amplification of Colossians 3:11.

In Christ there is neither French nor English: but the Frenchman is the Englishman's own self, and the English the Frenchman's own self. In Christ there is neither father, nor son: neither master nor servant: neither husband, nor wife: neither king, nor subject: but the father is the son's own self, and the subject is the king's own self and so forth. I am thou thyself and thou art I myself and can be no nearer or kin. We are all sons of God, all Christ's servants bought with his blood and every man to other Christ his own self.

I love thee not now, because thou art my father and hast done so much for me or my mother and hast borne me and given me suck of thy breasts (for so do Jews and Saracens) but because of the great love that Christ has showed me. I serve thee not because thou art my master or my king; for hope of reward or fear of pain, but for the love of Christ . . . Christ is all in all things to them that believe, and the cause of all love.

Here seest thou that we are Christ's brethren and even Christ himself, and whatsoever we do one to another that we do to Christ. If we be in Christ we work for no worldly purpose, but of love.[21]

Tyndale makes it personal. His Christ is personal. His is an accessible God—made palpable through my neighbor—a verbal God, a legible, English-speaking God. The plowboy is orphaned no longer.

When I first read these lines, it was difficult to imagine an opposing view, particularly by an institution that was supposed to cherish and teach this view. As baffling as it may seem, the Roman Church somehow read blasphemy in the above text. It threatened the old order of things, things that to them were unquestionable. It was an evil, therefore, to be exposed, routed, and destroyed along with its author. This chronic deafness was the going dis-ease of medieval Christianity.

So the church had no choice but to seek among them a champion who would do battle with the upstart-expatriate-translator-heretic. There was none better than Sir Thomas More.

10

Well Done

*And for heretics, as they be, the clergy doth denounce
them; and, as they be well worthy, the temporality doth
burn them; and after the fire of Smithfield hell doth
receive them, where the wretches burn forever.*

—Thomas More, *The Confutation of Tyndale's Answer*

IT WAS NO REAL SURPRISE TO DISCOVER THAT SIR THOMAS MORE
introduced the word *paradox* into English.[1] And, oddly enough, it made its
first appearance in his *Confutation of Tyndale's Answer*. For all his "champion
of the conscience" reputation, his "man for all seasons" fame, the reformers brought out something small and mean in Sir Thomas, something
vicious, merciless, and unrelenting.

Pope Paul II (1920–2005) praised More for defending the Church
against Henry VIII's "uncontrolled despotism . . . in the name of pri-
macy of conscience, of the individual's freedom vis-à-vis political power."[2]
Truth is, More "was intolerant of all dissident opinion."[3] He is renowned
as a martyr for individual conscience, and yet it was a right he denied to
those he persecuted as chancellor. The heretic, he said, was "damned and

135

defamed already by their own obstinate malice" and should "be kept but for the fire, first here, and after in hell."[4]

While the sentiment was not held by everyone, it had a particular friend in Sir Thomas. Monsters are a product of a monstrous age, certainly, but I suspect one has to have the monster in one already. At the trial of Thomas Bilney, More made it clear that the burning of heretics was justified by the violence they did to the Catholic Church.[5]

"What did Nature ever create milder, sweeter, and happier than the genius of Thomas More?" As William Manchester noted in his book, *A World Lit Only by Fire*, this statement by Erasmus perhaps said more about the Dutchman's generosity than it did More's true character. "It was not an age," Manchester wrote, "when men of mild and sweet disposition rose to power; a savage streak was almost prerequisite for achievement."[6]

> *{Thomas More} was the person of the greatest virtue these islands ever produced.*
>
> – DR. SAMUEL JOHNSON

At the burning of six heretics, More said it was "lawful, necessary, and well done."[7] I am almost certain that in spite of his reputation for humor, he meant that the execution itself was sufficiently carried out, that divine justice had been served.

Thomas More replaced Cardinal Wolsey as chancellor of England in October 1529. While Wolsey himself was anything but tolerant of the heretic, he was at least a "humane and often kindly man," and didn't quite have the appetite for burning that More did. John F. Davis, in an article in *The Historical Journal*, wrote that "More succeeded in halting the Reformation in England where Wolsey had largely condoned it." For one as savvy and relentless in a courtroom as More, the heretic was simply on the wrong side of that law, and had to be punished to its full limits.

Wolsey could be cruel. He had an indefatigable energy, and could slither among the best of his kind in the European courts. He burned his share of books, certainly, but burning flesh was a passion Wolsey never seemed to cultivate. And his time was cut short. The same could be said of Cuthbert Tunstall. For all his zeal against the reformer, Tunstall "stopped short of sending men to the stake."[8]

As we have already seen, following the rise in popularity of Tyndale's New Testament, Wolsey incited a severe persecution. But the fat chancellor fell from his great height and mismanaged the favor of his king within a year or so after. For all of Wolsey's achievement, and that he was able to change his stars (from a butcher's son in Ipswich to the second most powerful man in the kingdom); for all his acquisitions of wealth, property, and position; and all his

> ❧ *On 4 April 1519, in Coventry, England, six people were burned at the stake for teaching their children the Lord's Prayer and the Ten Commandments in English. The orphaned children were then dispersed to other homes with a severe warning.*
>
> – JOHN FOXE, *Actes and Monuments*

acts both great and infamous, at his end he put up no resistance. He knew his prince too well, and was almost docile against all his former greatness.[9] When the king needed a scapegoat, Wolsey was available. He had always been H8's "get it for me" guy.

Following More's replacement of Wolsey, John Stokesley replaced Cuthbert Tunstall as bishop of London the next year (1530). Unlike their immediate predecessors, More and Stokesley were men of like passion. Stokesley was known as the "hammer" of heretics. We will hear from Stokesley again at the end of our tale.

More, accepting the mantle from Wolsey, was now in a strategic position to do something permanent about the heretics, something more to his own tastes. He rallied the power of church and state behind him, "to crush them and their beliefs, and if need be to burn heresy out of England with fire."[10] (He was not speaking figuratively.) Beyond that, whatever he couldn't burn he would drown—with ink and vitriol.

England was threatening to implode from all the mounting pressure. Not to mention the events in the life of its prince. Unknown to itself at the time, English piety was moving steadily toward its inevitable rupture. And Henry was on a swift downward spiral toward insanity.

We are going to look now at a few men in England who burned in More's wrath. It is worth the moment's digression to note their names, what they believed, and what they suffered—Thomas Bilney, Richard Bainham, John Tewkesbury, and John Frith, men who burned *with* and ultimately *for* their faith.

The Gentle Scholar

"If English reform lacked a Luther or a Zwingli," one modern source suggested, "at least it had Thomas Bylney."[11] Bylney, or Bilney, the "gentle Cambridge scholar," was about the same age as Tyndale. He earned his degree at Trinity Hall and was ordained in 1519. His small compact frame may have earned him the epithet of "little Bilney," but he preached hot and loved Scripture more than life itself.

"Finally," Foxe wrote, in his *Actes and Monuments*, "as he [Bilney] himself was greatly inflamed with the love of true religion and godliness, even so again was in his heart an incredible desire to allure many unto the same, desiring nothing more, than that he might stir up and encourage any to the love of Christ, and sincere religion. Neither were his labours vain; for he converted many of his fellows unto the knowledge of the gospel."[12]

Some questioned whether or not he was a true Protestant. He accepted the Presence in the Eucharist, and yet he expressed doubts about the papacy. Like Tyndale, Bilney had been born under a Borgia pope. Paternity claims being what they are, both popular and spurious, some have called Bilney the "Father of the English Reformation," a claim for which there may be some truth. (As implied earlier, I tend to dismiss most "fatherhood" claims, whatever they might be. Such claims seem to vary from camp to camp. For instance, some will say that John Wycliffe was the "Father of the English Bible," others say Tyndale. In a way they are both true. But that only leaves the rest of us to imagine a joint custody, which can be confusing and messy.)

It was after reading the Greek New Testament by Erasmus that Bilney seems to have had a major inward conversion and turned toward reform. The Word of God became the chief study of his life. Bilney said,

> Scripture began to be more pleasant unto me than the honey or the honeycomb; wherein I learned that all my labours, my fasting and watching, all the redemption of masses and pardons, being done without truth in Christ, who alone saveth his people from their sins; these I say, I learned to be nothing else but even, as St. Augustine saith, a hasty and swift running out of the right way.[13]

He ate one meal a day. The other meal he took to those less fortunate than himself, either to the "lazar cots," that is, a home for lepers whom he not only fed but whom he helped with their sheets and clothing as well. He also ministered to those in prison.

Bilney and Tyndale and rare others like them took the priesthood the Church vested them with and lived as true priests, reaching out at the ragged hem of culture, among the detritus and wreckage, and general ruined life.

Thomas Bilney endured four trials for heresy. Unfortunately for Bilney, Thomas More argued for the prosecution. Bilney ultimately abjured, that is, he renounced any possible Protestant affiliation. He was then forced to copy the articles listed and sign them (this was a legal hook in case he changed his mind, for there was no mercy granted beyond that, no second chance). He was still punished, but the greater offence to Bilney and others like him was the disgrace, the forced humiliation, for which bearing the fagot (a bundle of sticks bound together) and throwing the heretical books (Tyndale's) into the fire was small.

Bilney's was an inward punishment of a much deeper sort.

The thought of abjuration eventually broke his heart. He had spent time in the Tower of London and had allowed Thomas More and others the satisfaction of his fallen music. He had even denounced Tyndale's New Testament and *The Obedience of a Christian Man*. But Bilney was suddenly altered. He began to rethink his denials. His preaching took on a renewed conviction, an incendiary charm that unsettled the nearby clergy, who succeeded at last in physically dragging Bilney from the pulpit.

The Church finally had enough of Master Bilney. For an abjured heretic to relapse was certain death. He had given out copies of Tyndale's Bible and *Obedience*, and told his friends that he was leaving Trinity to "go up to Jerusalem," a reference to Christ on his path to the cross. Brian Moynahan noted that this was the action of a "man who was seeking out his own death."[14]

Bilney was taken in March 1531 and made to stand before the bishop of Norwich. He was convicted of heresy and turned over to the secular power, but not before being degraded from the priesthood (the removing of vestments, scraping of the hands and other anointed body parts).

The following account from *Actes and Monuments* allows us to accompany Bilney to the scaffold. Even from Foxe, the scene is immediate.

> And so he, going forth in the streets, giving much alms by the way by the hands of one of his friends, and accompanied by one Dr. Warner, doctor of divinity, and parson of Winterton, whom he did choose, as his old acquaintance, to be with him for his ghostly comfort, came at the last to the place of execution, and descended down from the hill to the same, apparelled in a layman's gown, with his sleeves hanging down and his arms out, his hair being piteously mangled at his degradation (a little single body in person, but always of a good upright countenance,) and drew near to the stake prepared . . .
>
> Then the officers put reeds and faggots about his body, and set fire on the reeds, which made a very great flame, which sparkled and deformed the visor of his face; he holding up his hands, and knocking upon his breast, crying sometimes "Jesus!" sometimes, Credo! which flame was blown away from him by the violence of the wind, which was that day, and two or three days before, notably great; in which it was said, that the fields were marvellously plagued by the loss of corn; and so, for a little pause, he stood without flame, the flame departing and recoursing thrice ere the wood took strength to be the sharper to consume him; and then he gave up the ghost, and his body, being

withered, bowed downward upon the chain. Then one of the officers, with his halberd, smote out the staple in the stake behind him, and suffered his body to fall into the bottom of the fire, laying wood upon it; and so he was consumed.[15]

Supplication of the Beggars

In 1528, the year Tyndale printed *The Parable of the Wicked Mammon* and *The Obedience of a Christian Man*, Simon Fish published his *Supplication of the Beggars*, which was also printed in Antwerp. Fish, like Tyndale and others, was living in exile, being "compelled of force to voyde his owne house, and so fled over the sea to Tyndale."[16]

Though *Supplication* was a sizzling little book, it was not considered Reformation literature as much as it was a rant against the clergy, against the "ravenous wolves going in herds' clothing, devouring the flock, the Bishops, Abbots, Priors, Archdeacons, Suffraganes, Priests, Monks, Canons, Friars, Pardoners and Summoners."[17]

In the *Supplication*, Fish attacked the Church's "inventions" or those devices they had created for the purpose of gain—fees for masses, dirges, hallowings, indulgences, tithes—things that were used by the church to plunder the laity of their coin. (Fish calculated the amount almost to the penny. It came to "43 thousand pounds and £333 6s 8d sterling"[18] per year.)

The formula was easy. If you do *this*, *that* will be awarded to you. Salvation could be bought, or earned. It was the gospel they were fed. Fish argued that without the Word of God, how were they to know otherwise?

And Fish asked an even better question. If the pope could receive money and release a soul from purgatory, why couldn't he do it without the cash? It is a logical conclusion that echoed both Luther and Tyndale.

There is no purgatory, but that it is a thing invented by the covetousness of the spirituality, only to translate all kingdoms from the other princes unto them, and that there is not one word spoken of it in all Holy Scripture. They say also, that if there were a purgatory, and also if that the pope with his pardons for money may deliver one soul; he may deliver him as well without money: if he may deliver one, he may deliver a thousand: if he may deliver a thousand, he may deliver them all, and so destroy purgatory. And then is he a cruel tyrant without all charity if he keeps them there in prison and in pain, till men give him money.[19]

Anne Boleyn, the not-just-yet-but-almost Mrs. H8, at the urging of her brother George, showed a copy of *Supplication* to the king, and Henry was so taken with it he offered protection for Fish and his wife. When the king asked who made it, Anne answered, "A certain subject of your[s], one Fish, who was fled out of the Realm for fear of the Cardinall [Wolsey]."*

The king kept the book in his pocket for three or four days. He then asked that the wife send for her husband, and without danger. When she came to the king to sue for her husband's safety, he asked where her husband was.

"If it like your grace, not far off."

"Fetch him, and he shall come and go safe without peril, and no man shall do him harm."

Fish returned to England in 1530. By this time, Thomas More had succeeded Cardinal Wolsey as chancellor of England. Because of the king's favor, there was a shield of protection around Fish, which More acknowledged, and left him alone. The king even took Fish hunting and riding with him, and told Fish to go home to his wife because she had been so importunate in his behalf. Fish answered saying, "I durst not so do, for fear of Sir Thomas More and Stokesley, Bishop of London." The king supposedly gave Fish his signet ring as a further sign to More that he be not harmed.

Fish's wife, however, fell into More's gaze. He left Fish alone, but the

---

* Between the years 1525–26, while Fish was still in London, he took part in a saucy little play at Grey's Inn where he played the role of a cardinal, strangely reminiscent of Cardinal Wolsey. It was apparently a lavish production and well liked, by all except for Wolsey. When the cardinal found out, he raged against the play and Fish. Some of the players went to prison. Others were scolded severely. Fish fled. The play was a tragedy (no name is given). It was probably staged, literally, against the cardinal. Fish was the only one with daring enough to play the role.

wife enjoyed no such royal protection. The new chancellor called her on one offense. Mrs. Fish apparently would not allow a group of friars who were in her home to say the Gospels in Latin, even though she would have allowed them to say them in English. Here the courtly More shows his own ounce of slither. "Whereupon the Lord Chancellor [More] though[t] he had discharged the man, yet leaving not his grudge towards the wife, the next morning sent his man for her to appear before him: who, had it not been for her young daughter, who then lay sick of the plague, she would have come to much trouble."[20]

Simon Fish died of the plague shortly after that time, in 1531. Within six months, Mrs. Fish married James Bainham. But where the Fish story amuses, if but darkly, Bainham's weeps.

James Bainham

James Bainham was a "gentleman, son to one Master Bainham, a knight of Gloucestershire" a man of "virtuous disposition and godly conversation." He studied law, and was "addicted" to prayer. He was an "earnest reader of the Scriptures, a maintainer of the godly, a visitor of the prisoners, liberal to scholars, very merciful to his clients, using equity and justice to the poor, very diligent in giving counsel to all the needy, widows, fatherless, and afflicted, without money or reward; briefly, a singular example to all lawyers."[21]

Being married to the wife of the late Simon Fish, Bainham fell into the gaze of Thomas More as well, and of course More suspected Bainham of heresy and had him arrested on 15 December 1531. Bainham was carried to More's home at Chelsea. He was accused of denying transubstantiation, denying the value of confession, then remanded to a "free prison" which is like being an obligatory or confined houseguest.

After a small amount of time, though, his patience being what it was, More gave up trying to convert Bainham and imprisoned him at Chelsea, bound him to a tree in his own backyard, then whipped him. Bainham refused to name any names or tell More where any of the "heretical" books were. Bainham's wife was put in prison as well.

More sent Bainham to the Tower of London and had him racked in his presence. He was treated so severely that he was left lame. Still, he would admit to nothing. When no manner of "tortures and torments" would work, he was taken back to Chelsea before John Stokesley, the bishop of London. He was examined on more questions—purgatory, praying to the saints, confession, and whether or not the Scripture had been hidden for eight hundred years. To the last item Bainham said that the Scripture was never "these eight hundred years past, so plainly and expressly declared unto the people, as it hath been within these six years." He was referring to the emergence of Tyndale's New Testament in 1526.

Stokesley then asked Bainham why the Scriptures had been better declared these six years. Bainham told them plainly that the Church had abused the Scriptures, making it say what they wanted it to say, distorting it. "Moreover," he said, "that the New Testament now translated into English doth preach and teach the word of God, and before that time men did preach but only that folks should believe as the church did believe."[22]

It was rather like the canary singing for the cobra.

When asked what he thought of Martin Luther, Bainham replied, "I think nothing of it." He was asked about his books, and for a judgment of Tyndale. He said he had in his possession a copy of Tyndale's New Testament, and that he "thought he offended God not in using and keeping the same." He also admitted to owning and reading *The Wicked Mammon, The Obedience of a Christian Man, The Practice of Prelates*, the *Answer to Sir Thomas More's Dialogue*, and other works.

Bainham thought the New Testament to be "utterly good, and that the people should have it as it is." In response to an inquiry from More that is not documented, Bainham denied any knowledge whatsoever that Tyndale was ever "a naughty [morally bad, wicked] fellow."[23]

The next day at Chelsea, before Stokesley and More, Bainham was asked if he would return to the Catholic faith from whence he had fallen, and to which he would yet be received. The "bosom of his mother was open for him." Foxe wrote that Bainham, "wavering in a doubtful perplexity, between life on the one hand and death on the other,"[24] gave in to his tormentors and abjured the very faith he had just championed before them.

Bainham signed a bill of abjuration. If one abjures, or recants, then returns to their error, they can be persecuted to the strictest limit of the law. The document read, "I voluntarily, as a true penitent person returned from my heresies, utterly abjure." He hesitated, was imprisoned again, then stood before the authorities again until he finally signed the document renouncing all that he had formerly believed.

"I will forsake all my articles, and will meddle no more with them." Of course he had to pay a fine before he could walk away: twenty pounds to the king, and an act of penance. He had to stand at Paul's Cross with a fagot on his shoulder and listen as the sermon was preached. Part of his sentence was to return to prison occasionally and be appraised by the bishop. This was mid-February.

In less than a month, Bainham had a change of heart. He "bewailed" his abjuration and repented hard. He stood before his own church with Tyndale's Bible in his hand and a copy of *The Obedience of a Christian Man* in his pocket, and asked God and all the world to forgive him. He said, "For if I should not return again unto the truth, this word of God [in his hand] would damn me both body and soul at the day of judgment."[25]

Understanding clearly that there was no more mercy to be offered, he was arrested and sent to the Tower. On 19 April 1532 Bainham had to stand before Master Richard Foxford and a group of divines for interrogation. They showed him the bill he had signed and he admitted freely he had signed it. They asked him similar questions to those More and Stokesley had asked, to which he answered according to conscience.

What about the bread and wine, the sacraments, the body and blood of Christ? Bainham replied, "The bread is not Jesus Christ, for Christ's body is not chewed with the teeth. Therefore it is but bread."

When he would not turn, he was handed over to More and Stokesley again. Stokesley placed him in his coal bin with irons on his legs for just under a fortnight. From there he went to Chancellor More's and spent two nights chained to a post in More's backyard. He was brought back to Newgate Prison, abused some more, and on the last day of April 1532, he was taken to the scaffold at Smithfield.

Stokesley sent a Dr. Simons to escort Bainham to the scaffold. Simons did as he was told, but then slipped away for fear of the crowds who favored Bainham. Bainham was led to the stake, embraced it, stood upon a barrel of pitch and said, "I come here, good people, accused and condemned for a heretic, Sir Thomas More being my accuser and my judge. First I say it is lawful for every man and woman to have God's book in their mother tongue. Second, that the bishop of Rome is Antichrist . . . there is no purgatory, but the purgatory of Christ's blood, for our souls immediately go to heaven and rest with Jesus Christ for ever."

Upon hearing these words, a Master Pave said, "Thou liest, thou heretic! Thou deniest the blessed sacrament of the altar." Bainham replied to Master Pave saying that he did not deny the sacrament, only "your idolatry to the bread, and that Christ God and man should dwell in a piece of bread."[26]

Pave then gave the order: "Set fire to him and burn him." A trail of gunpowder sped in Bainham's direction and just before the flames ignited, he looked toward heaven, and said, "God forgive thee, and show thee more mercy than thou showest to me. The Lord forgive Sir Thomas More! And pray for me, all good people!"

Foxe wrote that in the "midst of the flaming fire," when Bainham's legs were half consumed, he spoke these words: "O ye papists behold, ye look for miracles, and here now you may see a miracle; for in this fire I feel no more pain, than if I were in a bed of my own: but it is to me a bed of roses."

Overcome with grief and not able to get Bainham's image or his words out of his head, Master Pave hung himself the next week while his wife was away.

John Tewkesbury

"John Tewkesbury was converted by the reading of Tyndale's Testament, and The Wicked Mammon."[27] He was arrested for the same reason. It is an old story by now, but John Tewkesbury, a London leather merchant, was arrested in April 1529 and examined by Bishop Tunstall and other bishops because he possessed the heretical books.

Questioning Tewkesbury, Tunstall and his bishops became aggravated and embarrassed, or as Foxe put it, "In the doctrine of justification and all other articles of his faith he [Tewkesbury] was very expert and prompt in his answers, in such sort that Tonstal [Tunstall], and all his learned men were ashamed that a leatherseller should so dispute with them, with such power of the Scriptures and heavenly wisdom, that they were not able to resist him."[28]

Tunstall warned Tewkesbury not to lean on his own wit for guidance but to trust "unto the doctrine of the holy mother church." Tewkesbury said that in his judgment he did not err from the teachings of the Church. When the topic of *The Wicked Mammon* came up and its many errors, Tewkesbury said, "Take ye the book and read it over, and I think in my conscience, ye shall find no fault in it."

The bishop responded saying, "I tell thee, before God and those which are here present, in examination of my conscience, that the articles above named, and many others contained in the same book, are false, heretical, and condemned by the holy church: how thinkest thou?"

The interrogation went this way until the good bishop insisted that Tewkesbury recant his evil, to which Tewkesbury denied there was any evil.

The leather seller was examined sometime later by Thomas More at More's house in Chelsea, where he was put in the stocks for six days. He was then taken to the Tower of London and racked until he, too, was lame. The tale is familiar, remembering both Bainham and Bilney. Getting their cues from the Inquisition perhaps (a formal institution of the papacy), apparently when a particular method of interrogation seemed to work, they stuck with it. Like Bainham and Bilney, Tewkesbury abjured.

On a Sunday, in Paul's Church, in open procession, he had to carry a fagot. He was then to stand before Paul's Cross with the same load of wood. "The Wednesday following, he should carry the same fagot about Newgate Market and Cheapside. That on Friday after, he should take the same fagot again at St. Peter's church in Cornhill, and carry it about the market of Leadenhall."

For the rest of his life he was told to wear an emblem of the fagot, one embroidered on his left sleeve, and the other on his right sleeve.

He was later found with the usual relapsed articles—Tyndale's books, believing in justification by faith, not believing in the literal presence of the Eucharist, and so on. Not to mention that he tore the embroidery off his arm. Stokesley was bishop of London by this time, and he and Thomas More had the poor leather merchant burned alive at Smithfield just before Christmas 1531. Thomas More, in his top lyric form, said of the poor leather seller that he had been "burned as there was never wretch I deemed better worthy."[29]

Mine Heart's Desire

For this cause have I sent unto you Timotheus, which is
my dear son, and faithful in the Lord, which shall put
you in remembrance of my ways which I have in Christ,
even as I teach everywhere in all congregations.

— I Corinthians 4:17 TNT

HE WAS TIMOTHY TO TYNDALE'S PAUL. HAVING REFERRED TO HIM as "my dear son in the faith," John Frith was the translator's most intimate and "dearly beloved" associate. A brief look at the life and martyrdom of John Frith will give us a more immediate glimpse of the testament Tyndale left there—the indelible print—and will instruct us at another level.

In Frith, Tyndale has a kindred spirit, a true mirror, which implies not only an all-consuming devotion to God and a gift of expression, an effervescent wit and a like passion for Scripture, but also an independence, as one called out—the fugitive-monk-priest-scholar-prophet living a self-imposed exile—one capable, like Tyndale, of keeping his own counsel, who does not fear the large counterspirits, and whose actions are not determined by the movement of the herd.

But for all their stealth, their abilities to outmaneuver the hunters, to *outMore* More, Tyndale and Frith shared a kind of tragic innocence. Within each of them was a heart that could be won over—piteous, ingenuous, tender, and unsuspecting. Frith and Tyndale were both betrayed preceding their deaths—Frith by a tailor, and Tyndale by a kind of English worm.

Born in 1503 to an innkeeper in Kent, Frith was nine years younger than Tyndale. He was educated at Eton, and then Cambridge (King's College). His achievement at King's was so impressive that in 1525 Cardinal Wolsey invited Frith to his new school at Oxford (Cardinal College, now Christ Church) as a junior canon. A man of "rare abilities, stainless life, and a gentleness of spirit," Frith was highly respected even among those who eventually became his enemies.

The Fish Cellar

After the arrival of Tyndale's New Testament in 1526, followed by *The Parable of the Wicked Mammon* in 1528, Cambridge was all abuzz with reformspeak, which obviously charmed Frith and others like him. So much so that he and six of his friends were arrested for suspicion of heresy (basically talking too much) by the dean of Cardinal College, John Higdon, who reported his actions to Wolsey. The six were cast into a prison "within a deep cave under the ground of the same college, where the salt fish was laid."[1] That is, the fish cellar.

Wolsey was still chancellor at this time, so the heat, while intense, was not of the deadly sort that came in More's chancellorship. Frith and the others remained in the cellar all summer where the conditions (not to mention the smell) proved too much for three of the youths who died of a fever that swept through Cardinal College that August. The remaining three were released on the condition that they stay within a ten-mile radius of the university.

Once released, however, Frith left England to join Tyndale in Antwerp. It is not known for certain when or where they first met, and it is possible they met at Cambridge while Tyndale was there (if he was there). Either way, Frith helped Tyndale with the revision of the New Testament and the Pentateuch.

Foxe made an observation about Tyndale's imprint on his young colleague, saying that in the sweep of his great learning, of which Frith was "addicted," he at last "fell into knowledge and acquaintance with William Tyndale, through whose instructions he first received into his heart the seed of the gospel and sincere godliness."[2]

Perhaps out of curiosity, or some other private motive, Frith went back to England three years later (at Lent 1531), only to return shortly after, before the hunters could track him. The conditions back home had changed. There was a new regime—Stokesley and More, both steely and less tolerant. It was Frith's report that convinced Tyndale that any thought of his own return to England was unwise.

To Wander in Phantasies

With refined instincts and an impossibly clear gaze into the Scripture, Frith absorbed the major writers and thinkers of the early Reformation, but, like Tyndale, found his way beyond them. He learned well, and perhaps surpassed his mentor in certain ways. One source said that "Tyndale was the first and best translator of the Bible into English, and Frith was the most talented theologian among the early Reformers."[3]

Frith was a gifted writer, articulate, precise. And, like Tyndale, he was capable of a significant bite when necessary—the artful bite, the intelligent nibble with its subtlety and afterburn. Writing of Simon Fish, for instance, Frith wrote, "whose eyes God had opened, not only to espy the wily walking of hypocrites and ruin of the realm, which through their means was nigh at hand, but also to mark and ponder the peril of mens' souls." Responding to Thomas More he wrote, "Verily, methinketh it a foul fault so sore to stumble even at the first."[4] I am personally not a big fan of alliteration, but Frith employed the device at times in a kind of mocking counter to the stylings of his enemies, those, like More, who tended to write with pomp, puff, and, well, pounce.

Like his mentor, Frith was a prolific writer, thinker, and argument maker, a caster down of imaginations. He is easier to read than either Tyndale or More. "His touch is lighter, he sticks to the point better, and repeats himself less."[5] His *Disputation of Purgatory* (1531) was his strongest assault and, of course, put a bounty on his head. *Disputation* is aimed in part at Thomas More and sets out to show the lack of biblical evidence of purgatory.

As an epigraph, Frith chose a passage from Colossians, one that seemed to snarl. "Beware lest any man come and spoil you through philosophy and deceitful vanity, through the traditions of men, and ordinances after the world, and not after Christ" (2:8 TNT). Frith made a point of addressing his youth. In 1531 he was twenty-eight. Thomas More was fifty-three. He chose to disarm his opponents with humility. In the preface "Unto the Christian Reader," Frith wrote:

> Grace and peace be with thee, Christian reader. I am sure there are many that will much marvel and count it a great presumption, that I, being so young and of so small learning, dare attempt to dispute this matter against these three personages [Thomas More, John Fisher, and John Rastell], of which number two, that is to say, my Lord of Rochester [Fisher] and Sir Thomas More, are ancient men, both of great wit and dignity. Notwithstanding, I will desire them patiently to hear mine answer, not advertising who speaketh the words, but rather what is said. And as concerning my youth, let them remember what Paul monisheth 1 Timothy iv. willing that Timotheus should instruct the congregation, and that no man should despise his youth; for as the Spirit of God is bound to no place, even so is he not addicted to any age or person, but inspireth when he will and where he will, making the young to see visions and espy the truth, and the elders to dream dreams, and to wander in phantasies. (Act ii. Joel ii.)
>
> And as touching my learning, I must needs acknowledge (as the truth is) that it is very small, nevertheless that little (as I am bound) have I determined by God's grace, to bestow to the edifying of Christ's congregation, which I pray god to increase in the knowledge of his word.[6]

Though Tyndale tried to talk him out of it, in July 1531, after writing his *Disputation*, Frith went back to England. Tyndale never saw him again. Frith made his way to Reading and was arrested as a vagabond (under More's vagrancy laws). He was put into the stocks. He was starving and desperate, and yet kept his identity a secret. After some negotiation with his keepers, he was allowed to contact the prior of Reading, Leonard Coxe, who recognized the dissembled wit (the candlestick hid under the basket), and befriended him. Coxe had once been a friend to Erasmus.

Frith trusted England in ways that Tyndale no longer did, and Tyndale failed to persuade Frith otherwise. England was not his friend. "Albeit, his safety continued not long, through the great hatred and deadly pursuit of Sir Thomas More, who at that time being Chancellor of England, persecuted him [Frith] both by land and sea, besetting all the ways, havens, and ports; yea, and promising great rewards if any man could bring him any news or tidings of him."[7]

When he was finally released, Frith made his way to London hoping to find passage back to Antwerp. But the price on his head was too attractive. Remaining, or attempting to remain invisible, he changed his clothes often and moved from place to place. More and Stokesley were well aware of his presence. All avenues were covered. Watchers were everywhere. After all, Frith was a prize, and of the first order. It was no secret that he was close to Tyndale, that he was a Timothy, dear to the translator and a formidable opponent in his own right.

To throw a lethal net around Frith was to wound Tyndale.

Frith was arrested at Milton Shore near Southend in Essex sometime in October. Frith and the merciful prior (of Reading) were both placed in the Tower. Advisor to the king and soon-to-be-chancellor Thomas Cromwell was impressed with the young man and allowed him to go about unshackled, though the other prisoners were in chains. He even allowed Frith to write, and told the lieutenant of the Tower that it would be a pity to lose Frith, if he could possibly be turned. The lieutenant agreed.

Frith remained in the Tower for five months. Action against him was slow, but it was certain. The peace was a false one. His book against purgatory weighed against him, certainly, and yet not enough to ultimately condemn him. A fellow prisoner asked Frith about the Eucharist, about transubstantiation. Frith told him what he believed, that it was a false and misleading doctrine. Not trusting his own memory, the man asked Frith to write down his thoughts. Frith hesitated, but complied. "Albeit, I was loath to take the matter in hand, yet to fulfill his instant intercession, I took upon me to touch this terrible tragedy, and wrote a treatise, which, besides my painful imprisonment, is like to purchase me a most cruel death."[8]

His Towered friend, nameless to us, gave the document to William Holt, a London tailor, who pretended to be a sympathizer. Holt took the document directly to Thomas More, who immediately wrote a reply. More began his text by stating his intention of treating Frith as a young man "misled by evil counselors."[9] But the chancellor found it difficult to keep up his charade and finally said that the devil himself could not have written a worse book than this. Frith said the sacrament was bread, and nothing but bread. Odd to us perhaps, this was enough to burn him.

There was no question about his guilt, or the verdict.

Abundance of Love Maketh Me Exceed in Babbling

While in the Tower, Frith received a letter from William Tyndale. In it, we are allowed to read Tyndale by a softer light. He is not arguing some grand point of theology. He is not translating from a foreign language. He is speaking to a friend.

In this first letter,[10] Tyndale calls Frith "Jacob." "Brother Jacob, beloved in my heart, there liveth not in whom I have so good hope and trust, and in whom mine heart rejoiceth, and my soul comforteth herself, as in you."

I am not only moved at the protection in Tyndale's voice, but also at how current his words are, how clear and direct he is, how luminous, and yet how he still manages to make his usual music.

> The grace of our Saviour Jesus Christ, his patience, meekness, humbleness, circumspection, and wisdom, be with your heart. Amen.
> Dearly beloved brother Jacob, mine heart's desire in our Saviour

Jesus is, that you arm yourself with patience, and be cold, sober, wise, and circumspect: and that you keep a-low by the ground, avoiding high questions that pass the common capacity. But expound the law truly . . . and then, as a faithful minister, set abroach the mercy of our Lord Jesus, and let the wounded consciences drink of the water of him. And then shall your preaching be with power, and not as the doctrine of the hypocrites; and the spirit of God shall work with you, and all consciences shall bear record unto you, and feel that it is so.

Tyndale has no illusions about the treachery of Thomas More. He warns Frith to "meddle as little" as possible with the presence of Christ in the sacrament. Be wary. Show restraint. Rely on Scripture, "and let them talk what they will." Do not tamper too liberally with the central nerve.

Finally, if there were in me any gift that could help at hand, and aid you if need required, I promise you I would not be far off, and commit the end to God: my soul is not faint, though my body be weary . . . Nature giveth age authority; but meekness is the glory of youth, and giveth them honour. Abundance of love maketh me exceed in babbling . . . The mighty God of Jacob be with you to supplant his enemies, and give you the favour of Joseph; and the wisdom and the spirit of Stephen be with your heart and with your mouth, and teach your lips what they shall say, and how to answer to all things. He is our God, if we despair in ourelves, and trust in him; and his is the glory. Amen.

WILLIAM TYNDALE

I hope our redemption is nigh.

A Poor Apostle's Life

Tyndale tried to warn Frith about allowing himself to become entrapped by his words, not to give speech to his deeper thoughts. He was in the power of the enemy. His warning ultimately went unheeded.

In a response to Thomas More, Frith speaks of his friend Tyndale (obviously because of some disparagement on More's part toward him). The following is an excerpt from Frith's hand, but it captures one of the more reliable images of his mentor.

And Tyndale, I trust, liveth, well content with such a poor apostle's life, as God gave his son Christ and his faithful ministers in this world, which is not sure of so many mites as ye [Thomas More] be yearly of pounds, although I am sure that for his learning and judgment in scripture he were more worthy to be promoted than all the bishops in England. I received a letter from him, which was written since Christmas, wherein among other matters he writeth thus: I call God to record . . . Judge, Christian reader, whether these words be not spoken of a faithful, clear, innocent heart. And as for his behaviour, [it] is such that I am sure no man can reprove him of any sin; howbeit no man is innocent before God, which beholdeth the heart.[11]

Mozley wrote, and it is worth repeating, "That Tyndale should have inspired this veneration in so rare a nature as Frith's, is perhaps the best proof that can be given of the greatness of his soul."[12]

More's response? Giving aggravation its full vent, More replied that if the reformers *must* write, why can't they keep their pernicious books to themselves instead of broadcasting them everywhere? Frith, of course, responded to More. His logic is as clear and as certain as his fate.

Until we see some means found, by which a reasonable reformation may be had, and sufficient instruction for the poor commoners, I assure you I neither will nor can cease to speak; for the word of God boileth in my body like a fervent fire, and will needs have an issue, and break out when occasion is given. But this hath been offered, is offered, and shall be offered: grant that the word of God, I mean the text of scripture, may go abroad in our English tongue, as other nations have it in their tongues, and my brother William Tyndale and I have done, and will promise you to write no more. If you will not grant this condition, then will we be doing while we have breath, and shew in few words that the scripture doth in many, and so at the least save some.[13]

If the Pain Be Above Your Strength

The following is Tyndale's second, and last, letter to his friend.[14] This letter would indeed have been a comfort, but it is doubtful that Frith ever received it before his death. Here Tyndale calls him John, which implies a closer proximity to his friend.

> Dearly beloved, howsoever the matter be, commit yourself wholly and only unto your most loving Father and most kind Lord, and fear not men that threat, nor trust men that speak fair: but trust him that is true of promise, and able to make his word good. Your cause is Christ's gospel, a light that must be fed with the blood of faith. The lamp must be dressed and snuffed daily, and that oil poured in every evening and morning, that the light go not out. Though we be sinners, yet is the cause right. If when we be buffeted for welldoing, we suffer patiently and endure, that is thankful with God.

Tyndale offers a word of encouragement against what he is now certain will be Frith's death: "For that end we are called. For Christ also suffered for us, leaving us an example . . . Hereby have we perceived love." It is difficult to imagine Tyndale writing this letter without great emotion. He continues, in deeper tones, as toward a glorious death. The words are those of one who has rehearsed the event again and again in his own mind.

> Dearly beloved, be of good courage, and comfort your soul with the hope of this high reward, and bear the image of Christ in your mortal body, that it may at his coming be made like to his, immortal: and follow the example of all your other dear brethren, which chose to suffer in hope of a better resurrection. Keep your conscience pure and

undefiled, and say against that nothing. Stick at necessary things . . . If you give yourself, cast yourself, yield yourself, commit yourself wholly and only to your loving Father; then shall this power be in you and make you strong, and that so strong that you shall feel no pain: and that shall be to another present death: and his Spirit shall speak in you, and teach you what to answer, according to his promise. He shall set out his truth by you wonderfully, and work for you above all that your heart can imagine. Yea, and you are not yet dead; though the hyprocrites all, with all they can make, have sworn your death . . . If the pain be above your strength, remember: "Whatsoever ye shall ask in my name, I will give it you." And pray to your Father in that name, and he will cease your pain, or shorten it. The Lord of Peace, of hope, and of faith, be with you. Amen.

WILLIAM TYNDALE

Most Helly and Cruel Death

John Frith was pronounced guilty on two counts: his denial of purgatory and his refusal to believe the sacrament of Christ's body (Eucharist) to be anything but bread, a memorial only. For these twin offenses he was to burn.

Here we see Thomas More in what has to be a form of madness. Possibly fearing some mercy from the king on Frith's behalf (at the urging of Anne Boleyn), More wrote to H8 reminding him of his title "Defender of the Faith," that it had been won for defending the very sacraments Frith was denying. By this time, More had resigned as chancellor, but he was eager that Frith should burn. Concerning Frith's opinion of the sacrament, More was so enraged he said,

[It] sholde cost hym [Frith] the beste bloude [blood] in hys body.

I fere me sore that Cryst wyll kyndle a fyre of fagottes for hym, & make hym therein swete [sweat] the bloude out of hys body here, and strayte frome hense send hys soule for euer into the fyre of hell.[15]

The Eucharist, in that it represented the physical presence of Christ in the material world, in a way represented the Church itself, therefore its denial was the worst of heresies.

Once Stokesley handed down the sentence, Frith was delivered to the mayor of the city (Sir Stephen Pecocke, said to be "a simple man") and the sheriff, who then took Frith to the notorious Newgate Prison in Cheapside. He was placed in the dungeon, and "laden with bolts and irons as many as he could bear." A collar of iron was placed around his neck, and the collar was attached to a post. The chains, the collar, and the post were so fixed that Frith could neither sit down nor stand upright. He was in this position for four days. There was no natural light in his cell but he was allowed a candle. In spite of the cruel geometry his body was forced to suffer, he continued to write.

On 4 July 1533 John Frith was escorted to the scaffold at Smithfield where "with great patience and constancy he suffered that most helly and cruel death of burning. And when the fire was set on the faggots he embraced the same in his arms, and with all patience committed his spirit unto Almighty God."[16]

Foxe wrote: "Amongst all other chances lamentable, there hath been none a great time which seemed unto me more grievous than the lamentable death and cruel handling of John Frith, so learned and excellent a young man."[17]

This isn't quite the whole story. Frith was bound to the stake back-to-back with a man named Andrew Hewet, a tailor who had been betrayed as well by Holt. Earlier, when asked by Stokesley about the sacrament, Hewet responded by saying he believed "even as John Frith doth."[18] But Frith "is a heretic, and already judged go be burned," Stokesley assured him, "and except thou revoke thine opinion, thou shalt be burned also with him." Apparently swept up in Frith's powerful influence, Hewet said, "Truly, I am content therewithal."

As the fire grew around the two men, Doctor Cooke, the vicar of All Hallows Church in Honey Lane (Cheapside) shouted to those gathered close by that they should pray for them "no more than they would do for a dog."[19] Hearing this, Frith asked God to forgive the good parson. The people were not as compliant with the parson's request as he had hoped.

And one more thing. Bainham had recanted. Tewkesbury and Bilney had recanted. Even Richard Baiford, a friend of Tyndale's, had recanted. But not Frith. Frith had no such denial in him. Mozley summarizes nicely: "The disciple is worthy of his master. There was no fear of him recanting; he had learnt his lesson too well."[20]

A Troubled Fascination: William Tyndale and Thomas More

We all talk a different language
Talking in defense

—Mike and the Mechanics, *"The Living Years"*

FOR ALL THAT WE FIND ATTRACTIVE ABOUT HIS WORDS, FOR ALL the plowspun rhapsody he authored into our conversational English, William Tyndale had sufficient bite as well, and was not afraid to use that bite when it was necessary to do so. He was equipped as few in the kingdom were equipped. Other than having a repentant king—for Henry is no David—Tyndale is the English Nathan, fearless and uncompromised.

As for Tudor vulgarity, while it was not an ornament Tyndale used very often, if at all, it was too much a part of the idiom of an angry age to avoid at times. Compared to his contemporaries Luther and More, Tyndale is the lamb when it comes to hard or indelicate language. His transgression is so rare it is hardly worth mentioning. In his *Obedience of a Christian Man* he speaks of bishops who denounce the preaching of the Word. "To preach is their duty only and not to offer their feet to be kissed or testicles or stones to be groped."[1]

In describing the death of Cardinal Wolsey, Tyndale mentioned a purgative given to the cardinal that just didn't seem to work (the purge actually brought about the cardinal's death following a prolonged sickness). Wolsey, Tyndale said, "took himself a medicine *ut emitteret spiritum per posteriora* [farted his spirit through his backside]." As Brian Moynahan observed, this is not the sort of prose expected of a translator. But, "to Tyndale, the Bible was a living book, with all the crudeness and vigour of everyday life. It excited him; it was a page turner."[2]

Tyndale's use of Latin to disguise the flatulence was pure taunt. Thomas More used English when he cursed. Tyndale chose Latin. It allowed him a double punch. He could mock Wolsey and the Church all in one swoop of toilet Latin.

In the *Obedience*, Tyndale wrote, "They pray in Latin, they christen in Latin, they bless in Latin, they give absolution in Latin; only curse they in the English tongue."[3]

Tyndale doesn't fight like More and Luther, Henry VIII or any of the noisemakers. What use of vulgarity he indulges is negligible, hardly an indictment against him. Nor does it throw a shadow over the translator of the New Testament.

As I read Tyndale, particularly his response to Thomas More's polemic, and in spite of the retaliation in his voice, I cannot help but notice the protection in his words, something he feels strongly for the plowboy, for the carpenter's apprentice, for the wheelwright, something he feels for me, the reader, and for you. He was ever the defender.

> I thought it my duty (most dear reader) to warn thee before, and to shew thee the right way in, and to give thee the true key to open it [Scripture], and to arm thee against false prophets and malicious hypocrites, whose perpetual study is to leaven the scripture with glosses [explanations], and there to lock it up where it should save thy soul, and to make us shoot at a wrong mark, to put our trust in those things that profit their bellies only and slay our souls.[4]

J. F. Mozley called it "a spice of sharpness in his nature."[5] Richard Ramius, in his biography of Thomas More, had a stronger opinion.

Tyndale, he said, "seems to have been a humorless and unpleasant man, seldom able to keep a friend for very long." Ramius used modifiers like "contentious" and "outspoken."[6] I cannot help but feel that in spite of his dedication to his subject and that Ramius does Tyndale the occasional injustice, this observation is not altogether unreasonable. Tyndale's defiance is hardly a secret. And defiance is, by definition, both contentious and outspoken, as I suppose it must be humorless and unpleasant as well.

Defiance is an unavoidable condition of Tyndale's life, and yet it leaves no stain on his nature. He is not mastered or diminished by it. He is not embittered. It does not alter him. On the contrary, not unlike his exile, it becomes his tutor—instructing, empowering. He listens well. His apprenticeship is wide and he misses nothing.

Like the artist, everything instructs him. He is a student of *all* languages.

Master of the pithy comeback, his application is casual. He is not rushed. I cannot read the following without small, suppressed laughter. "For we read of popes that have commanded the angels to set divers [some number of persons] out of Purgatory. Howbeit I am not yet certified whether they obey or no."[7]

For all his warmth, it is not difficult to imagine Tyndale with a caustic side. And he was fairly liberal in its application. He was also precise. Even Ramius admitted that Tyndale was "a genius with language, and he was brave, constant, and intelligent—so intelligent that he became Thomas More's most formidable intellectual adversary."[8]

In Tyndale's attachment *to* the Gospels, to the preservation *of* those Gospels, and most particularly, because of his identification *with* the Gospels, his ardor can be compared, albeit with restraint, to that of John the Baptist, the apostle Paul before the high priest, or even Jesus at the table of the moneylenders. The reference here (the point) is that it is not blind zealotry but an anger that to Tyndale is just, overdue, and above all righteous. Of this, Tyndale is convinced. There is no spoilage.

In his *Obedience*, in the midst of some of the most beautiful lines ever written on love and devotion to God, Tyndale is merciless with "the spirituality," that is, the pope and a whole lineup of bishops, friars, and priests, those "juggling spirits" he accuses of "belly love," that is, love that is appetite only, a one-sided affection that gives only for what it gets in return, love that is all about gain, which is no love at all.

Tyndale is menacingly deft with his verbal projectiles. It is impossible not to feel the heat, the deep aggravation. And if you prefer, the humor—mercilessly English.

His words have a very warm and eager metabolism. Still, his touch is weightless, light. He is not the blunt instrument of More, Luther, and King Harry. Very literally, he is the paper cut, the latent sting. The intelligence with which he does battle and the economy that allows him to take the most direct route makes him a dangerous adversary to the Church.

The *Oxford English Dictionary* credits William Tyndale with the first usage of the word *viper*, as in the deliciously militant "O generation of vipers" (Matthew 3:7, 12:34, 23:33; Luke 3:7). The Wycliffe Bible (1395) translates the same, "Generaciouns of eddris [adders]," but it lacks the ignition of Tyndale. And Tyndale adds the vocative *O*. There is an intensity in those few words that is not merely textual, though purely Tyndalian—elevated, well constructed, and yet gloriously hostile—a very speakable, orally satisfying English, shaped with the prophet in mind.

Yet for all his spice, for whatever seasoning Tyndale applies, his text remains calm and balanced throughout, as does his most polemical work, *The Answer to Thomas More's Dialogue*. Unlike More, Tyndale never rages, never loses control. Rant is not a part of his arsenal. It is just not his way. He never wishes More dead. He never condemns More or anyone else to an eternity in hell as was common for the "spirituality."

A Kind of Knowing

Tyndale possessed a gnosis, that is, a kind of knowing, a special kind of awareness outside the usual, a peculiar intelligence the artist possesses, which allows him to do and to act and to create according to his own vision. It implies a narcissism of sorts—a benign, controlled, nontoxic self-absorption—purged of the usual contaminants.

Art demands intensity from its makers, complete possession. It is a kind of bright madness, one that often begins as an unrest in the artist's center, the chaos from which order must be imagined. The artist must follow where this affliction leads him, where his fascination dictates. Tyndale would have given this a spiritual interpretation, but the dynamic is the same.

The point is, his vocation possessed him completely. There was nothing else. He had all the rare advantages of a man who was certain, both of his place in the world and his function within it. "His translation was no dead piece of learned labour: it was instinct with the life of the man that produced it: it was the Word of God transmitted through the agency of one to whom that Word was not an outward letter, but the very life of his soul."[9]

The artist, like the prophet, is an obsessive creature, single-minded, absorbed, always standing at a kind of remove from the humanity around him. Like Shakespeare, Tyndale is the gregarious loner. He must find and maintain a balance between his social interaction, what social interaction there is, and the severity his vocation demands. And this is where he is most often misinterpreted.

Though it is seldom arbitrary or random, you must allow him the occasional snap, the show of teeth. His vocation, or what he considers his duty to God, is above all other considerations. His love is that great, that thorough. It has a polish, not unlike his text.

This affliction, known to the greatest of artist/creators, implies an intolerance to any but his own method, his own application of his craft, the lines and dimensions of his own peculiar hearing.

What Ramius and most biographers miss in Tyndale is the artist, the creator. Even Tyndale misses this. He would not consider himself either artist or poet. Yet when you combine a powerful sense of calling to the virtuoso in him, you get a creature who is unique and unrepeatable, outside reason and comparison, who not only embraces the asceticism that both his art and his convictions demand of him, but who understands their necessity.

Tyndale is the ascetic, and for spiritual reasons, for an immovable sense of calling. And even the word *art* is somewhat of a paradox. While useful to us, it is also irrelevant. His desire was neither literary nor aesthetic.

Nevertheless, beauty, majesty, rhapsody, vitality, economy, all the components of the artistic imaginary were within Tyndale's power. The artistic, the prophetic, the headstrong, the expatriated, the exiled, all these come together in a confusion of living elements that render a single inimitable creature.

It was such a creature who gave us our English Bible.

Those who gathered to Tyndale, who befriended him, supported him, or discipled under him, understood his "spice," as we may now call it. He had devoted followers who loved him deeply and knowledgably, and were willing to share in his risk. The magnetism was a powerful one.

Mad Incantations

The Church in its wisdom, in order to quench the Lutheran heresy in England, allowed Thomas More not only to read Tyndale's work, but commissioned him to respond to it, to do battle with the renegade translator. England sought to engage its most formidable weapon, its "keenest champion" against its disinherited son. In a letter to More, Tunstall wrote,

> There are certain sons of iniquity, who by translating Lutheran books and printing them in great number are trying to infect the land with heresy, and there is much fear lest the catholic faith perish utterly, unless good and learned men meet the danger by quickly putting forth sound books in the vernacular on the catholic side. Now you can play the Demosthenes[10] both in English and Latin, and at every assembly you are wont to be the keenest champion of the truth. You cannot better bestow your leisure hours, if any you have, than in writing an English work, to shew to simpleminded people the crafty malignity of these impious heretics. Our illustrious king has set you a glorious example by his defense of the sacraments against Luther, thereby winning the immortal name of defender of the church. And that you may not fight blindfold, in ignorance of your opponents, I send you their mad follies in English, and also some of Luther's books [i.e., Latin]; from these you will learn the habits of these serpents, where they lurk, by what shifts and turns they seek to escape when grasped, and what they hope to

achieve. Go forward then to this holy work; succour the church, and win for yourself an immortal name, and eternal glory in heaven: and to this end I give you license to keep and to read books of that nature.[11]

It is not difficult to recognize William Tyndale as Tunstall's muse. And Martin Luther. At that time, Tyndale's New Testament, *The Obedience of a Christian Man*, *The Parable of the Wicked Mammon*, and his *Compendious Introduction to the Epistle of Paul to the Romans* were in circulation in England. And Tyndale dared to ask "where findest thou in all the Scriptures purgatory, shrift [confession], penance, pardon, *poena, culpa, hyperdoulia*, and a thousand feigned terms more?" *Show me.* The prelates had no response. They were certain that Sir Thomas would.

In fairness, it is only right to mention that Thomas More was offered a sum of up to five thousand pounds for this commission. In 1528 this was an impressive fortune. To his credit, More refused the offer.

In Tunstall's letter, we are also given some image of the strict controlling motherhood of the Catholic Church over its children, its "simpleminded," the "*simplicibus et idiotis hominibus,*"[12] as More had written.

This war of words may have been More's idea in the first place. C. S. Lewis suggested that the task was carried out not because More necessarily wanted to write a response, but because in his mind, it had to be written by someone.[13] Somebody had to do it.

With a detectable weariness over the task, in the *Confutation of Tyndale's Answer*, More said, "Would God, after all my laboure done, so that the remembrance of their pestilent errours were araced [erased] out of English mennes [men's] heartes and their abominable bookes burned up, myne owne were walked with them, and the name of these matters vtterly putte in oblivion."[14]

Still, the rebuttal of heresy became his chief thought. He remained busy as ever at court and in his responsibilities at Westminster, but said once that the issue was so pressing that a man might "wryte by candlellyght whyle he were halfe a slepe."[15] More was convinced that the time of antichrist was "very nere at hande,"[16] that Luther and Tyndale were no less than prophets of the great beast. This may account for More's urgency, his "feverish haste."[17]

To preface this bout between More and Tyndale, a quote from C. H. Williams provides a suitable context, validating my former claim that under an oppressive regime, the artist is, at best, muzzled.

In the first quarter of the sixteenth century English as a literary language was practically unformed. There was, it is true, no lack of official documents and even private correspondence, written in pain- fully cumbersome English, and to the modern eye looking very much like a foreign language, but the amount of literary prose of any sig- nificance appearing in those years was extremely small. It is hardly an exaggeration to say that the only exponents of true English prose during those years were Thomas More and William Tyndale.[18]

And so began the celebrated exchange between the two greatest minds England could boast, a literary brawl of close to a million words that brought out the best and perhaps the worst in both men, that clari- fied them both, and gave the dull world a bit of heat and spice.

Tom the Brawler

To Thomas More, William Tyndale was the arch-heretic, "the Captain of Englyshe heretikes." Tyndale represented the worst realization of his fears. He was the "son of iniquity," a "serpent." He had beating within his breast a "devilish, proud, dispitious heart." He had the "devil's mark on his forehead" and was a "hell-hound in the kennel of the devil . . . so puffed up with poison of pride, malice, and envy, that it is more than marvel that the skin can hold together."[19]

To Tyndale, More was a sellout, an otherwise honorable man who "knew the truth and forsook it."[20] He accused More of camouflaging error with ornamentation, that is, in his "poetry," his rich linguistic styling. Tyndale, in essence, accused More, the man of law, of falling back on the "it's not truth that matters but what you can prove, what you can make a jury believe" kind of courtroom dazzle and misdirec- tion. The more poetry, "where he erreth most," the more error he had to hide. In his *Answer to Thomas More's Dialogue*, Tyndale wrote, "M. More thinketh that his errors be so subtilly couched that no man can espy them. So blind he counteth all other men, in comparison of his great understanding."[21]

It is clear that the translator brought out something quite ugly in the great man. Thomas More the lawyer became Tom the Brawler, a taste More acquired in his response to Martin Luther.

Beyond Tyndale's theology, his desire to create a Bible in the vernacular, to bring God to the plowboy, and a few select issues we will look at in the next chapter, there is evidence to suggest another, more subtle reason why More had such lethal animosity toward Tyndale.

I am not sure anyone in England understood Tyndale, or what Tyndale's presence meant, as well as Thomas More. Sir Thomas not only recognized Tyndale's brilliance, he understood there was something unstoppable about the man, something determined, and by a knowledge that eluded even More, doubtless the finest mind in all of England (which is fair because Tyndale was not *in* England at the time).

It is a subtle distinction, written in the subtext of their debate perhaps, but here is an intelligence equivalent to More's own, though counter to all he believes. And yet Tyndale's convictions are not divided. His investment is complete. He is "all in," as might be said in a game of chance. His mind is single, his gaze fixed. He writes,

> To preach God's word is too much for half a man. And to minister to a temporal kingdom is too much for half a man also. Either or other requireth the whole man. One therefore cannot well do both. He that avengeth himself on every trifle is not meet to preach the patience of Christ, how that man out to forgive and to suffer all things. He that is overwhelmed with all manner of riches and doth but seek more daily is not meet to preach poverty.[22]

Tyndale was the man on the high wire, whose slightest misstep could be fatal. He had no choice but to pay close attention. He had no family to father, no state to manage, no heretics to worry, and no wife or king to pacify, no Alice or Henry. Fugitive, without country or king, Tyndale's only distraction was his personal safety and the well-being of his translation.

Tyndale could not be bought. Indeed, what money he had, if he had any—living "hand to mouth"[23] as he did—went back into his translation, into another revision, or to the needy, those even less fortunate than him. He owned nothing, and wanted nothing. Therefore, he could not be charmed or coerced by the usual means.

He did not seek fame or elevation, title or possession. He sought no place in court. He was not given to compromise. He was not bound to the same conventions More and others were. He had none of the ambitions of the eager young man of promise and wit common to the Renaissance.

What can you do with a man like that? There was no bargaining in him.

It was in William Tyndale that Thomas More saw not only the unquenchable, but worse, the inevitable. He saw the old world, his world, in decline, deflating. He saw a world he had no part of rising in ascent. Indeed, for More, Tyndale effected a kind of troubled fascination.

In response, More did what most men do when confronted by uncertainty, who fear the unknown. You hate. You strike. You pounce. You engage the medieval option of cruelty and annihilation. And Bully Tom went about his obligations with a medieval kind of street conviction, and with the full sanction and blessing of the Church. His many refinements, the high life he loved and maintained, all that was the saint in him, was in wide contrast to the fury with which he pursued and punished the heretic.

No Timid Friend to Truth

And afterward, from light to light, through heaven,
I have learned things which, if I repeat them,
Will give a bitter taste to many people.
Yet, should I be a timid friend to truth,
I fear I will not live among those who
Shall call this present time the ancient past.

—Dante Alighieri, *The Divine Comedy, Paradiso*

HE COULD NOT CALL WILLIAM TYNDALE ENOUGH NAMES OR CURSE HIM with more conviction. He could not write enough words or burn enough "heretics" to make it stop. He could not torment enough offenders in his own backyard. In his *Life of Thomas More*, Peter Ackroyd said that More "had reached such a pitch of nervous intensity that he could not rest from the fight; his whole life and duty lay now in his battle to protect the church."[1]

An examination of the literary clash between William Tyndale and Thomas More will not only allow us to measure the divide between the two men and their approaches to God as from camp to camp, but it will allow us to note Tyndale's theology as well—how he thinks, how he processes, how he measures, how he articulates, what he imposes on a text and what he does not, and so on. This exploration will also put to rest any notion that Tyndale is important only as a thorn or a foil to the sainted Thomas More.

A Lousy Little Friar

After Luther, Tyndale was a second thorn, and to the English spirituality it was insufferable. Thomas More, they were certain, had considerable pluck to make it go away.

But More's acid spew had a history long before his row with Tyndale. In 1523, he wrote a noxious little piece called *Responsio ad Lutherum* (Response to Luther). This action was initiated at the request of Henry VIII. The king himself had written *Assertio septem Sacrmentorum adversus Martin Lutherum*, that is, a defense of the seven sacraments acknowledged by the Catholic Church—Baptism, Eucharist, Confirmation, Penance, Matrimony, Holy Orders, and Anointing of the Sick. The "most insane scoundrel" and the most shameless buffoon"[2] that Luther was, allowed only two— Baptism and Eucharist.

As mentioned earlier, Henry's *Assertio* won him a title from a grateful Pope Leo X, that of *Fedei Defensor*, Defender of the Faith. Of course, a few years later, after Henry's little trouble, a less grateful Pope Paul III rescinded the title, and excommunicated the fractious king. Henry kept the title anyway, as every English monarch has since. It has been suggested that Thomas More may have assisted Henry in writing the *Assertio*.

Luther responded by calling

> *As a noun,* Harry *is the equivalent to the familiar Christian name* Henry. *As a verb,* harry *means "to make predatory raids or incursions; to commit ravages. To lay waste, sack, pillage, spoil. To harass (persons) by hostile attacks, forced exactions, or rapacity; to despoil. To worry, goad, torment, harass; to maltreat, ill-use, persecute; to worry mentally. To ravish, violate."*
>
> – OXFORD ENGLISH DICTIONARY

Henry a pig, a swine from hell. He called him a dolt and a liar who deserved to be covered in excrement. An outraged Henry then turned to Thomas More instructing him to answer Luther in kind, and trade "text for text and insult for insult."[3]

This commission might appear to excuse More's literary spleen, or his use of foul language, but I think not. He seems to have aptitude for this type of composition, which was called by one eighteenth-century writer "the greatest heap of nasty language that perhaps was ever put together."[4]

To maintain the hygiene of our present text, I have noted the Latin words More applied to Luther, whom he dubbed as *merda, stercus, lutum,* and *coenum* among other things. Each of these words is a variation on a theme I suppose, and each has its own colorful street slang equivalent, but they mean much the same thing, that is, feces, excrement.

In his *Responsio ad Lutherum,* More calls Luther an ape, an arch-dolt, a drunken pettifogger, a lousy little friar (lousy friarlet), a piece of scurf, a fogbrain, a pestilential buffoon.[5] He suggests that Luther celebrates Mass upon the toilet (*super foricam*) that he is an "arse-hole" the Antichrist has vomited onto the earth. Even Luther's flatulence is anathema.* Nothing is left out. "Who would not laugh at the most wretched scoundrel blasting out such frenzied boasts . . . Thence he farts and trumpets his splendid victories."[6]

Martin Luther was just as liberal in his return fire. The emotion was conspicuous. The two could make quite a mess.

In spite of the tedium, More's mockery has sharp teeth, and yet his usual refinements are absent. His vulgarity is "as wearing as the talk of small boys in the school washroom."[7] Though his laughter is not far off, all the calm possession of the moralist abandons him. This is London streetspeak, and More seems quite at home. "He is," said C. S. Lewis, "our first great Cockney humorist."[8] Peter Ackroyd included More in a host of "Cockney Visionaries" (Dickens, Blake, Milton, and Chaucer), being as he is, master of the Cockney invective.[9]

---

* Luther would often use flatulence as a way to rid himself of demons.

🌼 *It is not the language of a saint, perhaps, but it is the language of a Londoner.*

– PETER ACKROYD, *ALBION*

In spite of More's natural bent toward humor, and the laughter at times forced out of us, it is not difficult to get a sense of how far a man of otherwise refined character and reputation must go to satisfy the primal urge of hatred, or how deep the venom, with its power to destroy from inside. The Reformation indeed brought out the medieval in Thomas More.

And then, like a daisy rising in the midst of all the smear, More defends his beloved Church. She is the divinely inspired teacher, the preserver of the one true faith. She is flawless, errorless. As is his argument, which is both rational and convincing. Only through the Church is heaven possible. Only through her is the promise of God realized. Arguing for his Church and king, More writes:

> You have heard, reader, several passages from among many which the king has written, in which he points out that many things were said and done and taught by Christ which are not recorded by any of the *evangelists* [Gospels], which are not contained in any writings of the apostles, not related in any scriptural text. Since his associates held these details fresh in their memory, however, they have been passed on successively, as though from hand to hand, since the time of the apostles and have come all the way down to us. He also shows that the Catholic Church, in its sacraments and articles of faith, is taught and governed by the Holy Spirit. Moreover, he proves these statements, not only from the argument that otherwise the most absurd results would follow, but from the clear words of the evangelists, as well as the evident testimony of sacred writings, in addition to that of Christ himself. And what do you think Luther replies to these proofs? Set aside for a while, reader, the railing, the jeers, the mockery and the abuse; you will find nothing else but these two propositions: that nothing is true and certain apart from evident scriptures; that all other traditions are the work of men and are left to the free choice of each individual. But in the meantime,

to the reasons which the king presents; to the authority of the evange-
lists and of Christ Himself by which the king proves that other things
were done, taught, and commanded besides those which were set down
in writing; to these arguments which certainly should have received
some answer, Luther answers nothing at all.[10]

Remember that the above text is modernized in English. More is still
writing in Latin. That he so integrates the reasonable with the thuggish
makes for an odd, informative, and at times amusing read. As his polem-
ics evolve, the thuggish eclipses the reasonable altogether, as if the fight
has moved from the courtroom to the streets.

More's treatment of Tyndale sometime later was just as harsh, yet,
oddly, it lacked the foul language of his bout with Luther. This may say
more about William Tyndale than it does Thomas More. More observed
a restraint with Tyndale that he dismissed altogether with Luther. The
name-calling, the accusations, while no less raging, was at least sanitized.
It had no smell.

Luther and More created a genre of their own.

Tyndale doesn't give himself that kind of levity in his text. His muse
won't allow it. Again, he doesn't rage, he doesn't curse, and he certainly
doesn't throw fecal material. This restraint is consistent with his faith,
and with the beauty of his translation.

> *Let no filthy communication proceed out of your mouths: but that which is good to edify*
> *withal, when need is: that it may have favour with the hearers. And grieve not the Holy*
> *Spirit of God, by whom ye are sealed unto the day of redemption. Let all bitterness,*
> *fierceness and wrath, roaring and cursed speaking, be put away from you, with all*
> *maliciousness.* (Ephesians 4:29–30 TNT 1534)

There was certainly "fierceness and wrath, roaring and cursed speaking" aimed in his direction when these words (Scripture above) were first
translated. Tyndale never pretends to be the saint, but he *is* the adult. He has
fight in him, certainly, but he is never the bully, never the adolescent. He is
never reduced to primary urges, or to tantrum text.

If you stand at some distance from Thomas More and his fury, you may get the sense, as I did, of one trying too hard, fighting, as it were, a thing unbeatable, and by a Lilliputian resolve that is somewhat pointless. This is particularly true in his confrontation with Tyndale. To come undone and to jettison the usual graces with such wanton disregard is difficult to reckon, particularly with the legend posterity has attached to him.

What emerged in England was an energetic and male-dominated society of commerce and of progress, together with its own state church; it was a religion of the book and private prayer, eschewing all the ritual, public symbolism and spectacle which had marked late medieval Catholicism. The age of More was coming to a close.

– PETER ACKROYD, *THE LIFE OF THOMAS MORE*

According to the *Oxford English Dictionary*, Thomas More coined the word *utopia*—"an imagined place, an imagined perfection." Maybe it is true that a word lives in a man. It broods. It imprints itself upon his conscience.

I found it interesting that both William Tyndale and Thomas More are attributed with the first usage of the word *atonement*. According to the *OED*, More was attributed (1513 in *Richard III*) with the use of the word in a civil context, meaning "the condition of being at one with others; unity of feeling, harmony, concord, agreement. Restoration of friendly relations between persons who have been at variance; reconciliation." Here again, and though the irony may appear dense, we are given a way to perceive.

Tyndale, however, is attributed with the use of *atonement* in its spiritual context (1526 in 2 Corinthians 5:18), "reconciliation or restoration of friendly relations between God and sinners." What stands out, at least by first appearance in this dual attribution, is the notion of *the spirit* and *the law*. Two men. Two visions of life. Two faiths.

In spite of what liberties I may take with his name, none of this is to discount what is truly great about Thomas More—the depth of his belief, or his literary contribution, his peculiar intelligence, the martyrdom he suffered, the genuine nobility of his conscience. His greatness is not a sham. He had simply entered a game that C. S. Lewis said he had no real gift for.

Utopia

More's *Utopia* (1516) is considered a great work, maybe his greatest, although Lewis said, "hardly any two [scholars] agree as to its real significance."[11] The word *utopia* literally means "no place, land of nowhere." The name is often confused with *eutopia*, which means "a region of ideal happiness or good order." It is in the distance between the two forms that we hear More's laughter.

Utopia is an island that possesses a perfect social, legal, and political system. At a level somewhat beneath the visible surface, maybe even undetected or unnoticed by More himself, Utopia is perhaps a necessary imagination, an invention of one who knows by some oblique awareness that the plates are shifting beneath him, that perfection is, indeed, a dream, an impossible "land of nowhere."

A device we will see again in More, *Utopia* is written in the form of a dialogue, and in Latin, of course. The dialogue is a Platonic device, a lawyer's craft that allows More to say what he wants, however and to whomever he wants, in such a way that an illusion is created that softens the offensive. He can frame his argument strategically with all the right supports.

More's friend, Erasmus, thought of *Utopia* as a kind of comic book. Tyndale takes issue with it as "poetry." C. S. Lewis suggested that it is best received when it is taken exactly for what it is, "a holiday work, a spontaneous overflow of intellectual high spirits, a revel of debate, paradox, comedy and (above all) of invention, which starts many hares and kills none."[12] Later in life More himself thought "it fitter too be burned."

Of interest to us, prying into men's heads as we might do, is that *Utopia* belonged to More in the first place—the ideal suspended in one's thoughts, the dream of what might be. A reimagining. It was born perhaps out of a man's hope of something *other*, something better, purer, more perfect, and much kinder than what is.

Unfortunately, such a place existed for neither More nor Tyndale.

Utopia was, ironically, More's last great work. The polemical works were all that were left to him, a regretful use of a truly great mind. C. S. Lewis lamented a Thomas More who never really had the chance to materialize.

> To rebuke magnificently is one of the duties of a great polemical writer. More often attempts it but he always fails. He loses himself in a wilderness of opprobrious [shameful, disgraceful] adjectives. He cannot denounce like a prophet; he can only scold and grumble like a father in an old fashioned comedy . . . In obedience to his conscience he spent what might have been the best years of his literary life on work which demanded talents that he lacked and gave very limited scope to those he had. It may well have been no easy sacrifice.[13]

One of More's earlier works was *The History of King Richard III*. Having served in the court of Henry VII, father of Henry VIII (both Henries had an eye for talent), More's *Richard III* has been considered Tudor propaganda (Henry VII became the first Tudor monarch at the death of Richard III, the last Plantagenet). Historian Richard Ramius considered More's *Richard III* the best thing he ever wrote. In it "we find the mature man, a genius at setting a scene, a wizard at depicting character, a believer in a fundamental order of things that gave events meaning and provided a moral context that allowed reasonable men to recognize virtue when they saw it and to condemn vice on the intuitive perception of the vicious act."[14]

Written both in Latin and in very readable English, More's Richard was transformed a few generations later into Shakespeare's "bunchbak'd toad," the "elvish-mark'd, abortive, rooting hog," the villain's villain, deformed, "rudely stamped," the homicidal Gloucester who kills his wife, his brother, his nephews (the princes in the Tower), his first-in-arms Buckingham, and the slow, sweet, and quite insane Henry VI.

With all the name-calling and crude references, Shakespeare's Richard is treated with the same thuggish handling More's Richard is. It sounds oddly like the tone of the *Responsio*, though it is a much more enjoyable read.

Having long been acquainted with Shakespeare's *Richard III* myself, More's version was a delight.

Shakespeare was first and always a showman. And he wrote his plays under a Tudor monarch. The Elizabethan playgoer loved his *Richard III*. Death, weirdness, and high position were big entertainment.

Posterity has given poor Richard a sincere apology for the abuse. Always the lawyer, More said that much of what he wrote was hearsay, that there was nothing certain, "and whoso divineth upon conjectures, may as well shoot too far as too short."[15] More's Richard was born, among other ghastly attachments, with teeth.

> [He was] little of stature, ill featured of limbs, crooked-backed, his left shoulder much higher than his right, hard-favored in appearance, and such as is in the case of lords called warlike, in other men called otherwise. He was malicious, wrathful, envious, and from before his birth, ever perverse. It is for truth reported that the Duchess his mother had so much ado in her travail to birth him that she could not be delivered of him uncut, and he came into the world with the feet forward, as men be borne outward, and (as the story runs) also not untoothed.[16]

The narrative is enticing. Richard III is a villain and More does justice to the tale. Had More stayed on this particular literary path and not attempted to champion England against the reformers, English would have had its first fine prose (that honor goes to his nemesis, William Tyndale). More's *History of King Richard III* was left unfinished, abandoned. In the greater evaluation this, too, is neither arbitrary nor random. A greatness unmet, a great writer unmade.

Argument is the tincture in a lawyer's blood, a charm too powerful to shake off.

In the end of the Shakespeare play, it is a conquering Richmond (Henry VII, a Tudor, and a Lancastrian) who ends the so-called War of the Roses, marries Elizabeth of York, and so combines the divided houses of York and Lancaster. It is a lovely dark fabrication extracted from More's *Richard III*. Of course, nothing ever stopped Shakespeare from putting a great line in a villain's mouth. "Now is the winter of our discontent, made glorious summer by this son of York," or "a horse, a horse, my kingdom for a horse," and my favorite, "I have set my life upon a cast, and I will stand the hazard of the die."

Shakespeare's *Richard III* is useful as well because it is a perfect example of translation, of interpretation, of that delicate step from Nabokov's *Fromish* to *Toish*. More's *Richard III* is just as English as Shakespeare's, but when translated, or processed through genius, it eclipses its former state. William Tyndale had the same effect with the original Hebrew and Greek manuscripts when he imagined them in English. He, too, in a sense, played to the crowd, to the plowperson.

Both Tyndale and Shakespeare worked with text that did not originate with them, but was nonetheless animated by them, brought to life in a most deathless and unrepeatable way. That migration a text makes from mere explanation to art. Also, and this is a subtle distinction, English is absorptive. It is promiscuous. It borrows and it steals from other tongues and makes them her own, so it is no real surprise that her first poets were endowed with her peculiar genius.

As we now look at the polemical works that passed between More and Tyndale, the deeper issues will become evident, primarily the nature and authority of the Church, and the translation of the Bible into the vernacular. All other arguments were in one way or another relative to these two volatile points of contention.

Hackwork

Thomas More's *A Dialogue Concerning Heresies* was published the year he became Lord Chancellor of England (1529). More decided it was important enough that he would "put business aside, and rob himself of time and sleep to defend the most essential thing in his life—the Catholic Church."[17]

Not unlike the *Assertio*, his words are well chosen, the cut precise. For the moment, More still has command of his usual bright faculties, but the slip is imminent. He is "still the artist and the man of letters . . . he has not yet sunk to the hack-work of controversy; he has not yet become the mere grinder out of arguments, the overwhelmer of the enemy with sheer length and strength of words."[18] The *Dialogue* was made up of four books, 184 folio pages, and 170,000 words.

Here is More the lawyer; More the rational, the logician, the tactician; More the argument maker. And yet, while the legal side was doubtless his best side, it didn't seem to help him in certain types of composition. The law not only had the "worst influence on his style,"[19] but in much of his polemical work he simply did not convince, or at least as a lawyer of his magnitude should convince by mere treatment of evidence. He is reduced in the end to endless repetition and what seems like pounding.

The Dialogue, as it was called, was written in the form of a conversation between More and a curious young fellow, the Messenger, who would bring up an issue and More would reply with an entire arsenal of convincing text. The Messenger, conveniently, was somewhat dull-witted.

David Daniell tries to be merciful toward More's *Dialogue*, but fails. "There is no new theological truth, just insistent reiteration that the Church can never be wrong . . . More is trying to demonstrate the patience of the Church: he can try the patience of his reader beyond endurance."[20] The following is from a man renowned as a great writer.

> I am quod I very glad that it hath been your hap to be there. Not so much for any thing that ye have shewed them of our communication already, concerning the praying of saints, worshiping of images and relics, and going in pilgrimage, wherein I think ye told them no newelte [novelty], for I doubt not but they could have told you more of the matters them self than ye have heard or could hear of me, ye have either heard somewhat whereby ye be in some part of these matters (that we shall speak of) already satisfied, wherein our business therein may be the shorter, or else ye be the more strongly instructed for the other part whereby our disputation shall be the fuller, and the matters the more plainly touched, for the more ample satisfaction of such as yourself or your master shall hereafter happen to find in any doubt of these things that we shall now touch and treat of.[21]

Reading More's English is often like attempting to run in deep sand. More, for once, to address the unrefined, the *simplicibus et idiotis hominibus*, is writing in English, not in his beloved Latin. And yet, far from being great writing, it is tedium. It wears. Maybe he is thinking in Latin and writing in English. Again, and worst of all, it condescends.

Here is an observation we might make: As you read Tyndale, you get a different register of language altogether. Tyndale would have said the above text in half the time, or less. Tyndale will seem more familiar to your ear than Thomas More—the result of being exposed to five hundred years of Bible English, which is essentially Tyndale English, Tyndale motion, Tyndale economy distilled into the conversations of everyday life. He is immensely readable.

If More's pace is leisurely, even somewhat rambling in the *Dialogue*, in the books to follow, toward the end of their debate, his pitch rises, and he is reduced to something more savage. His master, H8, has grown even more unpredictable. His transformation from spoiled boy to hideous monster, or "monstrous baby,"[22] is accelerating rapidly. And as the tie between Rome and England has begun to show signs of stress, indeed, as they threaten to snap altogether, More may suspect the undoing of his entire world.

Except for a brief flare of blood and insanity in the reign of Mary Tudor, England would never be Catholic again. According to David Starkey, there is something intrinsically English about *not* being Catholic.

The central question of More's *Dialogue* was that of authority. Did authority belong to the Church or did it belong to the Scripture? More argued that the Church was above the Scripture, that it was the Church who made the Scripture and not the other way around. This has been Catholic Church doctrine since its very inception.

To More, the Church was the ultimate authority, and the pope's interpretation of the Scripture was, and is, infallible. Indeed, there is no salvation outside the Church—*extra ecclesiam nulla salus*. This belief remains unchanged to this day, and not only in the Roman West, but in the Orthodox East (Rome's estranged sister).

More did not deny the authority of the Bible, he simply maintained that the Church was above Scripture because it was the Church who decided which books made up the canon of Scripture in the first place, what went in and what was left out. According to More, the visible* Church, or the *church revealed*, is the guardian of the true Christian faith. "Without a single, living, authoritative Church, there would be no reliable means of living the faith, much less any standard for disproving heretical doctrine."[23] The Scripture is "not the source of knowledge or the end of thinking, but rather a means to understanding."[24]

For Tyndale and the reformists, Scripture was the ultimate authority in the life of faith. It gave design and empowerment to the Church. It was not merely a prop, the third leg to support the Church (the other two being Holy Tradition—those traditions and beliefs practiced by all Christians from one generation to the next—and the teaching of the Church Fathers handed down orally beginning with the apostles). What was necessary was written. The rest is spurious, doubtful. Tyndale explains,

> The pith and substance in general of every thing necessary unto our souls' health, both of what we ought to believe, and what we ought to do, was written; and of the miracles done to confirm it, as many as were needful: so that whatsoever we ought to believe or do, that same is written expressly, or drawn out of that which is written.[25]

As the debate thickened, Tyndale returned the volley with *An Answer to Thomas More's Dialogue*. In the *Answer*, Tyndale defines the church, who, and what it is. He also defends his use of certain words that More found odious. Tyndale substitutes *elder* for *priest*, *love* for *charity*, *congregation* for *church*, *repentance* for *penance*, *knowledge* for *confession*, *favour* for *grace*. In these substitutions, Tyndale was not only tampering with language, but with a way of understanding that had been unchallenged for centuries.

---

* Luther and others argued the presence of an "invisible" church, known only to God.

Talk Softly and Write One Ridiculously Long Book

He that hath a good heart toward the word of God, and a set purpose to fashion his deeds thereafter and to garnish it with godly living and to testify it to others, the same shall increase more and more daily in the grace of Christ. But he that loveth it not, to live thereafter and to edify others, the same shall lose the grace of true knowledge and be blinded again and every day wax worse and worse and blinder and blinder, till he be an utter enemy of the word of God, and his heart so hardened, that it shall be impossible to convert him.

—William Tyndale, "W. T. unto the Reader" TNT 1534

WILLIAM TYNDALE WAS CONVINCED THAT IF YOU MISPERCEIVE God at the most primary level, your entire perception leans out of center, out of plumb. And if an entire living architecture, that is, the church, is founded on such a misperception, if the entire apparatus of faith operates by a flawed mathematic, and over a great length of time, the spoil becomes complete, and all is askew. Nothing can be right. The state of belief is merely gross misbelief.

The logical substitute for such a condition can only be superstition and myth. A saccharine faith. An imagination. Add to that what amounts to, in essence, a low-grade contempt for Scripture, and the result is predictable. That is, a religious system that is both "beetle blind" and "bedlam mad" (to borrow Tyndale's own adjectives).

Challenge is all that is left; for the established Church, at its best, misrepresents the very deity it claims to serve. For the reformer, the Church had strayed from its original formula, and therefore all of its components were flawed. Only severe rethinking would alter its course. And with no access to the Scriptures, the blindness was complete. Until men and women "could read the scriptures for themselves in their own language, the authority of the church was relatively uncontested."[1]

This chapter will consider the argument, those particular grievances between Tyndale and More.

By the way, the voice of complaint is hardly ever attractive. All the attacking and counter-attacking quickly lose their gloss and fail to amuse after a period of time. The comic abuses, the foul language, the *theatre excremental*, may entertain for a moment, then a kind of drab tedium sets in. So we will consider the issues, employ a bit of Tyndalian economics, and move on.

> *As I err in my wit, so err I in my will. When I judge that to be evil, which in deed is good, then hate I that which is good. And when I suppose that good which is evil indeed then love I evil.*
>
> – WILLIAM TYNDALE, THE OBEDIENCE OF A CHRISTIAN MAN

Out of obligation to the bigger picture, that is, the whole life of Tyndale, these arguments cannot be avoided. The list is a short one.

The first complaint, already noted, was that of *authority*. For Tyndale, the authority was the Scripture. For More and the Catholics, authority was vested solely in the Church.

Tyndale begins his *Answer* with a definition of "the church." He says the word *church* itself has many meanings. At first it was a place, a house perhaps, where people in ancient times gathered to listen to the "word of doctrine and the law of God."[2] Here they learned how to live godly in the faith of Christ. The officers "preached the pure word of God only, and prayed in a tongue all men could understand."[3]

Something changed. In time, the old guard was gone.

Tyndale, never shy, comes right to the point in the first few pages. (The word *dumb* is used in the sense of "unintelligible, mute to the general congregation.")

> Judge, therefore, reader, whether the pope with his be the church; whether their authority be above the scripture; whether all they teach without scripture be equal with the scripture . . . Judge whether it be possible that any good should come out of their dumb ceremonies and sacraments into thy soul. Judge their penance, pilgrimages, pardons, purgatory, praying to posts, dumb blessings, dumb absolutions, their dumb pattering, and howling, their dumb strange holy gestures, with all their dumb disguisings, their satisfactions and justifyings. And because thou findest them false in so many things, trust them in nothing; but judge them in all things. Mark at the last the practice of our fleshly spirituality and their ways, by which they have walked above eight hundred years; how they stablish their lies, first, with falsifying the scripture; then through corrupting with their riches, whereof they have infinite treasure in store; and last of all, with the sword.[4]

For all his modesty concerning literary style, or his denial of style altogether, the above excerpt is doubtless the voice of the preacher. However painful it might be for its hostility, here we get a rare glimpse of Tyndale the pulpiteer. The parallel construction, the alliteration, the pounding rhythm, the rhetorical punch that feels as good in the pulpit as on the printed page: "And because thou findest them false in so *many* things, trust them in *no*-thing; but judge them in *all* things." (Emphasis, mine. Charm, all Tyndale's.)

To Tyndale, the Church lost its original footing and became something quite different than was first intended. "Holy Church" in Tyndale's day meant only the pope, bishops, cardinals, legates, patriarchs, archbishops, abbots, priors, priests, monks, and so on. Or, as Tyndale gibed, that "multitude of shaven, shorn, and oiled," those of the spirituality, "the shaven flock of them that shore the world."[5]

Tyndale argued that when addressing the Church, it was to this "multitude" you spoke. In rebuttal, he cited Galatians 1:13. "For Paul saith, 'I persecuted the church of God above measure:' which was not the preachers only, but all that believed generally: as it is to see Acts xxii, where he saith: 'I persecuted this way even unto death, binding and putting in prison both men and women.'"[6]

The taste for the word *church* having gone sour in his mouth, having been reimagined as it was, Tyndale chose to use the word *congregation* instead. The church (*ecclesia*), he said, "is a multitude of all them that believe in Christ, wheresoever they be gathered together." For Tyndale's word, *congregation*, the King James translators used *assembly*.

The word ΕΚΚΛΕΣΙΑ (*ekklesia*) is defined as "a gathering of citizens called out from their homes into some public place, an assembly."[7] The *Oxford English Dictionary* defines *ecclesia* as "a Greek word for a regularly convoked assembly. On the introduction of Christianity it became the regular word for CHURCH." The KJV translates *ecclesia* as "church," and in some instances "assembly." It's not that Tyndale has issue so much with the word itself as what has been done with and to the word. Like that which lies at the heart of his complaint, it has become a distortion, a ghost, a relic, lifeless and unrecognizable.

> ❀ *Bytwene Tyndale and me no thynge ellys {else} in effecte, but to fynde out whyche chyrche is the very chyrche.*
>
> – THOMAS MORE

> Christ's elect church is the whole multitude of all repenting sinners that believe in Christ, and put all their trust and confidence in the mercy of God; feeling in their hearts that God for Christ's sake loveth

them, and will be, or rather is, merciful unto them, for forgiveth their sins of which they repent . . . And this faith is the foundation laid of the apostles and prophets; whereupon Paul saith (Ephesian ii) that we are built, and thereby of the household of God. And this faith is the rock, whereon Christ built his congregation.[8]

Not only was he clarifying what and who the church is, but the reference to "the rock" is not one that More was apt to miss. The whole papal mythology depended on a few lines of Scripture:

> He [Jesus] said unto them, But whom say ye that I am? Simon Peter answered and said, Thou art Christ, the Son of the living God. And Jesus answered and said to him: happy art thou, Simon the son of Jonas: for flesh and blood hath not opened unto thee that, but my Father which is in heaven. And I say also unto thee, That thou art Peter, and upon this rock I will build my congregation. And the gates of hell shall not prevail against it. And I will give unto thee the keys of the kingdom of heaven: and whatsoever thou bindest upon earth, shall be bound in heaven: and whatsoever thou loosest on earth shall be loosed in heaven. (Matthew 16:15–19 TNT 1534)

To the Roman, Peter himself was the "rock" upon which Christ would build his church, making him the first pope. To Tyndale, the "foundation" was not Simon Peter, but the very faith Peter expressed in his confession. Upon *this rock, this foundation,* upon *this confession, this revelation,* upon *this thing revealed to you by my Father* in heaven I will build my congregation, my church. In *The Practice of Prelates,* Tyndale wrote,

> This faith is the rock whereon Christ's church is built. For who is of Christ's church, but he only that believeth that Christ is God's Son, come into the world to save sinners? This faith is it, against which hell-gates cannot prevail. This faith is it, which saveth the congregation of Christ; and not Peter.[9]

Thomas More took issue with Tyndale on the substitution of this and other words in his translation of the New Testament. Tyndale, he said, "mistranslated three words of great weight . . . the word *Priest*; the other, the *Church*; the third, *Charity*."[10] An examination of these words will give us a view of the bigger picture—not only the specific gripe between Tyndale and More on Tyndale's translating skill, but also the divide between the reformer and the Church that refused him.

The Kingdom of God Standeth Not in Words But in Power

Writing about conflict between two people or two opposing perceptions of faith is often flypaper tacky. With hardly any effort the writer finds himself stumbling about on pasty surfaces. Objective clarity is at stake. Belief touches all of us. Even unbelief demands a kind of faith. Either way, the tread is sticky and it slows both rhythm and progress. Forgive the preamble, but after almost five hundred years, the argument is still warm.

Tyndale's taste, and that of other reformers, had long spoiled with the use of words like *church, priest, charity, favor, purgatory, penance,* and *confession* (shrift). In their place he chose what he thought was the better word—*congregation* for *church, elder* for *priest, love* for *charity,* and *favor* for *grace.* The remaining words—*purgatory, penance,* and *confession*—Tyndale dismissed altogether. He stated his objections and why he felt they had no place in genuine Christian spirituality.

Tyndale translated the Greek word *presbyter* πρεσβυτερό (presbuteros) as *senior.* He admitted that *senior* was not the best word, but at the time he couldn't think of a better one. More called him out on it, and Tyndale actually agreed. In short time he found, as Flaubert might say, *le mot juste,* the right word. "I spied my fault since, long ere M. More told it me, and have mended it in all the works which I since made, and call it an *elder.* And in that he [More] maketh heresy of it."[11] More insisted the word for the Christian minister should be *priest,* though Tyndale used the word only in reference to Jewish rabbis. He was correct in doing so. The Greek ιερεύ *hiereus* (hee-er-yooce'), referred to Jewish Levitical priests.

An infuriated More accused Tyndale, saying that he would "make us

189

to believe that we need no priest to offer up daily the same sacrifice that our savior offered once . . . And that a priest is nothing else but a man chosen among the people to preach."[12] More was stating exactly what the reformers believed.

Tyndale noted that even in More's Latin Bible the word is *presbuteros* (elder). When he asked More why Jerome and the apostles never call the Christian ministers priests (*sacerdos* or *hiereus*), More sidestepped Tyndale, and said he never had spoken with those old men so he was unable to ask them.

We have mentioned the use of *love* instead of the Vulgate *charity*. Mozley called this particular usage Tyndale's "crowning offense." As with the other word substitutes, there is much more at stake than mere semantics. To use *love* for *charity* is no less than a change of deity itself, a redefining.

It was worth the trouble of the Reformation, Tyndale would have argued, for this clarification alone. Tyndale was fond of the word *love* not only for its accuracy, but also for its flexibility. Both noun and verb, it suggested possibilities about the nature of God himself. In the word lies both *being* and *doing*, the harmony of *faith* and *works*, *spirit* and *the law*.

> *Without God's word do nothing. And to his word add nothing, neither pull anything therefrom . . . Serve God in the spirit, and thy neighbor with all outward service.*
>
> —WILLIAM TYNDALE, *THE OBEDIENCE OF A CHRISTIAN MAN*

The argument between More and Tyndale on this issue of faith and works might be addressed this way: For More, a man may have good faith and live wickedly. For Tyndale, this was all wrong. "Wicked deeds prove that a heart is unfaithful. Unless you are hitting the mark with your deeds, the aim or your soul must be crooked. Your faith should inform every activity of your being."[13]

This and other word substitutes upset the order. It gnawed at the threads and filaments that held the great myth together. To satisfy the severe demands of salvation by works alone, by merit, or by any other means of exchange, is to imply a conditional God, a conditional kind of love, which is no love.

Tyndale's substitution of *favor* for *grace* touched another deep nerve. *Grace*, for Tyndale, though he did not dismiss the word altogether, where it seemed right and where the translation seemed to suggest it, he used the word *favor* in its place. Still, in the final revision of his New Testament, he reverted back to *grace* in all but five places. No translator after Tyndale revived the use of *favor*.

For the words *purgatory, penance,* and *confession,* Tyndale showed no mercy whatsoever. Concerning such things, he said, Scripture "maketh no mention" and "knoweth not of it."

Penance is defined as "the performance of some act of self-mortification or the undergoing of some penalty as an expression of sorrow for sin or wrongdoing; religious discipline, either imposed by ecclesiastical authority or voluntarily undertaken, as a token of repentance and as a means of satisfaction for sin; (also) such discipline or observance imposed by a priest upon a penitent after confession, as an integral part of the sacrament of penance" (*OED*).

Thomas More was fond of the word. He wore a "hair shirt," that is, a garment that chafed his flesh as a reminder of his unworthiness. More also used a knotted rope to punish his sinful flesh (flagellation). This was a normal practice among pious Catholics. This punishment was a payment made to satisfy sin. For Tyndale, however, the word *penance* "is a word of their own forging to deceive us withal."[14]

> In the scripture we find *penitentia*, repentance. *Agite penitentiam*, do penance: *peniteat vos*, let it repent you. *Metanoiete* in Greek, forthink [change direction of one's thoughts] ye, or let it forthink you. Of *repentance* they have made *penance*, to blind the people and to make them think that they must take pain and do some holy deeds to make satisfaction for their sins . . . Repentance goeth before faith and prepareth the way to Christ and to the promises. For Christ cometh not, but unto them that see their sins in the law and repent. Repentance that is to say, this mourning and sorrow of the heart, lasteth all our lives long.[15]

Comic Abuse

More's final literary assault against William Tyndale, his *Confutation of Tyndale's Answer*, weighed in at a half-million words. That is more than two *Moby Dicks* or a single *War and Peace*. Most of it is just angry spew, not worthy of More's usual fare.

His text was reduced to repetition, name-calling, the same rhetorical pounce that he used against Martin Luther. He promises to draw Tyndale into the "light which illumineth every man," meaning that he will expose the reformer, and make the "matter so lightsome and so clear to every man, that I shall leave Tyndale never a dark corner to creep into, able to hide his head."[16]

There are admirers of Thomas More who wish he had never written the *Confutation of Tyndale's Answer*. It is not uncertain that Thomas More himself wished he had never written the *Confutation*. David Daniell said that "his [More's] hatred of Tyndale can be seen to be quite out of hand, and More's unhappy private obsessions appear on every page."[17] "Near-rabid" is one modifier Daniell used.

You get the feeling that More could do no worse than hurl his huge *Confutation* at the translator, beat him down with sheer mass of words. It is doubtful that anyone was about to read it, at least not in its entirety.

The Confutation of Tyndale's Answer is more of the same acid rant—only much much more. The repetition is maddening. Sir Thomas is still the lawyer, but the tactic is now exasperation. He uses excess to fill all possible gaps. Almost every page has a reiteration of the main arguments, so the reader can pick up in the middle if he desires. "The man who sits down and reads fairly fifty pages of More will find many phrases to admire; but he will also find an invertabrate length of sentence, a fumbling multiplication of eptithets, and an almost complete lack of rhythmical vitality."[18]

C. S. Lewis suggested the reason for this is because More "never really rose from a legal to a literary conception of clarity and complete-ness. He multiplies words in a vain endeavour to stop up all possible chinks, where a better artist forces his conceptions on us by the light and heat of intellect and emotion in which they burn."[19] And More was once again writing in English, to the "vulgar," playing to the gallery. At a half-million words, who cares? I doubt that the gallery was paying attention.

More took off the gloves completely. All former graces are mute. It was all pounce. C. S. Lewis said that of all More's writing, *Confutation* is "the longest, the harshest, and the dullest."[20] If More would talk "a little less about faggots and Smithfield and about Luther's 'abominable bichery,' a theme that almost obsesses him, I for one should have no quarrel with his comic abuse."[21]

Having fulfilled his daytime duties as chancellor, More worked on the *Confutation* at night. As evident in the text, he wrote swiftly, "almost furiously," composing thousands of words a week throughout summer and winter. It is written in More's favorite lawyerly style, the dialogue (the most efficient setting for dispute). He took passages from the *The Obedience* or *The Wicked Mammon* (often paraphrased, seasoned to his taste) and answered them. The following is a sampling of the general tone (spelling modernized).

WILLIAM TYNDALE: Mark whether it be not true in the highest degree . . .

THOMAS MORE: Tyndale is a great marker. There is nothing with him now but mark, mark, mark. It is a pity that the man were not made a marker of chases in some tennis play.

The text is belittling. Evidence that Tyndale's argument is well made, that Tyndale himself has grown formidable.

WILLIAM TYNDALE: Judge whether it be possible that any good should come out of their dumb [silent] ceremonies and sacraments.

THOMAS MORE: Judge good Christian reader whether it be possible that he be any better than a beast out of whose brutish beastly mouth, cometh such a filthy foam.

More was obviously depending on the faithful Catholic to receive his good pelting of the heretic translator with applause. He used current phrases, common proverbs, anecdotes, and stories to drive his thuggish humor.

> **WILLIAM TYNDALE**: More must needs grant that church is
> as common as ecclesia.
> **THOMAS MORE**: First I say that master More must not needs
> grant this to Tyndale never a whit.

Tyndale attacked More as a poet, a juggler of words, who "rageth, and fareth exceeding foul with himself . . . he biteth, sucketh, gnaweth, towseth [to ransack] and mowseth [to master by romping] Tyndale."[22] While unattractive, if not entertaining, such a climate is unavoidable where strong passions collide. "In scurrility [coarseness of speech, esp. in invective and jesting]," C. S. Lewis said of the pair, "they are about equals."

At a more civil pitch, the literary approach of Tyndale and More begs comparison. The following excerpt by Lewis is both clear and insightful, and summarizes subtleties of shading between them. It is also too rich to ignore or dismiss.

> Where Tyndale is most continuously and obviously superior to More is in style. He is, beyond comparison, lighter, swifter, more economical. He is very unadorned (an occasional alliteration, some rhetorical repetitions, some asyndeton) but not at all jejune [uninteresting]. The rhythm is excellent, the sort of rhythm which is always underlining the argument . . . What we miss in Tyndale is the manysidedness, the elbow-room of More's mind; what we miss in More is the joyous, lyric quality of Tyndale. The sentences that stick to mind from Tyndale's work are half way to poetry—"Who taught eagles to spy out their prey? Even so the children of God spy out their father"—"that they might love and love again"—"Where the Spirit is, it is always summer." In More we feel all the "smoke and stir" of London; the very plodding of his sentences is like horse traffic in the streets. In Tyndale we breathe the mountain air. Amid all More's jokes I feel a melancholy in the background; amid all

Tyndale's severities there is something like laughter, that laughter which he speaks of as coming from "the low bottom of the heart."[23]

We have noted the differences between More and Tyndale, including temper and doctrine, but if you look closer, there was much about them that was very similar. They were both contemptuous of the Middle Ages and were both men of the "new learning." Lewis also suggested that "if the view be accepted that a feudal world was at this time being replaced by something harsher in the social and economic sphere, that More and Tyndale belonged to the Old."[24]

Together, More and Tyndale introduced more than five hundred new words into the English language. We have already been acquainted with many of William Tyndale's contributions to the language, and appendix B presents the list of first usage as indexed in the *Oxford English Dictionary*.

For a small sample, and to cite words you and I use every day, the *Oxford English Dictionary* credits Thomas More with the following: *absurdity, accumulate, addict, aloof, alternate, ambiguous, anticipate, anxiety, audible, banker, bankrupt, circumvention, circumscribe, deliberately, event, exact, exaggerate, explain, foreseen, forthcoming, function, heretical, hyperbole, immediate, incidently, indelible, indifference, insinuate, invite, limited, logical, meanness, meat market, monopoly, mutilate, necessitate, obstruction, paradox, perniciously, political, precision, pretext, reprobate, reprove, resuscitate, revealed, saintly, slavery, smug, substitute, suppression, Talmud, tongue-tied, ultra-*[prefix], *uncontrolled, unloving, vehemence, warmly, well-spent,* and *utopia.*

More introduced the word *vocabulary* itself into the language.

Beyond their native intelligence, their academic pedigree, their zeal for faith, and that they were both literary men, there are other similarities we might note between William Tyndale and Thomas More. They were, as the great often are, both tragic men who shared a similar end.

In the Power of Leviathan

Both William Tyndale and Thomas More spent their last days in prison. High profile prisoners, they were both secluded, kept behind castle walls—More in the Tower of London, and Tyndale in Vilvoorde Castle near Brussels. More's cell was a pentagonal stone chamber, eighteen by twenty feet in dimension, with a vaulted ceiling and walls nine to thirteen feet thick, an accommodation reserved for the privileged. For a time he was allowed books and writing instruments, to take exercise and have guests. He even had a servant.

Tyndale was not so fortunate. We will cover the details of Tyndale's imprisonment in a final chapter, but he was confined to a dungeon, and with all the adjectives your darker imagination can supply.

The captivity for both Tyndale and More was extensive, the length of days almost identical, to the number. Tyndale was captive 500 days; More 445. They were separated by a couple of hundred miles, and by the conditions of their internment, but there was actually a small window of time, between May and July of 1535, that the two men were in prison at the same time.

Thomas More refused to acknowledge H8 as Supreme Head of the Church of England (a term More thought contradictory and impossible). He did not attend the wedding of H8 and Anne Boleyn—forgivable for a lesser mortal perhaps, but not for one with a presence as large as More's and one with such close proximity to the king. Meaning was too prevalent, too vocal.

Relieving himself of the chain of office, More thought he might simply recede from public life, return to his beloved Chelsea—a kind of self-imposed banishment. But H8 would have none of it. Charged with treason, all of More's lands were confiscated, and his head was required of him.

Both Tyndale and More were martyrs for their respective faiths. They were equally defiant, Tyndale toward the pope, to Roman custom, to the silence between God and the plowboy, to a stubborn English spirituality; and More ultimately to the passions of his king and a changing England.

England has since reclaimed both More and Tyndale, as nations will do in quieter times and upon reflection of their own greatness.[*]

---

[*] Between More and Tyndale, Thomas More has received the greater share of honor. He is on the calendar of saints in both the Anglican and Roman Catholic Church. More was canonized (created a saint) by Pope Pius XI 19 May 1935. William Tyndale is officially recognized in the Anglican Church with a Collect Proper on 6 October.

Thomas More and William Tyndale never met, in spite of the small-ness of the circles they trafficked. By 1535, Humphrey Monmouth, Tyndale's patron during his year in London, was one of the sheriffs of London. As if irony could be anything but strange, it was Monmouth who led Thomas More to the scaffold on the day of his execution. More had arrested Monmouth and thrown him in the Tower for suspicion of heresy just years before. It was an awkward justice, and yet it is doubtful that Monmouth found much joy in it.

Edward Halle, whose *Chronicles* was the source for much of John Foxe's account of Tyndale, was one of the many under-sheriffs in London at the time. He was present at More's beheading as well. In his account of the event, Halle wrote that one of the last requests Thomas More made at the block was that his beard not be severed, for it had done nothing to deserve punishment. "Thus with a mock," Halle said, "he ended his life."[25] It took one stroke of the axe to separate his head from his body. As custom dictated, the executioner lifted the head and cried out, "Behold the head of a traitor!"*

None of this is to imply that Sir Thomas More's imprisonment was easy or that he did not pay a heavy cost emotionally and physically. By 1535, Henry VIII had begun to show signs of mental undoing, and the fallout was monstrous. By the time More was arrested, he had been emotionally drawn and quartered, and by men he had been friends with for years.

But it is his behavior in those last days that assure Thomas More of greatness. And whatever this book may suggest, or whatever you may read into my words, this greatness cannot be sullied or denied.

---

* Thomas More's head was boiled (customary) and set upon a pike on London Bridge. Sometime later, More's daughter Margaret got possession of the head. Her use for it is undocumented, and legend has contaminated the small evidences available.

15

The Medicine of Scripture

For the nature of God's word is, that whosoever read it or hear it reasoned and disputed before him, it will begin immediately to make him every day better and better, till he be grown into a perfect man in the knowledge of Christ and love of the law of God.

—William Tyndale, *Preface to The Obedience of a Christian Man*

I AM AS VULNERABLE AS THE NEXT GUY WHEN IT COMES TO BEING swept up by a metaphor, by that delicate art of resemblance, where one image allows you to visualize another by a trick of linguistic misdirection. When the music is just right, there is nothing finer in the world. Nothing. Still, that Thomas More became chancellor of England the same year Tyndale shipwrecked, although a natural disaster, it is a frighteningly accurate image.

Marten de Keyser printed Tyndale's translation of the Pentateuch in Antwerp, January 1530, though the work of translation itself was done in Hamburg. Things had heated up in Antwerp. On 7 December 1530 an edict was issued that warned against writing or printing any new book "upon what subject soever" without a license. The offender would be "pilloried, and marked besides with a red-hot iron, or to have an eye put out or a hand cut off at the discretion of the judge, who was to see that sentence to be executed without delay." Back home, a royal injunction in that same year forbid anyone to buy or own an English Bible.[1]

Hamburg was an ideal location for a translator (again, *ideal* is relative). The German Reformation had claimed the city. There was sufficient Hebrew there as well. Tyndale had no Hebrew when he left England in 1524. Germany is the most likely place he would have learned it. Wittenberg, Hamburg, Marburg, and Worms all had teachers, and the odd rabbi or two.

Neither Europe nor England were friends of the Jews by anyone's measure. Edward I had routed them out of England in the thirteenth century (Edict of Expulsion, 1290). Thomas More and Martin Luther were unkind to them as well. The Jews were, Luther said, "a base, and whoring people," and not a people of God. But their Hebrew was necessary for Bible translation.

There is no such xenophobia to be detected in Tyndale. It was not in him to hate. He did not *hate* the corrupt prelate. He did not *hate* Thomas More. He neither wished for nor delighted in anyone's death as More and others had. Hate was simply not a way Tyndale chose to regulate his passion. He lived by a higher rule. It was one of the many things he did not have in common with the age.

He had powerful emotions, certainly, and his words had intelligent bite, but to him the word *reform* meant just what it appeared to mean. He would have loved nothing more than to see a kind of repentance or a turning on the part of the English spirituality. But he also knew them too well to be optimistic.

Myles Coverdale was waiting for Tyndale when he arrived in Hamburg. They lived and worked together at the home of Margaret Emerson.

> Thus, having lost by that ship, both money, his copies, and his time, he came in another ship to Hamburgh, where, at his appointment, Master Coverdale tarried for him, and helped him in the translating of the whole five books of Moses, from Easter till December, in the house of a worshipful widow, Mistress Margaret Van Emmerson, A.D. 1529; a great sweating sickness being at the same time in the town. So,

having despatched his business at Hamburgh, he returned afterwards
to Antwerp again.[2]

Myles (or Miles) Coverdale (1488–1569) was a few years older than
Tyndale. The two of them most likely met at Cambridge. Little is known
of their correspondence, but it is certain that Tyndale requested his help
in Hamburg.

Years later, in the reign of Edward VI, Coverdale was made bishop of
Exeter. His tenure was a short one. When Mary Tudor became queen in
1553, she returned (or attempted to return) England to Rome. Coverdale
fled England for Denmark and other places, and returned in the reign
of Elizabeth in 1558. Fortunately, and unlike many of Tyndale's friends,
Coverdale died of natural causes at eighty-one—very, very old in those days.

A Hebrew Heart and Mind

If Tyndale actually shipwrecked, having lost everything he would have
needed to replenish his small library of books necessary to translate the
Old Testament—the Septuagint (LXX), Martin Luther's German translation of the Bible, and Jerome's Vulgate, not to mention his Hebrew and
Greek grammar. According to Foxe's account already cited, the printed
version of the Pentateuch would have been the restored version, the original having been lost at sea.

Since Tyndale had learned, and was continuing to learn Hebrew,
there were reasons to revise his 1526 New Testament. His understanding
of Hebrew gave him new information about the Greek. One informed the
other in certain ways. This was a new consideration at the time.

His 1534 New Testament had more than five thousand changes,
reflecting this renewed perception of *the whole*. Tyndale's Bible possesses a
unity not only of language, but also of Hebrew thought and conscience, in
both testaments. For all its New Testament Greek, and the unveiling of its
Christ, Tyndale's New Testament is still offspring of the Hebrews. It has a
Hebrew heart and mind.

Half of the changes made to the translation were designed to "bring the English nearer to the Greek original. Connecting particles are inserted, loose renderings made more precise; sometimes a new interpretation is adopted, or a sentence completely rewritten."[3] It was simply a more polished, seasoned, and corrected version. Mozley noted that "roughnesses are smoothed away, paraphrases are pruned, and a number of heavy or antique words disappear." "O ye *endued with* little faith" became "O ye *of* little faith" (Matthew 8:26). "And ye shall find *ease* unto your souls" became "And ye shall find *rest* unto your souls" (Matthew 11:29). By some measure these changes may seem small, but Tyndale invested seven or more years on such detail.

The colophon (printer's identification) on the 1534 revised New Testament says "Imprinted at Antwerp by Martin Emperor Anno 1534." As mentioned earlier, because of the nature of the outlawed texts and the irresistible profitability attached to them, printers used many aliases. Martin Emperor, or L' Empereur, is, in fact, Martin (sometimes Marten) de Keyser. If you look closely at the two names, the disguise is amusing. *Kaiser*, in German, means emperor (adopted from *Caesar*). The age, indeed, had a sense of humor if you knew where to look for it. Like Tyndale, it chose to remain hidden. The title page of the 1534 New Testament reads:

THE NEW TESTAMENT
diligently corrected and compared with the Greek
By
WILLIAM TYNDALE
and finished in the year of our Lord God
A. 1534
in the month of November

In *Obedience*, Tyndale noted how the Hebrew and the English work more fluently and more promisingly together than they do with the Latin. "And the properties of the Hebrew tongue agreeth a thousand times more with the English than with the Latin. The manner of speaking is both one, so that in a thousand places thou needest not but to translate it into the English word for word."[4]

Tyndale had a sense of the Hebrew language, rare for the times. He understood it at depths necessary for a clear and simple translation. "His [Tyndale's] ability to catch the Hebrew spirit, and his boldness with English, are remarkable and are now at last becoming more appreciated."[5] His Pentateuch was the first English translation from the original Hebrew, and was the model for all English translations to follow.

To make any subject clear and simple takes command, but especially language, as elusive and malleable as it can be. To speculate, if language affects the way we think and perceive, if it affects cognition as theorized, Tyndale's mastery of eight languages would certainly have given him the necessary tools to compare the subtleties that exist between tongues—the nuance, the delicate shifts of pitch and mood, the rise and fall of its music.

An Impertinent Joye

In his 1534 revised New Testament, Tyndale included a lengthy preface (*W. T. Unto the Reader*), which was followed by yet a second preface reasonably titled *William Tyndale, Yet Once More to the Christian Reader*. George Joye, another Tyndale underling, a Cambridge man, worked for a season with Tyndale in Antwerp on the revision of the New Testament, before its 1534 release.

But what may have started as a promising arrangement between Joye and Tyndale eventually soured. Before Tyndale published his 1534 revision, Joye took the manuscript, quietly made changes to Tyndale's work, then published it himself. "I was astonied [astonished]," Tyndale wrote, "and wondered not a little what fury had driven him [Joye] to make such change and to call it a diligent translation."[6]

To add to the injury, Joye did not attach his own name to the altered manuscript. Tyndale agreed that to translate is any man's right. Do all the translating you want, certainly, just put your own name on it. Joye's tampering implied Tyndale authorship.

The complaint ignited over the treatment of the word *resurrection* (αναστασί *anastasis*). Every place Tyndale used the word, Joye substituted the phrase "the life after this life" or some variation. Tyndale said that for a long time Joye had "marvellous imaginations about this word *resurrection*."[7] Among the English reformers in 1533, the resurrection was a hot topic.

Tyndale felt obligated not only to voice his complaint about George Joye, but to part company with him as well. Tyndale could no longer tolerate Joye's "unquiet curiosity." Once again the integrity of the translation was at stake, and Joye would only undermine Tyndale's effort.

Joye had not "used the office of an honest man," Tyndale wrote, "seeing he knew that I was correcting in [the New Testament] myself: neither did he walk after the rules of the love and softness which Christ and his disciples teach us."[8] In his *Yet Once More* preface, Tyndale included a well-informed argument about the word *resurrection*.

At the conclusion of this second preface, Tyndale restated that this New Testament was "diligently corrected." And once again, if there be fault in it, "let them show it me, if they be nigh, or write to me, if they be far off, or write openly against it and improve it, and I promise them, if I shall perceive that their reasons conclude, I will confess mine ignorance openly."[9]

Both William Roye and George Joye pressed Tyndale to publicize his complaints—against Roye in the preface of *The Parable of the Wicked Mammon* and against Joye in the *Yet Once More to the Christian Reader* preface to the 1534 revision of the New Testament. This is unfortunate on both accounts. For all that was lovely and life-altering about *The Wicked Mammon*, for all its generosity and innovation, and for the grand second act of Tyndale's New Testament, the complaint that filled its first pages left a blemish.

One last note about George Joye. He translated many of the Old Testament books, including Jeremiah, Isaiah, Lamentations, Proverbs, Ecclesiastes, and Psalms (1530). Though it is difficult to determine percentage of use, the Myles Coverdale Bible (1535) included Joye's translations. The Matthew's Bible (1537) included Joye's translation as well. But as a translator, Joye worked with a formidable handicap. He knew no Hebrew. What he translated, he translated from the Latin. There is a touch of the plagiarist in Joye. He brought no innovation to the field, no heat of genius.

W T

The Old Testament came together in three parts. First was the Pentateuch in 1530 (a second edition of Genesis in 1534); Tyndale's book of Jonah came out in May 1531; the books of Joshua through 2 Chronicles were included in John Rogers' Matthew's Bible of July 1537 (the name Thomas Matthew is itself an alias for Rogers).

Though some are doubtful that Tyndale actually translated these books, his presence is evident. Mozley wrote, "In these unnamed books we find also the little peculiarities, the unusual habits, the tricks and inconsistencies, which we have learnt to know in Tyndale's New Testament and Pentateuch. No one would dream of imitating these, or could succeed if he tried."[10]

There is no reason to doubt Tyndale's translation of these books.

In Matthew's Bible, the first approved English Bible, between the Old Testament and the New is a page imprinted with the initials W T. In that span between Malachi and the Gospel of Matthew, Rogers gives us the identity of its true father.

Printed in Antwerp in 1537, the Matthew's Bible contained Tyndale's New Testament, his translation of the Pentateuch, the books from Joshua through 2 Chronicles, and the book of Jonah. Coverdale's translation filled in the rest. The historian Edward Halle wrote:

> This man [Tyndale] translated the New Testament into English, and first put it in print, and likewise he translated the five books of Moses, Joshua, Judges, Ruth, the books of the Kings [Samuel and 1–2 Kings] and the books of Paralipomenon [Chronicles], Nehemiah or the first of Esdras, the prophet Jonas, and no more of the holy scripture.[11]

The Apple of His Eye

Unlike his 1526 New Testament, included in both the Pentateuch and the 1534 revised New Testament are prologues and prefaces to the reader. In these many introductions and reader guides, Tyndale is part teacher, part explorer, part shepherd, part sentinel. In the prefaces that introduce the Old Testament and the New Testament, there is the occasional stab of heated text—his lunge toward Joye, and the usual suspects (the pope and his minions, More, Wolsey, and others). But in his prologues to the separate books of the Bible he stays focused on the Scripture.

Tyndale is infinitely quotable. In the *Prologue upon the First Epistle of St. Paul to the Corinthians*, he wrote, "Where love is not, there is nothing that pleaseth God. For that one should love another, is all that God requireth of us."[12]

His prologue to the book of Jonah is five times longer than the Scripture it prologues. Following is a brief excerpt from that prologue:

> And of the gospel or promises which thou meetest in the scripture, believe fast that God will fulfil them unto thee, and that unto the uttermost jot, at the repentance of thine heart, when thou turnest to him and forsakest evil, even of his goodness and fatherly mercy unto thee, and not for thy flattering him with hypocritish works of thine own feigning.[13]

Exodus 15 of the William Tyndale Old Testament begins, "Then Moses and the children of Israel sang this song unto the Lord." In this passage we find: "The Lord is my strength and my song, and is become my salvation." Psalm 118:4 in the King James Version repeats Tyndale word for word (after the Myles Coverdale Bible or possibly the translation of the Psalms by George Joye). The familiar "My God, my God, why hast thou forsaken me?" of Psalm 22:1 is another Tyndale translation (from Matthew 27:46 in the 1526 TNT).

Tyndale ran out of time before he could translate the entire Old Testament, and yet we must credit him with the lyrical blueprint of the Psalms, the weight and movement of its music. Listen to the passage from his translation of Exodus 15:

> *The Lord is my strength and my song, and is become my salvation.*
> *He is my God and I will glorify him,*

he is my father's God and I will lift him up on high.
The Lord is a man of war, Jehovah is his name:
Pharao's chariots and his host hath he cast into the sea.
His jolly captains are drowned in the Red Sea,
the deep waters have covered them: they sank to the bottom as a stone.
Thine hand Lord is glorious in power,
thine hand Lord hath all to-dashed the enemy.[14]

The Lord is my strength and my song . . . I will glorify him . . . I will lift him up on high. William Tyndale gave the Psalms its recognizable sound, though his contribution is indirect. He essentially gave future translators a sonic template, and taught what to listen for. The following excerpt is from Deuteronomy 32 (the song of Moses).

Hear O heaven and I shall speak
And hear O earth the words of my mouth.
My doctrine drop as doth the rain, and my speech flow as doth the dew . . .
He found him [Israel] in a desert land, in a void ground and a roaring
   wilderness.
He led him about and gave him understanding,
and kept him as the apple of his eye.
As an eagle that stirreth up her nest and fluttereth over her young,
he stretched out his wings and took him up and bare him on his shoulders.

As it is with all that he translated, it is not enough to say that he merely Englished the text before him (whether Hebrew or Greek). It needed the right negotiator, the broker of "authentic genius."[15] In *The Shadow of a Great Rock: A Literary Appreciation of the King James Bible,* Harold Bloom said that "Tyndale's New Testament is so vast an aesthetic improvement upon the Greek text that I am perpetually delighted."[16] "Nearly everything memorable in the English New Testament is the achievement of the matchless William Tyndale," Bloom noted, "and not of the early Christian authors."[17]

The Soft Internal Tissue

Consistent with Tyndale's belief that the Scripture is a living thing, in *A Prologue Showing the Use of the Scripture* that introduces his translation of the Pentateuch, he informs the reader how to perceive what they are about to read.

Not only does Tyndale's language make it a personal experience with God, he also encourages the reader to see themselves in the text, to perceive the Scripture as a kind of mirror, or as Tyndale said it himself, "when thou seest thyself in the glass of God's word." "As thou readest," he said, "therefore think that every syllable pertaineth to thine own self, and suck out the pith of the scripture and arm thyself against all assaults."[18]

In the subtext of all Tyndale believed and taught was his conviction that Scripture, far from being mere text or inanimate components of expression, was alive and vibrant. In the *Prologue to the Book of Jonas* (Jonah), he wrote, "The scripture has a body without, and within a soul, spirit and life . . . And within it hath a pith, kernel, marrow, and all sweetness for God's elect."

> *Read God's word diligently and with a good heart and it shall teach you all things.*
>
> – WILLIAM TYNDALE, *A PROLOGUE INTO THE FOURTH BOOK OF MOSES CALLED NUMBERS*

Not only does Tyndale's translation have a great orality, that is, a pleasing aesthetic of sound, it has *interiority* as well, that rare ability for a text to penetrate and inspire movement beneath the common surfaces.

> Though a man had a precious jewel and a rich, yet if he wist [know] not the value thereof nor wherefore it served, he were neither the better nor richer of a straw. Even so though we read the scripture and babble of it never so much, yet if we know not the use of it, and wherefore it was given, and what is therein to be sought, it profiteth us nothing at all. It is not enough therefore to read and talk of it only, but we must

also desire God day and night instantly to open our eyes, and to make us understand and feel wherefore [why] the scripture was given, that we may apply the medicine of the scripture, every man to his own sores, unless that we intend to be idle disputers, and brawlers about vain words, ever gnawing upon the bitter bark without and never attaining unto the sweet pith within, and persecuting one another for defending of lewd imaginations and fanstasies of our own invention.[19]

Tyndale clearly loved the bustling inner life of Scripture. The word *pith*, perhaps his favorite word, means "the innermost or central part of a thing; the essential or vital part; the spirit or essence; the core, the nub."[20] Of a plant, it is "the soft internal tissue." As a translator, Tyndale meddled with the interior life of a word. He loved this type of interrogation, particularly where meaning and sound could agree.

According to the excerpt above, desiring God is the key to the "sweet pith within," the soft internal tissue. It is the code that unlocks the deep medicines of Scripture. Looking into the Scripture, therefore, is not a one-sided enterprise. It implies a kind of mutual exploration.

While *meaning* can be elusive, Tyndale approached Scripture by two avenues, *feeling* and *study*. He gave priority to feeling. He referred to Christianity itself as a "feeling" faith. In the prologue to Exodus he wrote:

If any man ask me, seeing that faith justifieth me why I work? I answer love compelleth me. For as long as my soul feeleth what love God hath shewed me in Christ, I cannot but love God again and his will and commandments and of love work them, nor can they seem hard unto me.[21]

Feeling is a distinction only possible with a living Scripture, one that interacts with its readers and hearers. "Where the Spirit is there is feeling," he wrote, "for the Spirit maketh us feel all things. Where the Spirit is not there is no feeling, but a vain opinion or imagination."[22] It is not enough to know about God, to read and talk about God (which profits little), but *desire* is essential, a *feeling desire* for God, to engage with God not only in the Scriptures, but in the work of love. "And let love interpret the law," he said. The Pentateuch is the essence of the law, handed down to

Moses, and therefore it may be interpreted, or perceived, from its New Testament Christ.

> And let love interpret the law that thou understand this to be the final end of the law, and the whole cause why the law was given: even to bring thee to the knowledge of God, how that he hath done all things for thee, that thou mightest love him again and with all thine heart and thy neighbor for his sake as thyself and as Christ loved thee. Because thy neighbor is the son of God also and created unto his likeness as thou art, and bought with as dear blood as art thou.[23]

A Small Still Voice

The following samples from Genesis to 2 Chronicles are classic Tyndale. Each one has the old sound, the old music, the old familiar authority. From "Let my people go" to "after the fire, came a small still voice." The Old Testament had just as much punch at its debut as the New Testament in 1526.

Because Tyndale only numbered the chapters and not the verses, I will cite chapter only. (It wasn't until the advent of the Geneva Bible in 1557 that the chapters were divided into verses.) As with the Christmas story or the parables of Jesus with their deep reminiscence, their homespun solemnity, this small sampling is chosen primarily for something that endures in a certain line of text or a certain music—a word or phrase of note.

Then said Adam: this is once bone of my bones, and flesh of my flesh. This shall be called woman: because she was taken of the man. For this cause shall a man leave his father and mother and cleave unto his wife, and they shall be one flesh. And they were either of them naked, both Adam and his wife, and were not ashamed. (Genesis 2)

And they heard the voice of the Lord as he walked in the garden in the cool of the day. (Genesis 3)

And the Lord said unto Cain: where is Abel they brother? And he said: I cannot tell, am I my brother's keeper? (Genesis 4)

And he said: come not hither, but put thy shoes off thy feet: for the place whereon thou standest is holy ground. (Exodus 3)

Then Moses and Aaron went and told Pharao, thus saith the Lord God of Israel. Let my people go. (Exodus 5)

For I know their sorrow and am come down to deliver them out of the hands of the Egyptians, and to bring them out of that land unto a good land and a large, and unto a land that floweth with milk and honey. (Exodus 3)

And the Lord said: behold, there is a place by me, and thou shalt stand upon a rock, and while my glory goeth forth I will put thee in a cleft of the rock, and will put mine hand upon thee while I pass by. And then I will take away mine hand, and thou shalt see my back parts: but my face shall not be seen. (Exodus 33)

The Lord bless thee and keep thee.
The Lord make his face shine upon thee and be merciful unto thee.
The Lord lift up his countenance upon thee, and give thee peace. (Numbers 6)

But if it seem evil unto you to serve the Lord, then choose you this day whom you will serve. (Joshua 24)

Entreat me not to leave thee,
and to return from after thee,
for whither thou goest, I will go,
and where thou dwellest, there I will dwell:
thy people are my people, and thy God is my God.
where thou diest, I will die, and there will be buried. (Ruth 1)

But now thy kingdom shall not continue. The Lord hath sought him a man after his own heart, and hath commanded him to be a captain over his people: because thou hast not kept that which the Lord commanded thee. (1 Samuel 13)

Then Nathan said to David: thou art the man. (2 Samuel 12)

And behold, the Lord went by and a mighty strong wind that rent the mountains and brake the mountains before him. But the Lord was not in the wind. And after the wind came an earthquake. But the Lord was not in the earthquake. And after the earthquake, came fire: but the Lord was not in the fire. And after the fire, came a small still voice. (I Kings 19)

Innovation

Before Tyndale's Genesis there was John Wycliffe's Bible and the Latin Vulgate. But only the educated could read *"In principio creavit Deus coelum et terram. Terra autem erat inanis et vacua, et tenebrae erant super faciem abyssi, et spiritus Dei ferebatur super aquas. Dixitque Deus: Fiat lux! et fact est lux."* If you had a copy of the Wycliffe Bible at the time, you would be a bit more fortunate. Still, Wycliffe is a world away from Tyndale.

> *In the bigynnyng God made of nouyt heuene and erthe. Forsothe the erthe was idel and voide, and derknessis weren on the face of depthe; and the Spiryt of the Lord was borun on the watris. And God seide, Liyt be maad, and liyt was maad.* (Wycliffe Bible 1395)

> *In the beginning God created heaven and earth. The earth was void and empty, and darkness was upon the deep, and the spirit of God moved upon the water. Then God said: let there be light and there was light.* (William Tyndale Old Testament)

Mentioned earlier, according to the *Oxford English Dictionary*, William Tyndale was credited with the first usage of the word *Jehovah*. This was his response to YHWH (known elsewhere as Yahweh), the four-consonant name of God, otherwise known as the *tetragrammaton*. The name was held by the ancients to be unspeakable. The Vulgate used the word *Adonai* (*nomen meum Adonai*). Wycliffe's English Bible, which was translated from the Latin and not the Hebrew, did the same (my great name Adonai).

Another Tyndale innovation is *the* + *noun* + *of* + *the* + *noun* construct, found in phrases like "beasts of the field," "the word of the Lord," and so on. "State of the union" is an example of modern usage of this same construct, as is "law of the land." In the above sampling of Old Testament Scripture we are introduced to "bone of my bones," and "flesh of my flesh," and "the voice of the Lord."

Adapting the Hebrew to the English, as Tyndale did, gave us "the Book of Moses" instead of "Moses' Book," "the children of Israel" instead of "Israel's children." While these seem so familiar to you and me for their assimilation into our religious idiom, they were introduced in Tyndale.

So Why Jonah?

Is it random? Is there some message within the message? Tyndale translated all the New Testament, including a second revision. He translated the Pentateuch, the books of Joshua to 2 Chronicles, then curiously jumped to the book Jonah (Jonas). This small book was obviously an important inclusion to Tyndale. The title itself is a sermonette.

> The Prophet Jonas, with an introduction before teaching to understand him and the right use also of all the scripture, and why it was written, and what is therein to be sought, and showing wherewith the scripture is locked up that he which readeth it, cannot understand it, though he study therein never so much: and again with what keys it is so opened, that the reader can be stopped out with no subtlety or false doctrine of man, from the true sense and understanding thereof.[24]

In *The Prologue to the Book of Jonas*, he retells the story how Jonas (Jonah), after being commanded to go to Nineveh and preach repentance, was as willing as a woman "commanded to leap into a tub of living snakes and adders." Jonah said, "I will get me another way." God had other plans for Jonah, of course. The image was a huge fish, but Jonah was swallowed up by the monster of his own resistance. In his confinement, when his imaginations had somewhat cooled, he prayed (the prayer between God and Jonah will remain sealed, for only his thanksgiving is recorded). But Tyndale's explanation anticipates a more modern perception.

When Jonah had been in the fish's belly a space and the rage of his conscience was somewhat quieted and suaged and he come to himself again and had received a little hope, the qualms and pangs of desperation which went over his heart, half overcome, he prayed, as he maketh mention in the text saying Jonas prayed unto the Lord his God out of the belly of the fish. But the words of that prayer are not here set. The prayer that here standeth in the text, is the prayer of praise and thanksgiving which he prayed and wrote when he was escaped and past all jeopardy. In the end of which prayer he saith, I will sacrifice with the voice of thanksgiving and pay that I have vowed that saving cometh of the Lord. For verily to confess out of the heart, that all benefits come of God, even out of the goodness his mercy and not deserving of our deeds, is the only sacrifice that pleaseth God.[25]

Tyndale said Jonas had been educated in "a new school," in a furnace where "he was purged of much refuse and dross of fleshly wisdom, which resisted the wisdom of God and led Jonas's will contrary to the will of God." That is a lot of imagery for being consigned to the belly of a fish. Tyndale's point is that as we are blind in Adam, we "cannot but seek and will our own profit, pleasure and glory." However, if we are taught in the Spirit, "we cannot but seek and will the pleasure and glory of God only."[26]

Jonas continued his "repent or perish" message to the Ninevites.

Behind his lesson of Jonas was a reluctant England that Tyndale felt commanded to preach to, if but from a remove (he was on the continent). Tyndale was convinced, even as he suggested in the *Prologue to the Exposition upon the First Epistle of John* that even as it was not enough for the parents to conceive a child and to birth a child, they had to take care of that child until it could take care of itself. In the same way Tyndale said, "Even so it is not enough to have translated the scripture into the vulgar and common tongue, except we also brought again the light to understand it."[27] He took this responsibility unto himself. It was not enough to give them a Bible. A lamp was necessary to read it by.

It is to the repentant soul, the soul that thirsts and longs after God, and after the promises of God (the evangelion) that the Scripture opens itself, and comes to flower in the heart.

> Thou must search diligently for the promises of mercy which God hath promised thee again . . . and that the promises be given unto a repenting soul that thirsteth and longeth after them, of the pure and fatherly mercy of God through our faith only without all the deserving of our deeds or merits or works, but for Christ's sake alone and for the merits and deservings of his works, death, and passions that he suffered altogether for us, and not for himself . . . If they [the promises of God] be written in thine heart, are the keys which so open all the scripture unto thee, that no creature can lock thee out, and with which thou shalt go in and out, and find pasture and food everywhere. And if these lessons be not written in thine heart, then is all the scripture shut up, as a kernel in the shell, so that thou mayest read it and commune of it and rehearse all the stories of it and dispute subtly and be a profound sophister, and yet understand not one jot thereof.[28]

The book of Jonah—powerful, brief, and moved along by a dramatic narrative—was of great interest and use to the reformers. Luther translated it in 1526 as a separate work, before completing an entire Old Testament in 1534. The heart of the message is the necessity to preach salvation to a sinful people, in spite of the weakness of the preacher himself.

For Tyndale, it was still about a vernacular Scripture, about a hoarding prelacy, a false church. A people threatened by their own sinfulness, and yet ignorant of a gospel they are hardly aware of, need an interpreter, someone to hold up the "glass of God's word."

16

Now We See in a Glass
Even in a Dark Speaking

*The cause is verily, that except a man cast away his own
imagination and reason, he cannot perceive God, and
understand the virtue and power of the blood of Christ.*

—William Tyndale, *A Pathway into the Holy Scripture*

HE WAS AMIABLE, SYMPATHETIC. RELIGION HAD NOT YET HARDENED
in him. Stephen Vaughn was a friend of Thomas Cromwell's and had
been in his service since 1524. His business took him back and forth to
Antwerp and his nature was suitable to the delicate work Cromwell had
in mind.

Cromwell started thinking that perhaps bringing William Tyndale
back to England might not be such a bad idea. He imagined some advantage
to his continuing propaganda efforts. Tyndale had grown in stature, and
would perhaps be the only mind capable of any challenge, or counterbalance,
to Chancellor More.

Vaughn sent a series of letters to Henry and to Cromwell. In these letters it was clear that he was having difficulty finding the translator. He had sent letters to Tyndale—to Frankfurt, Hamburg, and Marburg—assuring him of safe passage, and by royal sanction. Through his own agents, Tyndale finally responded to Vaughn, and from Vaughn's correspondence home it was clear that Tyndale did not trust the situation. He had heard disturbing things, and he was certain Thomas More would honor no pledge made to a "heretic."

In time, and again through a mediator (Tyndale was ever cautious), Vaughn was given a portion of a book Tyndale was writing at the time, *Tyndale's Answer to Thomas More's Dialogue.* Tyndale did not want to publish the manuscript until he had some idea how the king was going to react. Vaughn was aware also that Tyndale had drafted a letter to the king that would accompany the book. He spoke with Cromwell about it, doubting the king was going to be too pleased with any letter from Tyndale at the moment. The king was still chafing about Tyndale's *Practice of Prelates.*

For all that pleased the king with *Obedience,* Henry steamed at *Prelates.*

As for Tyndale's yet-to-be-published book, Vaughn told Cromwell, "He maketh my Lord Chancellor [Thomas More] such an answer as I am loth to praise or dispraise. No work that ever he made is written in so gentle a style." It was an honest appraisal. *The Answer* was direct, and it was the last work of its kind. Vaughn was stunned by it.

> God hath created us and made us into his own likeness; and our Saviour Christ hath bought us with his blood. And therefore are we God's possession, of duty and right; and Christ's servants only, to wait on his will and pleasure, and ought therefore to move neither hand nor foot, nor any other member, either heart or mind, otherwise than he hath appointed. God is honoured in his own person, when we receive all things, both good and bad, at his hand; and love his law with all our hearts; and believe, hope, and long for all that he promiseth.
>
> If I hate the law, so I break it in mine heart; and both hate and dishonour God, the maker thereof. If I break it outwardly, then I dishonour God before the world, and the officer that ministereth it. If I hurt my neighbor, then I dishonour my neighbour and him that made

him, and him also that bought him with his blood. And even so, if I
hate my neighbour in mine heart, then I hate him that commandeth
me to love him, and him that deserved that I should at the least way
for his sake love him.[1]

Stokesley and More shared a mutual passion toward the heretic, a
powerful union of intent that made them quite a lethal force. This was
the year (1530) John Tyndale was humiliated on the wrong side of a
horse. He escaped death himself only by inches.

Vaughn wrote another letter to the king reporting that he had actually
spoken to Tyndale in a field. This was the *Do you not know me? My name is
Tyndale* moment between them, mentioned in the prologue. A clandestine
meeting, it was held in shadows and in voices and whispers. Once they
greeted and Vaughn assured Tyndale who he was, Tyndale asked Vaughn
about his book *Practice of Prelates*. He understood that the king was displeased with it, yet he could not understand the king's fury. All he had
wanted to do, he said, was to warn the king about the clergy around him,
particularly Wolsey, that their activities were harmful to the realm and to
the king.

> Take heed, therefore, wicked prelates, blind leaders of the blind; indu-
> rate and obstinate hypocrites, take heed. For if the Pharisees for their
> resisting the Holy Ghost, that is to say, persecuting the open and man-
> ifest truth, and slaying the preachers thereof, escaped not the wrath
> and vengeance of God; how shall ye escape, which are far worse than
> the Pharisees?[2]

Had Tyndale left it at that, with a stand against corrupt and schem-
ing bishops, he would have fared much better. What upset the king about
Prelates was Tyndale's opinion of the divorce. Brian Moynahan attributed
Tyndale's "staggering simple-mindedness" to his tendency toward political
blunder. Tyndale's opinion on the divorce was based entirely on Scripture,
and he spilled it all. Thinking it was Wolsey and his bishops who were
pushing the divorce for their own ends and not the king himself, he wrote:

If the king's most noble grace will needs have another wife, then let them search the laws of God, whether it be lawful nor not . . . If we care to keep his [God's] laws, he will care for the keeping of us, for the truth of his promises. If it be found unlawful, then let his grace fear God, and cease to shame himself and his blood, his lords, his subjects, and his realm, and specially the blessed name of our Saviour Jesus Christ, and his holy doctrine, and the profession of our faith: for whosoever professeth the faith of Christ, and liveth contrary unto his doctrine, shameth the name of our Saviour Jesus Christ. Moreover whatsoever God coupled, man may not loose, no, though he name himself pope. Wherefore, if this marriage be of God, the pope cannot dispense with it: for God hath given no power against himself; but to preach the ordinances only hath he given power. Therefore if we will see what is right and what is wrong, let us bring in unto the light of God's law, and let us submit our causes unto the judgment thereof, and be content to have our appetites slain thereby, that we lust no farther than God's ordinance giveth us liberty.[3]

Between the king's renowned lust and his wit, there was little contest, the former having the greater rule over the latter. Henry was well heated, or as one writer said it, he was a "boar in a rut."[4] (A sexual distinction, of which, with Henry, we must make allowances for many.) The Venetian ambassador reported that Henry was already treating Anne Boleyn "as if she was his wife."

Rage? Of course he raged. Should we expect anything else?

And Tyndale might have chosen a better subtitle than "Whether the Kinge's Grace maye be separated from hys quene because she was his brother's wyfe." Tyndale argued in favor of Catherine of Aragon. Anne Boleyn wasn't really in question. He simply concluded that Henry could not divorce Catherine. Scripturally, it was unlawful.

A generation or so later, Elizabethan printers simply took out the part about the divorce because it questioned the legitimacy of their own queen.

Tyndale was not a political creature. He had the clarity of mind for it, certainly, but he just didn't have the necessary stretch and elasticity, nor did he compromise well. And again, Tyndale was so intensely focused, his life was so given to a vernacular Scripture and to being "the voice of one crying in the wilderness," it is doubtful that he would have been able to read such a mind as his king's or have the patience to yield to its vacillations.

Does This Deserve Hatred?

Vaughn was moved by the translator. His letter to Cromwell repeated Tyndale's words (introduced earlier): "If for my pains therein taken, if for my poverty, if for mine exile out of my natural country and bitter absence from my friends . . ."[5] In the beginning of the letter, Tyndale said that what he sacrificed, he sacrificed for the good of the king and his people. But why, Tyndale asked, was his Grace so dissatisfied? Vaughn continued his account of Tyndale's words:

> Was there in me any such mind, when I warned his Grace to beware of his cardinal, whose iniquity he shortly after proved according to my writing? Doth this deserve hatred? Again, may his Grace, being a Christian prince, be so unkind to God, which hath commanded His Word to be spread throughout the world, to give more faith to the wicked persuasions of men, which, presuming above God's wisdom, and contrary to that which Christ expressly commandeth in His Testament, dare say that it is not lawful for the people to have the same in a tongue that they understand, because the purity thereof should open men's eyes to see their wickedness? Is there more danger in the King's subjects than in the subjects of all other princes, which in every of their tongues have the same, under privilege of their sovereigns? As I now am, very death were more pleasant to me than life, considering man's nature to be such as can bear no truth.[6]

Tyndale's passion for an English Scripture is conspicuous, but he wouldn't publish his *Answer to Thomas More* until he heard from the king. Vaughn did his best to persuade Tyndale to return to England, but toward the end of their conversation Tyndale said that he "neither would nor durst [dared] come into England albeit your Grace would promise him never so much surety: fearing lest, as he hath before written your promise made should shortly be broken by the persuasion of the clergy, which would affirm that promises made unto heretics ought not to be kept." This was Vaughn's report that he said he gave "word for word as near as I could by any possible means to remembrance."[7]

With night coming on, parting from Tyndale in that field brought on the sudden awareness of danger. Tyndale just slipped away into the night, and so lightly and with such practiced steps as to become untraceable. Vaughn marveled at the intelligence of Tyndale's stealth and realized perhaps that this is what Tyndale lived with all the time.

> After these words he then, being something fearful of me lest I would have pursued him, and drawing also towards night, he took his leave of me, and departed from the town, and I toward the town saying I should shortly peradventure see him again, or if not, hear from him. Howbeit I suppose he afterwards returned to the town by another way: for there is no likelihood that he should lodge without the town. Hasty to pursue him I was not, because I had some likelihood to speak shortly again with him: and in pursuing him I might perchance have failed of my purpose, and put myself in danger.[8]

The letter continues, then ends abruptly, midsentence. It was thought that the king, in his rage, tore it up. For all that he might have meant to Henry VIII, Tyndale's return was not going to happen. After his *Practice of Prelates*, Henry had notices placed in public denouncing the book. Eustace Chapuys noted correctly that the king's denunciation would only make the book much more appealing.

Thomas More was delighted.

As capricious as ever, Henry later wanted Tyndale back in England. Chapuys said that Henry blamed the change of policy on Cromwell.

The Great Wager

There was one more attempt to persuade Tyndale to come home. Cromwell sent a letter to Vaughn in May 1531. The document is littered with stray marks, corrections, and second thoughts. Cromwell obviously had a difficult time sending this to Vaughn. It was a defeat. The king had instructed him at last to end the operation, though Cromwell was still convinced Tyndale would be of value to the king.

Cromwell was, as Wolsey had been, as More was, and as anyone close to the tantrum king was, working with an emotionally unstable monarch. Cromwell learned what Wolsey had known well, that his job was basically to do whatever the king wanted him to do, to get whatever he was asked to get. Cromwell wrote:

> His highness nothing liked the said book [didn't like Tyndale's *Answer to Thomas More*], being filled with seditious, slanderous lies and fantastical opinions, showing therein neither learning nor truth: and further communing with his Grace I might well conceive that he thought that ye bare much affection towards the said Tyndale, whom in his manners and knowledge in worldly things ye undoubtedly in your letters do much allow and commend: whose works being replete with so abominable slanders and lies imagined and only feigned to infect the people, declareth him both to lack grace, virtue, learning, discretion, and all other good qualities nothing else pretending in all his works but to seduce and deceive.[9]

The letter then ordered Vaughn to desist his attention to Tyndale and leave the matter of his return alone. He advised Vaughn to obey, lest his future advancement be thwarted and disappoint the hopes he and others had for him.

Then, in a postscript Cromwell essentially did an about-face and advised Vaughn to continue pressing for Tyndale's return. On the condition that the translator might abandon his "opinions and fantasies surely rooted in him." If he did so, "I doubt not," Cromwell assured, "but the King's Highness would be much joyous of his conversion and amendment: and so being converted, if then he would return into this realm, undoubtedly the King's royal majesty is so inclined to mercy, pity, and compassion that he refuseth none which he seeth to submit themselves to the obedience and good order of the world."[10]

It is not known how Vaughn reacted to Cromwell other than to carry out his order, whether he was bewildered or elated, but when the letter was read to Tyndale, the translator himself was overcome. He was not as close to the tangle of English politics, and his considerations were fewer and much more refined than Vaughn's, Cromwell's or anyone else's. Vaughn wrote, "I perceived that man to be exceedingly altered." Tyndale, with tears in his eyes, said:

> What gracious words are these! I assure you, if it would stand with the king's most gracious pleasure to grant only a bare text of the Scriptures to be put forth among his people, like is put forth among the subjects of the Emperor in these parts, and of other Christian princes, be it of the translation of what person soever shall please his Majesty, I shall immediately make faithful promise never to write more, nor abide two days in these parts after the same; but immediately to repair [return] into his realm, and there most humbly submit myself at the feet of his royal Majesty, offering my body to suffer what pain or torture, yea, what death his Grace will, so that this be obtained.[11]

It would have been one thing for his words to end there, for the king to soften his position, for Tyndale to return, and on and on. But it didn't happen that way. If only his Majesty would allow the Scripture in English, he urged, even some small portion of it, whether or not it was his own translation, he would write no more.

Behind his oath, however, is the awareness that Henry is who Henry is, that Thomas More is who Thomas More is, and that change is not going to come without severe overthrow. That change would come, certainly, though not in time to save Tyndale. The letter continues.

> And till that time I will abide the asperity of all chances, whatsoever shall come, and endure my life in as much pains as it is able to bear and suffer. And as concerning my reconciliation, his Grace may be assured that whatsoever I have said or written in all my life against the honor of God's Word, and it be so proved, the same shall I before his

Majesty and all the world utterly renounce and forsake, and with most humble and meek mind embrace the truth, abhorring all error soever at the most gracious and benign request of his royal majesty, of whose wisdom, prudence, and learning I hear so great praise and commendation than of any other creature living. But if these things which I have written be true, and stand with God's Word, why should his Majesty, having so excellent gift of knowledge in the scriptures, move me to do anything against my conscience?[12]

This is not the resolve of a pauper translator. It has the backbone of Luther's "Here I stand" moment at Worms.[13] Tyndale will admit he is wrong if indeed it may be proven that he is wrong. We have seen that already. But if he is right, if what he has written is agreeable with the Scripture, it is beyond the jurisdiction even of a king. And Tyndale knew the English king too well. Until a promise could turn into action, Tyndale would not forfeit his life to the caprice of such a mind as Henry's.

After this, Vaughn made one more attempt to persuade Tyndale, but by that time all parties knew it was futile. Vaughn reported back to Cromwell that he found Tyndale, as always, "singing one note." An English Scripture, always an English Scripture.

It is difficult for those who live and move in the political ooze to understand someone like Tyndale.

> *He {Tyndale} was a man without any spot or blemish or rancor or malice, full of mercy and compassion, so that no man living was able to reprove him of any sin or crime.*
>
> – JOHN FOXE, *ACTES AND MONUMENTS*

The fact that he sang only "one note" made him who he was. This singularity, this impenetrable will separated Tyndale from the others. To deny an English Scripture was to deny all that he believed, to deny the great wager of his life.

The king had many affairs to tend to. He was stretched the way sovereigns must stretch. He had a kingdom. He had one wife he must dispose of. He would turn over an entire world to take another one. January 1533 he married Anne Boleyn secretly because she was with child. And there were other distractions. Thomas More had the English religious apparatus to watch after, and of late he was having to negotiate his way along "the slippery precipice of royal favor."[14] Like Wolsey, like Cromwell, like Anne Boleyn, like English Catholicism, Thomas More's fall was at hand.

Whatsoever the World Babble of Me

Thomas More had agents watching Vaughn's movements while he was in Antwerp. They were to inform More about anyone Vaughn had contact with. This was all for the sake of the prize Vaughn might lead them to.

About this same time, another English reformer, George Constantine, a renegade priest and Tyndale sympathizer, was captured by More and taken to More's Chelsea home and put in the stocks, where he was interrogated for several days. More reported that Constantine "uttered and disclosed dyvers of hys companyons." Constantine also told More about the smuggling operation of "those develyshe bokes [Tyndale's books] whyche hym self and other of hys fellows hadde brought and shypped."[15]

Because of the assistance Constantine had given to a grateful More, Richard Necton was committed to Newgate Prison. Unless Necton died in prison, More said, he "standeth in peryll to be [dead] ere long, for hys fallynge agayne to Tindales heryses burned."[16]

Constantine somehow managed to free himself from More's stocks and climbed over the wall and made his escape. He then returned to Antwerp. As compensation for his help, it is likely that More allowed him to escape. A "small fish for a bigger fish" kind of courtesy.

More was not even angry that Constantine had escaped. Typical of More humor, he told his porter to repair the stocks and lock them up well "lest the prisoner try to steal back in."

Constantine told More all about Vaughn's mission with Tyndale. He added, "For that Englishman which shall be found to be familiar with him there [Vaughn], may thereby bring himself in suspicion of heresy, and haply hear thereof at his returning hither."[17] Vaughn found out about Constantine's report and that he had said things against him. He understood clearly that he was in More's gaze. He also realized that the king was being informed. Vaughn finally claimed, in his own defense, that "whatsoever the world babble of me, that I am neither Lutheran nor *yet* Tyndalian"[18] (italics mine, hint of optimism, Vaughn's). In a letter to Cromwell, Vaughn wrote,

> I am unkindly handled to have such sharp inquisitions made of me in mine absence; I am unkindly handled for my service. Such stripes and bitter rewards would faint and make weak the hearts of some men towards their prince; but I am the stronger, because I know the truth . . .
>
> I hear everywhere how diligently my lord chancellor [More] inquireth, of all those he examineth in cases of heresy, for me—what are my manners, my opinions, my conversation, my faith; and others are deputed to make like inquisitions. Why take they so great pains? What think they to hear? I am a man as they are; a sinner too . . . among Christians I have been a Christian, among Jews like to them, among Lutherans a Lutheran also. What can I do here withoug such policy?
>
> . . . George Constantine came to Antwerp after his breaking from my lord chancellor, the 6th of December. With him nor with none other such will I meddle or have to do [have anything to do with], considering I am beaten with mine own labours.[19]

The whole point is that More was not to be taken lightly, in spite of any appearance of safety from the king. More's zeal for the heretic, and particularly for Tyndale, was quite advanced. Vaughn's letter implied that More was England's chief inquisitor.

Another Tyndale friendly, Richard Bayfield, wasn't so lucky. Bayfield was a Cambridge graduate and a former Benedictine monk who came to believe as Tyndale and the other reformers. He abjured in front of Tunstall in 1528. Bayfield was a major smuggler of Tyndale Bibles and books. He made three major runs, but on the third was betrayed and captured into More's hands. He was taken to the Tower and shackled to the wall by his neck, waist, and legs. More said Bayfield "fell to heresy and was abjured, and after that like a dog returning to his vomit." Bayfield "monk and apostate" was "well and worthily burned in Smithfield."

More also said, "Of Bayfields burning hath Tyndale no cause to glory, though Tyndale's books brought him to burning."[20]

Of Thomas More, Foxe concluded in his treatment of Bayfield that More was "so blinded in the zeal of popery, so deadly set against the one side, and so partially affectionate unto the other, that in them whom he favoureth he can see nothing but all fair roses and sweet virtue; in the other which he hateth, there is never a thing can please his fantasy, but all is as black as pitch, vice, abomination, heresy, and folly, whatsoever they do, or intend to do."[21]

Stephen Vaughn never saw Tyndale again. The king found other work for him to do. He thought Vaughn had come too close to the translator and was possibly infected with the man, so he kept him at a distance.

Henry attempted to have Tyndale sent home by request to the emperor, but the emperor was rather cool to Henry and did nothing. The emperor, who had had enough of Harry, reasoned that "Tyndale is only being prosecuted for his attachment to the Queen's [Catherine, the emperor's aunt] cause, which, it is thought, all the best men in England favor."[22]

Henry then did what was natural for a thwarted king. He would have Tyndale kidnapped. He sent Thomas Elyot to do the job. Elyot was the new English ambassador in the imperial court. The plan was to have Tyndale taken by force and brought back to London for punishment. On 14 March 1532 Elyot wrote the following to the Duke of Norfolk.

> The king willeth me, by his grace's letters, to remain at Brussels some space of time for the apprehension of William Tyndale, which somewhat minisheth my hope of a soon return [to England]; considering that, like as he is in with movable, semblably so is his person uncertain to come by; and as far as I can perceive, hearing of the king's diligence in the apprehension of him, he withdraweth him into such places where he thinketh to be farthest out of danger.[23]

Elyot put out money for bribes, but his efforts went nowhere. By June he was back in England, bankrupt by his efforts on the continent. Tyndale's abilities at concealment were far beyond Elyot's depth. For the moment he was still Teflon coated.

Let Not Thine Heart Fail Thee

The year is 1532, the latter end. It is difficult to imagine the weight Tyndale has on him. He will at last be betrayed, but even now betrayal is all around him. He has had almost a decade to look into its heart. And religious treachery is perhaps the most cunning, the most insidious of all types of treachery. Money is fertilizing all of Antwerp for Tyndale's blood.

It is just not his time yet. Even he knows this.

This is the year Tyndale wrote his *Exposition upon the Fifth, Sixth and Seventh Chapters of Matthew*, his treatment of the Sermon on the Mount. He is in crescendo. His life is reaching toward a summit. "Yet let not thine heart fail thee," he would write, "neither despair, as though God had forsaken thee, or loved thee not."

> Bless are ye when men revile you, and persecute you, and shall falsely say all manner of evil sayings against you for my sake. Rejoice, and be glad, for great is your reward in heaven. For so persecuted they the prophets which were before your days. [Matthew 5:11–12 TNT 1526]
>
> Here seest thou the uttermost, what a Christian man must look for. It is not enough to suffer for righteousness; but that no bitterness or poison be left out of thy cup, thou shalt be reviled and railed upon; and even when thou art condemned to death, then be excommunicate and delivered to Satan, deprived of the fellowship of the holy church, the company of angels, and of thy part in Christ's blood; and shalt be cursed to hell, defied, detested, and execrate with all the blasphemous railings, that the poisonful heart of hypocrites can think or imagine; and shalt see before thy face when thou goest to they death, that all the world is persuaded and brought in belief, that thou hast said and done that thou never thoughtest, and that thou diest for that, thou art as guiltless of as the child that is unborn.
>
> Well, though iniquity so highly prevail, and the truth for which thou diest be so low kept under, and be not once known before the

world, insomuch that it seemeth rather to be hindered by thy death than furthered (which is of all griefs the greatest) yet let not thine heart fail thee neither despair, as though God had forsaken thee, or loved thee not: but comfort thyself with old ensamples [examples], how God hath suffered all his old friends to be so entreated, and also his only and dear son Jesus; whose ensample, above all other, set before thine eyes, because thou art sure he was beloved above all other, that thou doubt not but thou art loved also, and so much the more beloved, the more thou art like to the image of his ensample in suffering . . . he was beloved of God; and so art thou. His cause came to light also, and so shall thine at the last; yea, and thy reward is great in heaven with him for thy deep suffering.[24]

It is one thing to say "Jesus loves you" in our twenty-first-century bumper sticker kind of way, particularly in a time of relative prosperity and peace, where the demands are minimal. It is an altogether different thing when the world is on fire.

17

Do Thou the Worst Thou Canst unto Me

I have striven to be Thine, more than to be this world's, or mine own. Yet this is nothing; I leave eternity to Thee; for what is man that he should live out the lifetime of his God?

— Herman Melville, *Moby Dick*

THE VILLAIN WAS AN ENGLISHMAN NAMED HENRY PHILLIPS. HE might have been Fagin (from *Oliver Twist*), or Quilp (the elfish little devil from *The Old Curiosity Shop* whose name sounds like a kind of troubled swallow). He was easily Uriah Heep. Either way, he was a Dickens character—dark, slithering, exaggerated, an English caricature.

Phillips will always be remembered as a Judas, and yet one who had no repentance in him, no remorse. He would not have hung himself on anyone's account, nor given back the coin. He was a whining, squandering, thankless gentleman's son with no thought of reform.

Phillips was a cliché, an agent, a hireling of the Catholic Church, or at least its English guard. For all their dominion, all their influence in the world, this silly creature was the best they could do. And he performed flawlessly.

In his midtwenties, he had just received a bachelor's degree in civil law from Oxford. His father, Richard Phillips, a Dorset landowner, was a three-time member of Parliament and twice a sheriff who held a position of authority as a customhouse officer of the Port of Poole. The senior Phillips had attended the London wedding of Anne Boleyn and Henry VIII in January 1533—no small honor. A generation or so later, under James I, Edward Phillips, our villain's nephew, would become Master of the Rolls (a judge whose importance is next to that of Lord Chief Justice).

But even the best of families have the occasional Henry.

In spite of his beginnings, after leaving Oxford in 1533, young Harry, as he liked to be called, began to live loosely and wildly, without limits. The result was poverty and opprobrium. His father had entrusted him with money to settle a debt. Henry had other thoughts on how to invest his father's money. He told his mother afterward, while "piteously begging" her to intercede with his father, that he had "chanced to fall into play,"[1] and lost it all.

In all his letters that have survived, he is "both fawning and full of self-pitying complaint." He whined that "by fortune he was driven he whist not whither."[2] Fortune eventually drove Phillips to Louvain (present day Louven), in Belgium, the center of Catholic sentiment.

And in another part of that same country, less than thirty miles from Louvain, was William Tyndale—warm, trusting, idealistic, naïve. As wary as he had been, as cautious, as hidden and apparitionlike as he remained throughout his years of exile and translation, William Tyndale proved to be no match for the streetwise Phillips.

At the Edge of a Phrase

In 1535, William Tyndale had been living for at least a year at the English House. An Englishman named Thomas Poyntz, and his wife, managed the house. Poyntz was a discerning man with a good heart, and loyal to his idealistic and outspoken friend. He was the cousin of

Lady Walsh at Little Sodbury Manor in Gloucestershire. There was safety in Thomas. In Poyntz, Tyndale "had a good, shrewd friend and loyal sympathizer."[3]

Though he knew better than to relax his guard, Tyndale felt as secure as one could feel as an outlaw in Antwerp. Then again, he had suffered alienation for just over a decade. How unsafe can a little conversation be, and with an Englishman, the son of a gentleman? It is possible that due to the changes in English spirituality, with Thomas More arrested for treason and in the Tower, and with Henry VIII proclaimed as supreme head of the new Anglican church, a Protestant church at that, Tyndale might have been caught up in a sweep of optimism.

In May, there was news of a plot to apprehend three Englishmen. Just days before Tyndale was arrested, a letter was sent by a visiting English merchant in Antwerp to a friend in London saying, "There is commission come from the procuror-general of Brussels to take three Englishmen."[4] The three Englishmen were thought to be Robert Barnes, George Joye, and William Tyndale.

Not wanting to annoy the English merchants in Antwerp, no action moved forward just yet. Joye fled to Calais. Barnes had not been in Antwerp for some time. Which left only Tyndale, and he didn't seem that alarmed. Though it was meant for the merchant and not necessarily the outspoken writer-heretic, there was also a kind of immunity for those living at the English House. A resident of the English House could only be arrested within the limits of the building "for a grave crime for which evidence of guilt already existed."[5]

And in comes Phillips, whom John Foxe described as a "comely fellow, like as he had been a gentleman with a servant with him: but wherefore [why] he came, or for what purpose he was sent thither, no one could tell."[6] It is not known how Phillips discovered Tyndale. For those who labor in shadows, who understand its mind, this would have been small work. Doubtless Phillips had planned well.

Personable and with a generous spirit, Tyndale was most agreeable company and the merchants liked him. They had given him a regular stipend as support. They were his friends, and Tyndale had, of late, begun to dine out with them—often. Evidence of a less strenuous watch. It was during one of these casual meals that Phillips entered into his life.

> Master Tyndale divers times was desired forth to dinner and supper amongst merchants: by means whereof this Henry Phillips became acquainted with him, so that within a short space Master Tyndale had a great confidence in him, and brought him to his lodging, to the house of Thomas Poyntz: and had him also once or twice with him to dinner and supper, and further entered such friendship with him, that through his procurement he lay in the same house of the said Pointz: to whom he showed moreover his books, and other secrets of his study, so little did Tyndale then mistrust this traitor.[7]

Perhaps the youth filled a vacancy, some unmet paternal craving, against which Tyndale is defenseless and unguarded. John Frith, Tyndale's Timothy, is dead. Phillips would have been armed with all the necessary information, all the detail he needed to work the charm. Tyndale took to him instantly, and with honest affection. Phillips had all the right references, all the right personal effects. He was from Tyndale's England, the West country. It was in his voice. He went to Oxford and was well studied in languages.

Tyndale escorted Phillips into his private quarters, showed him his books and the unfinished works—pen, ink, papers, the odd scribble of thought.

It is certain that Phillips was under a secret commission from someone in England, someone with a lot of power, a lot of cash, and a real grinding vendetta against William Tyndale. Suddenly and mysteriously, having no money, having been turned away by his family and friends, Phillips had money, and lots of it.

Phillips was patient. And profitability being what it was in Antwerp among the English merchants, the authorities had no real cause to raid the English House just yet.

Whoever it was that set Phillips in play was well practiced in the conspirator's art. By all inferences, it was John Stokesley, the bishop of

London who commissioned Phillips, and with the backing of Sir Thomas More. Though Stokesley denied having anything to do with the burning of Tyndale, he had worked closely with Thomas More in the routing, examination, and punishment of Lutherans prior to More's trouble. Whoever it was had carefully studied both predator and prey and knew the match to be a good one.

Stokesley didn't have near the sagacity or the zeal for the chase that Thomas More had. Few did. But Stokesley was both cruel and loyal. He also had More's validation, whether More was present or not. More set a rather nasty prece-

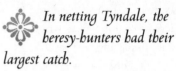 *In netting Tyndale, the heresy-hunters had their largest catch.*

– DAVID DANIELL, *WILLIAM TYNDALE: A BIOGRAPHY*

dent. He certainly had the mind to establish an effective spy trap, and he knew William Tyndale better than anyone else. He would have delighted in the pairing of Tyndale and Phillips. There was no reason More could not run any operation he wished from his height in the Bell Tower.

Henry VIII could not be blamed for Tyndale's arrest either. Phillips despised his king. Nor could Cromwell be blamed. As we have already seen, Cromwell made formidable attempts to save Tyndale, even with the help of his master. Besides, Cromwell is chancellor now. He and the king are distracted with affairs of state that are of much larger consequence than Tyndale.

From letters that passed back and forth across the channel it is clear that the English government had nothing to do with Tyndale's arrest and execution. But that doesn't dismiss Stokesley, who represented the Church, the government among all governments. A servant of Stokesley, John Tisen, a former student of Tyndale's, who would be able to recognize the translator, had been seen in Antwerp on assignment from his master.

> All this, together with the cruelty of his [Stokesley's] character, his zeal for persecution, his boasts on his deathbed of the number of heretics whom he had robbed of life, makes it reasonable enough to see him the chief backer, if not the prime engineer, of the plot which destroyed Tyndale.[8]

Tyndale took Phillips into his confidence, and not only invited him to dine with him, as he did often, but eventually secured a place for him to lodge at the English House.

Phillips was a kind of weasel, but he was good at it. Having no understanding of weaselese—trusting, believing the best, artless and unworldly—Tyndale was an easy target. He suspected nothing. To be as wary as he had been and for so long, he left himself unguarded and accessible. John Foxe wrote, "For in the wily subtleties of this world he was simple and inexpert."[9]

The only one who had any suspicions was Thomas Poyntz. Poyntz could not quite put a finger on it or prove anything, nor would it clarify in his thoughts, but he could not shake his suspicion of the dissembling Phillips. It was something you might catch at the edge of a phrase, a slight ping of recognition that registers in the middle of you somehow, at the margin of sense. Either way, his radar sounded even if Tyndale's had not. Poyntz detected something, some activity, and being proficient at his trade, Phillips knew it.

> But Pointz, having no great confidence in the fellow, asked Master Tyndale how he came acquainted with this Philips. Master Tyndale answered, that he [Phillips] was an honest man, handsomely learned, and very conformable. Then Pointz, perceiving that he bare such favour to him, said no more.[10]

On one occasion Phillips asked Poyntz to walk with him. During this little walk the lubricious Harry let Poyntz know that he had money. Poyntz wasn't sure what to think until it was all over. We might imagine a silent spot in the conversation, a small window of opportunity, Phillips baiting the suspicious Poyntz with a become-my-friend-or-become-my-enemy kind of dirty-money choice.

> The said Phillips, being in the town three or four days, upon a time desired Pointz to walk with him forth of the town to show him the commodities thereof, and in walking together without the town, had

communication of divers things, and some of the king's affairs: by which talks Pointz as yet suspected nothing, but after, by the sequel of the matter, he perceived more what was intended.[11]

After dining often with Tyndale, entering into his confidence, and sifting Poyntz, Phillips left Antwerp for the court in Brussels, who were hostile to the English. When he returned to Antwerp he brought back with him the procurator-general (the emperor's attorney) and other officers.

Such As the Market Will Give

Having some business in the town of Barrois, eighteen miles away, Poyntz left Antwerp, and was not expected back for at least six weeks. Agitated at the presence of Phillips but still powerless against his weasel charm, the general opacity, and the sorcery he had over his friend, Poyntz was hesitant to leave.

For Phillips, exercising animal patience, Poyntz's absence created an opportunity.

With Poyntz safely out of the way, one evening Phillips came to the English House and asked Mrs. Poyntz if Tyndale happened to be in. The very odd but brief conversation between Phillips and Mrs. Poyntz is in Foxe. Asking for Master Tyndale, and whether he should dine there with him, he asked the lady of the house:

PHILLIPS: What good meat shall we have?
MRS. POYNTZ: Such as the market will give.

This little discourse between Harry and the unsuspecting Mrs. Poyntz is too good to pass up. The first time I read it, having some idea the treachery that was to follow, it was like a touch of ice, or some other deadly metaphorical interpretation. As if Tyndale was the meal about to be served.

When Phillips returned to the English House he asked Tyndale to loan him forty shillings. He has money. This is pure staging.

PHILLIPS: I lost my purse this morning.[12]

Tyndale gave him the forty shillings, with a lot of warm flattery and goodwill.

PHILLIPS: Master Tyndale, you shall be my guest here this day.
TYNDALE: No, I go forth this day to dinner, and you shall go with me, and be my guest, where you shall be welcome.

I insist. I insist. Said the mouse to the cat.
By dinnertime, Phillips had secured two officers in the narrow street adjacent to the English House. More of an alley, the entrance to the house was narrow enough that two could not walk side by side comfortably. Tyndale insisted that Phillips go first, and Phillips would not have it, gentleman that he was. *I insist. I insist. No, no, after you. Please.*

> Phillips, a tall, comely person, followed behind him; who had set offi-cers on either side of the door upon two seats, which, being there, might see who came in the entry; and coming through the same entry, Philips pointed with his finger over Master Tyndale's head down to him, that the officers who sat at the door might see that it was he whom they should take, as the officers that took Master Tyndale afterwards told Pointz, and said to Pointz, when they had laid him in prison, that they pitied to see his simplicity when they took him. Then they took him, and brought him to the emperor's attorney, or procuror-general, where he dined. Then came the procuror-general to the house of Pointz, and sent away all that was there of Master Tyndale's, as well his books as other things; and from thence Tyndale was had to the castle of Filford, eighteen English miles from Antwerp, and there he remained until he was put to death.[13]

No further description is given in Foxe's account of the arrest. It is doubtful that the officers' pity moved Phillips at all. What we have is a tragi-comic villain and his unsuspecting prey. We are given no satisfaction—no look of astonishment on the translator's face, no cry for help, no attempt at escape. Nothing. It was not Tyndale's style. Just something sunken, deflated, and fallen.

From there, Foxe wrote four short paragraphs on Tyndale's imprisonment at Vilvorde Castle and his execution.

Though he had managed to elude capture for more than ten years, Tyndale knew the street was smarter than he was. He may have known that Phillips was his Judas. My guess is that he did not.

Tyndale was arrested on 21 May 1535 (some sources say 23 or 24 May), then taken to Vilvorde Castle and placed in the dungeon. He was charged with heresy.

Vilvorde Castle

Tyndale spent the next sixteen months in Vilvorde prison, a term of five hundred days. There is an entry in the archives at Brussels of a payment to Adolfe van Wesele, the lieutenant of the castle at Vilvorde in reimbursement of money he spent "in the keeping of a certain prisoner, named William Tintalus, Lutheran . . . for a year and one hundred and thirty five days, at forty stivers a day."[14] This entry is found under the heading: "Account of the confiscated goods of the Lutherans and heretical sects."

Vilvorde is six miles from Brussels. Built in 1374 and modeled after the Bastille in Paris, Vilvorde had been the residence of Edward III and other English kings. It had seven towers, was surrounded by a moat, and was spanned by three drawbridges. In spite of the immediate image this description might arouse, the enchantment had long departed from it. Mozley's word is "gloomy." The next five hundred days of Tyndale's life were cruel and unforgiving.

His exile deepened.

All his goods, what little he had, were impounded. If Anne Poyntz had been alerted, she may have been able to salvage a small portion of Tyndale's possessions. His book on the sacraments and William Tracey's Testament were found by friends and printed sometime later. These documents were probably hidden to avoid confiscation.

At the time of his arrest the mood against the Lutheran was becoming more severe, and not only in Europe. Just days after Tyndale's arrest, fourteen Anabaptists were burned at the stake in England.

Charles V, upstaged by Luther some years before, was ready to muzzle the whole movement if he could. Tyndale's luck could hardly be worse.

Thomas More would be executed in two months time (July 4).

Tyndale would not ultimately burn for the translation, which was an offense, certainly, but as a heretic whose ideas were too contaminated for him to live. Tyndale's main injury to God was that he did not think like a Catholic. His opinion of the sacrament, his deafness to the pope, his insistence on justification by faith—these were the issues that condemned him.

Thomas Cromwell, the political animal that he was, servant and first minister to the king, with More about to be dispatched, had to keep watch over Henry's mood against his own desire to see Tyndale released. Not to mention that by now, the king had begun to cool toward his once-beloved Anne Boleyn. Within a year of Tyndale's arrest, she would be dead, her head sliced off with a French sword, making way a fortnight later for H8 to marry Ms. Seymour, plain Jane.

Cromwell's godson, Thomas Theobold, who was on the continent and on Cromwell's payroll, sent a letter to Thomas Cranmer, archbishop of Canterbury and friend to Cromwell. It is dated 31 July 1535. The following starts in the middle of the letter.

> All succour that I can perceive them to have, is only by him which hath taken Tyndale, called Harry Phillips, with whom I had long and familiar communication; for I made him believe that I was minded to tarry and study at Louvain. I could not perceive the contrary by his communication, but that Tyndale shall die, which he doth follow [urge] and procureth with all diligent endeavour, rejoicing much therein, saying that he had a commission out also for to have taken Dr. Barnes and George Joye with other [Tyndale].[15]

No one seemed to "urge" Tyndale's death with as much persistence or hawkish vigilance as Phillips. Working on a kind of commission basis, he was surely looking at a bonus for his efforts. He seemed driven. David Daniell uses the word psychopathic to describe Phillips. Either way, Tyndale is unlucky in the match. "But that Tyndale shall die" has a chill determination about it.[16]

> This said Phillips is greatly afraid (in so much as I can perceive) that the English merchants that be in Antwerp will lay watch to do him some displeasure privily . . . Either this Phillips hath great friends in England to maintain him here, or else, as he showed me, he is well beneficed in the bishopric of Exeter. He raileth at Louvain and in the queen of Hungary's court most shamefully against our king his highness tyrannum, expilatorem republicae [tyrant, spoiler of the commonwealth], with many other railing words, rejoicing that he trusteth to see the emperor to scourge his highness with his council and friends . . .
>
> Written at Antwerp the last day of July by your bedeman and servant, ever to my small power.
>
> Thomas Tebold

I, for one, am glad we don't speak that way anymore (the genteel formality that counterfeits the raw emotion behind it). That Phillips is "greatly afraid" some of the merchants "will lay watch to do him some displeasure privily" is a bit much. Phillips knows the injury he has done and is wise to be wary. He won't rest until Tyndale is finished. Even during the interrogation in Tyndale's cell, Phillips is within hearing distance. He is death's editor, the finisher, watching that every detail is perfectly attended.

For the weasel, to snuff out the life of one like Tyndale is an affront to God, a punishing of sorts against the providence that allowed his life to spoil so irrevocably.

There Be Not Many Perfecter Men This Day Living

When Thomas Poyntz returned, he found the English merchants a bit anxious. With Tyndale's arrest there had been an uncomfortable breach in their assumed immunity. There was some attempt in England to appeal to the emperor, but there was little chance of success. And England was experiencing a sea change, an overturning of an old order.

The Act of Supremacy passed in November 1534, which declared Henry VIII supreme head of the new Church of England (*Anglicana Ecclesia*). A wave of arrests had been implemented because of the Act. The Treason Act made it illegal to "maliciously wish, will, or desire, by words or by writing" or to deny the king any of his new titles or call him a heretic, schismatic, tyrant, or infidel. Thomas More was arrested 17 April 1534 and sent to the Tower for his refusal to take the oath of supremacy.

The English merchants in Antwerp rallied in support of Tyndale. A letter was sent to the court at Brussels and the English government. Tyndale was important to them, certainly, but the manner of his arrest violated their corporate diplomatic privilege. To be expected, the court was unmoved.

In August, a desperate Poyntz wrote to his brother John who was the lord of the manor of North Ockenden in Essex. John had been in the court of Henry VIII for some time. The letter provides a valuable window into the moment. The following excerpt represents the essentials of the letter, but the ambience and the fleeting images of Tyndale are too rich to dismiss.

> Brother, I write to you on a matter greatly concerning the king. My love of my country and my duty to my prince compels me to speak, lest the king be misled and brought into injury by men, yes traitors, who, under colour of forwarding his honour, seek to bring their own purposes to pass. I do not name them, but it is clear that it must be the papists who are at the bottom of it. For whereas it was said here of one William Tyndale, for to have been sent hither; the which is in prison and like to suffer death, except it be through his gracious help; it is thought those letters be stopped.
>
> This man was lodged with me three quarters of a year, and was taken out of my house by a sergeant-at-arms, otherwise called a door-warder, and the procurer-general of Brabant; the which was done by

procurement out of England, and, as I suppose, unknown to the king's grace till it was done. For I know well, if it had pleased his grace to have sent him a commandment to come into England, he would not have disobeyed it, to have put his life in jeopardy [even at the risk of his life]. But these privy lurkers, perceiving that the king meant to send for Tyndale, and fearing that he would hear him charitably, as no doubt he would, wished to hinder a thing so unfavourable to their interests, and therefore—so it is supposed—they have represented to the king or the council, that Tyndale's death in Brabant would be to the king's high honor and profit. In fact however Tyndale's death would hurt the king in several ways, as they very well know. Whatever be the method they have used, these crafty fellows ought to be ashamed of their deed: but they merely desire the king's favour and their own promotions and power, and are past shame.

The death of this man will be a great hindrance to the gospel, and to the enemies of it one of the highest pleasures. And it would please the king's highness to send for this man, so that he might dispute his articles with them at large, which they lay to him, it might, by the mean thereof, be so opened to the court and the council of this country, that they would be at another point with the Bishop of Rome within a short space. And I think he shall shortly be at a point to be condemned; for there are two Englishmen at Louvain that do and have applied it sore, taking great pains to translate out of English into Latin in those things that may make against him, so that the clergy here may understand it, and to condemn him, as they have done all others, for keeping opinions contrary to their business, the which they call the order of holy church.

Brother, the knowledge that I have of this man causes me to write as my conscience bids me; for the king's grace should have him at this day as high a treasure as of any one man living, that has been of no greater reputation. Therefore I desire you that this matter may be solicited to his grace for this man, with as good effect as shall lie in you, or by your means to be done, for in my conscience there be not many perfecter men this day living, as knows God.[17]

"As high a treasure as of any one man living." Poyntz has his moments, certainly, and though he is not the wordsmith his beloved friend is, Mozley said, "His heart is in the right place."[18] Poyntz is being too optimistic in assuming the king will do anything, or that the king's influence in the Low Countries is sufficient enough if he actually *could* do anything. But what is important to us is that Poyntz has crossed some line. Like many others, he has been altered under Tyndale's influence, infected with Tyndale's own brand of selflessness, with his interpretation of the Gospels, the Christian's obligation to his neighbor and to God through his neighbor, with Tyndale's I-am-thou-thyself-and-thou-art-I-myself-and-can-be-no-nearer-or-kin kind of service to his friend.

With an ardor matched only by Phillips, Thomas Poyntz was willing to risk his life for his friend.

Brother John sent the letter to Cromwell on 21 September. Cromwell then composed two letters to be sent to the two leading members of the privy council of Brabant—the president, Carondolet (the archbishop of Palermo), and to the marquis of Bergen-op-Zoom. The letters no longer exist but they asked that Tyndale be released and sent back to England as a matter of grace. Stephen Vaughn, who privately hoped for Tyndale's release, delivered the letters.

The details of what happened next are a bit tangled, but in short, Thomas Poyntz got involved once again to move the letters along, only one of which was delivered. By the end of October, Poyntz had an answer to Cromwell's letter from the marquis. He returned to Brussels and delivered the letters to the emperor's council. Waiting three days for a reply, he was told that Tyndale would be released to him.

Then Phillips slithered in, quite agitated.

Some Dark Genius

Henry Phillips heard that Tyndale was to be released into the custody of Thomas Poyntz and sent to England. It was his business to know everything about Tyndale. If Tyndale was released, Phillips would forfeit his thirty pieces of silver. And if Tyndale somehow got an audience with Cromwell or, heaven forbid, the king, Phillips could be ruined.

Phillips reacted the way we might expect him to react, the way his nature obligated him to react. He lied even harder, more convincingly. After all, nothing was certain. England was far away, and the supports beneath Tyndale were fragile, ailing.

To the authorities in Brussels, Phillips claimed that Thomas Poyntz had been Tyndale's protector, that he was ever the heretic the translator was, and that they shared the same opinion. He convinced them that the letters were an invention of Poyntz, that they were of no value, and that no one else was involved but Poyntz himself.

It worked.

Poyntz was arrested at Hallowtide (around November 1) by the procurer-general, the one who had arrested Tyndale months earlier. He was not delivered to prison, but into the custody of two sergeants at arms under a kind of strict house arrest. One of these keepers stayed in the home of Poyntz and his wife. The same day as his arrest, the procurer-general with a member of the chancery visited him and demanded a written statement of his opinions so there would be no need to examine him in person anymore. The next day they came again. They did the same for the next six days.

Poyntz dithered and delayed.

There were more than one hundred items counted against him, twenty-three of which were drawn up and given to the commissioners. This lengthy document was then given to Poyntz for his answer. He was permitted to have counsel. His reply was to be ready in eight days. Then in another eight days the prosecution would reply to his answer. This went on in eight-day cycles "till the process were ended."

Poyntz strategically put the commissioners off and refused to give them an answer saying that his own counselors could not come to him without a license from the commissioners and he couldn't leave the premises to meet with them. Every eight-day cycle offered another excuse until, finally, he was threatened. "Bring your answer this day or else ye shall be put from it."[19] In other words, he would pay for his delays with his flesh. But the process continued until tedium won out.

During all this time he was allowed no communication. And whatever letters he did write had to be written in Flemish only, so the procurer-general could read them. Likewise he was not allowed to talk except in Flemish, so his jailers could understand anything he might have said.

This process is complicated and dull, but we may assume that Tyndale's case would have followed in a like, yet stricter, fashion.

This odd punishment went on from November to January. Every time the commissioners came to Poyntz, Harry Phillips was close by. He kept a jealous watch over his interests. It may be assumed that Poyntz did not fear that his life was in danger until Phillips became a part of his nightmare.

It is worth something perhaps to note that for all the slime that sticks to his name, Phillips must have been an incredibly persuasive individual. From his family he had learned the way of nobility, and from some void of nobility in his own nature, some dark genius, persuasion seemed to be a particular art of his.

After being confined for about thirteen weeks, Poyntz realized that if he remained there he would be put to death. His confinement was strict, but he wasn't behind a stone wall just yet. He was about to be moved to a more secure prison. Something had to give.

At the beginning of February, he escaped. He knew the lay of the land well enough to elude capture, and eventually made his way to England.

Poyntz was officially banished from the Netherlands. His business was left in ruins, as were all his domestic interests. Even his wife Anna, a native of Antwerp, refused to join him in England. He finally saw his children again, but it was many years later.

In 1547, his brother John died. Thomas succeeded him at the manor of North Ockenden, but by this time, he was too poor to afford to live there. Four years after his brother's death he received a royal order, authorizing collections to be made to defray his heavy debts and losses dating from the time of his imprisonment.

Thomas Poyntz died in 1562. Mozley summarized nicely.

In a worldly way his life was ruined by his generous championship of Tyndale: but the luster of his deed is his perpetual possession. The poor fools of this world sometime turn out to have a higher wisdom than the prudent; and in the long line of tablets in the Poyntz family, which is the glory of North Ockenden church, none awakes so lively an interest in the visitor as that of this simple and warm-hearted man.[20]

The epitaph of Thomas Poyntz reads:

He, for faithful service to his prince and ardent profession of evangelical truth, suffered bonds and imprisonment beyond the sea, and would plainly have been destined to death, had he not, trusting in divine providence, saved himself in a wonderful manner by breaking his prison. In this chapel he now sleeps peacefully in the Lord, 1562.

On 13 April 1536 Stephen Vaughn wrote a letter to Cromwell from the Low Countries. In a postscript he wrote, "If now you send me but your letter to the privy council, I could deliver Tyndale from the fire, so it come by time, for else it would be too late."[21] Cromwell did nothing. Mozley suggested that Vaughn was deluded and that Cromwell perhaps judged the matter with a bit more clarity.

From this point, any thought of Tyndale's release was mere optimism.

And had Tyndale been released to England he still may not have escaped burning. He had powerful enemies. There was no longer a Thomas More, but More had left a deadly spirit behind him. And Tyndale was too powerful, too large a figure to leave uncharred. "His radical opinions, his outspoken nature, his outstanding abilities would soon have brought him into trouble."[22]

If Henry and Cromwell failed to save Tyndale, they had even less good fortune prosecuting Henry Phillips. They were better off chasing a ghost. And it hardly mattered. Phillips was the author of his own decline, as might be expected. It is not known how he died. Foxe reported a rumor that Phillips "was consumed at last with lice."[23] If this is true, consider the justice of it, one small creature's ultimate conquest over another. A nibbling end.

A few years after Tyndale's execution, Phillips was supposedly arrested

as a traitor to both the kings of Vienna and Hungary, threatened with losing his eyes or his life. The last we hear of Phillips is in 1542. History
quits him after so much time and wasted text.

So will we.

18

And the Peace of God, Which Passeth All Understanding

*At my first answering, no man assisted me, but all forsook me. I
pray God, that it may not be laid to their charges: not withstanding
the Lord assisted me, and strengthened me, that by me the preaching
should be fulfilled to the utmost, and that all the gentiles should
hear. And I was delivered out of the mouth of the lion. And the
Lord shall deliver me from all evil doing, and shall keep me unto
his heavenly kingdom. To whom be praise for ever and ever. Amen.*

—2 Timothy 4:16–21 TNT

THE TRIAL WILL DRAG ON. IN ONE SENSE, IT IS ALL OVER. THE REST
is just argument, loud words, noise, the wait. Tyndale is no longer on the
run. He is no longer fugitive. For the first time since leaving England, he
is settled in one place. He is offered legal assistance, a mouthpiece, but
chooses to answer for himself. It is his nature to do so. And his captors
prefer it.

He is not alarmed. He is not desperate. Though the excess Latin is a kind of punishment. He longs to hear an English voice. Everything is Latin, French, or Flemish. Anything for English. Someone. Anyone. But he is denied guests.

He is going nowhere, and he seems to be the only one certain of it. Though his friends do everything they can to have him released, especially Poyntz, it is doubtful that Tyndale was ever aware of their efforts. His calm is an inspired calm—thorough and impregnable.

As for the trial, like so much of Tyndale lore, there is very little documentation of the event, but enough is known about heresy trials, and about the methods of the Inquisition to create an informed image of the proceedings.

There are two parts to every trial. First, the inquiry, the interrogation. (Oddly enough, John Wycliffe is credited with the first use of the word *inquisition*.)[1] This process determines if the accused has opinions that are indeed heretical. In Tyndale's case, this meant continuous visits to his cell, endless questioning, and in a language he had come to despise. The tedium, the pretense, the riddling wordcraft of the arguments, is as cruel as the intent that drives it.

There is no rack, no medieval torture device. Just the Latin. And the injustice, the lack of courtesies.

Immediately after Tyndale's arrest, the procurator-general, the emperor's attorney, Pierre Dufief, confiscated all of his belongings—papers, books, clothing, personal items, everything. It is doubtful that Tyndale was allowed any access to his possessions after that. Much of it was sold as "payment" for his confinement.

History has cast Dufief as a vicious prosecutor, a "magistrate of evil reputation."[2] We know how much he was paid for his part in what Mozley calls "destroying the arch-enemy [Tyndale]." At £128, he was the highest-paid official in the entire affair. All of them were paid handsomely, but Dufief's high payment suggests his role as facilitator, the man to move it along.

In his defense, for all his nastiness, Dufief, like Vaughn, softened after spending time with Tyndale. Tyndale was *"Homo doctus,"* Dufief said of him, *"pius et bonus* [a learned, good, and godly man]." Foxe even mentioned that Tyndale, once again very Pauline in his manner and effect, converted both the jailer [nameless] and his daughter.

> Such was the power of his doctrine, and the sincerity of his life, that during the time of his imprisonment, (which endured a year and a half,) it is said, he converted his keeper, the keeper's daughter, and others of his household. Also the rest that were with Tyndale conversant in the castle, reported of him that if he were not a good Christian man, they could not tell whom to trust.[3]

A commission was nominated to carry out the trial—Dufief, three theologians (doctors in divinity), three canons (clergymen) from Louvain, William van Caverschoen, secretary to the Inquisitor Apostolic for the Low Countries, and four members of the Council of Regency. Altogether there were seventeen, none of whom spoke any English, and only a few could speak Latin.

The only one not mentioned perhaps was Henry Phillips, officially a nobody, but a nobody who somehow managed to have all access. He was necessary somehow. Phillips was, in many ways, Tyndale's assassin. He missed nothing. He was always within hearing distance. He stood outside the cell when Tyndale was being questioned.

Of all these, there were two commissioners who stood out, and who conducted most of the interview/debates with Tyndale. They were James Masson (Latin name—*Latomus,* which means a worker in stone) and Ruard Tupper (or Tapper), also known as *Enchusanus.*

Both Masson and Tapper were theologians from Louvain. Giving one's self a Latin name was a popular convention among academics. The pretension was a shared one. If you look at their names, Tapper and Masson, both imply a wearing away of stone.

Latomus (Masson) was trained in theology at Paris and Louvain and was a specialist in debating, or controverting, with the enemies of Rome. Tapper was also a theologian, but he was not the gentle debater Masson was. He was the brawler. Their style with Tyndale might be described as an early form of good cop/bad cop. Tapper was merciless with the heretic. But they had a formidable opponent in Tyndale. He was not easy to rattle.

Foxe said that "there was much writing and great disputation to and fro, between him [Tyndale] and them of the university of Louvain . . . in such a sort, that they all had enough to do, and more than they could well wield, to answer the authorities and testimonies of the scripture, whereupon he most pithily grounded his doctrine."[4] Tyndale was big news. The bustle around his cage might be comic were it not so deadly.

As expected, Tyndale held his own with the Scripture. Whether it was More, Stokesley, Masson, Tapper, or any of the intervening personalities, none had the desire or command of Scripture that Tyndale had.

It is unlikely that he had any books or papers other than the ones demanded of the interrogation (by the rules of the Inquisition he was obligated to write down his defense). What Scripture he had was kept in the reserve of his memory. The entire affair was conducted in Latin, and after some time Tyndale had had enough, and requested someone who spoke English.

The process would continue until the Inquisition was convinced of the crime. Thomas Poyntz wrote that Tyndale's opinions had to be translated from English into Latin "so that the clergy here may understand it, and to condemn him, as they have done all others, for keeping opinions contrary to their business, the which they call 'the order of Holy Church.'"[5]

The Art of Argument

Mozley called it "paper-warfare." The writing that passed between Tyndale and the opposition was considerable. Unfortunately, none of Tyndale's words survived, other than the artifacts found in Masson's response, or in his correspondence. The following is an excerpt from a letter Masson wrote to a friend about Tyndale and his insistence on *sola fides* (faith alone). From this letter we can note the tenor of the debate and what Tyndale was up against.

When William Tyndale (he says) was in prison for Lutheranism, he wrote a book on the theme: *Sola fides justificat apud Deum*, faith alone justifies before God; this he called his key to healthy understanding of sacred scripture. We replied in three books. In the first we took away his key, and put another in its place. To this Tyndale, though he had no reasonable answer to make, yet preferred to make a show of replying rather than to acknowledge his error, and he wrote a second book against us, enlarging on the same theme, and also treating of nearly all the other matters of contention between us and them. We had therefore to answer him again in a second book of ours; and we plainly overturned his foundations and demonstrated the absurdity of his opinion. But we also added a third book, going shortly and clearly into the other points of dispute: "for this had Tyndale requested, that he might be able not only to hear, but also to read what we hold on these matters; and we were unwilling to decline any request of his." We feared indeed that our labor would not profit him: yet we hoped it might be a help to others.

There was nothing harsh in Masson's report, only the legal skirmish between opposing intellects, between two rigid and immovable opinions. Demaus suggested that Masson had been disarmed by Tyndale's "nobility and candour"[6] even as Dufief and others. The debates between the two men were conducted with mutual respect. The usual bleat and pounce doesn't work with a party of two. "If you are talking with a man in the privacy of an inner chamber, for his ear alone, and not for the mob in the market place, you cannot rail upon him perpetually, though he be your bitterest enemy."[7]

Masson privately nursed the hope that he might turn Tyndale. Unturnable, Tyndale made his argument as he did anything else he wrote, with precision and clarity (in spite of the Latin he had to frame it in). Tyndale was at his "one note" again, by now a familiar and comforting music. Exercising his immense singularity. (It is odd that Vaughn, a decent man among monsters, a discerning man who in the right ways "got" Tyndale, made his "one note" comment as if it were almost a bad thing.)

To continue the account, Tyndale asked Masson to make a written reply to his theme of *sola fide* (faith alone). Masson then listed several ways he and Tyndale agreed. It was all tactical—the art of argument. He arrived at the inevitable, where it was all leading in the first place—faith versus works. Reading the following brings the translator a step forward. It is Masson to Tyndale.

> Your use of scripture is onesided and unsound. If, as you write, you desire to be instructed, be careful not to regard the sacred text as a store-house of arguments for your part. You omit passages that tell against you, and which imply that our good acts merit reward from God. It is true that St. Paul says that our works have no merit and do not justify us, but he is speaking only of the time before we believe in Christ. Our first faith certainly is a free gift of God, in which we play no part at all, but as soon as we receive that faith and are justified through Christ, then we become for the first time capable of merit, partakers of the divine operation. You say that good works simply declare a man's goodness and do not make him good, just as the fruit of a tree shews, and does not create, the healthiness of the stock. The simile is a bad one; for the bearing of fruit weakens the tree, but good acts strengthen the mind: a fountain and its water would suit your purpose better. Our good works, you say again, are not needed by God nor do they benefit him, any more than the bitter draught, drunk by a patient, benefits the physician who prescribes it. I agree with you here: nevertheless God rewards us as if he needed our works, he rewards us merely for doing his will. Lastly, if good men merit no reward for doing his will. Lastly, if good men merit no reward of God, what are we to say of sinners? Is it reason to say that a reward can be given only to an evil act and not to a good one?[8]

This is the drone Tyndale had to endure. The same dull music, the opposition singing their one note. It was recorded in a document appropriately titled *Three Books with Confutations against William Tyndale* [Confutationum adversus Guilielmum Tindalum libri tres]. We will look at one more entry from Masson/Latomus. Tyndale misunderstood the meaning of faith, Latomus argued, made it a "weak and stunted" thing, belittling the work of grace in the heart.

Against all the wind and heat, Tyndale refused to be contentious. Masson, showing signs of exasperation, would have preferred a more combatant Tyndale. "Would that you meant it!" he said, thinking Tyndale's serenity to be tactical, contrived. Tyndale's resolve and its attending calm were too firmly settled, and far beyond the reach of his accusers. Here, Masson quotes Tyndale.

> Reflect upon all this, and you will clearly see that absurdity in which you are landed. Let me quote your statement of the case in your own words, so that "all readers may see its absurdity, and if you—which God forbid—shut your eyes, yet they may shun the mark of an obstinate heart. Works (you say) are the last things required in the law, and they do not fulfil the law before God. In work we ever sin, and our thoughts are impure. The love, *caritas*, which should fulfil the law, is colder in us than ice. Therefore we live by faith as long as we are in the flesh; and by faith we overcometh the world. This is the victory, which overcometh the world, even our faith (I John v), our faith in God through Christ; for the love of him who overcame all the temptations of the devil shall be imputed to us. By faith therefore is all the promise that it may be firm to every seed of them that believe; for by the works of the law shall no flesh be justified before him. Thus far you recognize your own words. Here you seem to open the secrets of your heart." Yet when we come to examine this position, it cannot stand; it is riddled with difficulties. Consider, I beg you, Tyndale, to what absurdity you are come by leaving the well trodden paths and the teaching of the fathers.[9]

"At the end of your treatise," Masson said, "you say that you have with a good conscience put forth your opinions. We believe your opinions are even as you say. Wherefore if your belief is true, you are rightly displeased with those that imprison you in the name of the pope and emperor, and treat you as a malefactor. Now since you ask to hear from us, nay to read, what our opinion is on the controversy, I will not disappoint your desire, in hope of thus recalling you from that error to catholic and true doctrine."[10]

Masson then argues his full case. He quotes from the fathers. He appeals to Church authority. Tyndale is surprised by none of it. Masson is less at ease when speaking about justification. He circumnavigates and attempts redirection. He has none of the scriptural brawn of his opponent. The goal is to convince the accused of the error of his ways. If this is not achieved, conviction follows, and a charge of heresy.

In the end, it was a stalemate. From the beginning it had been a stalemate. Tyndale had no shadow of turning in him, and Latomus had no power to convince. This comedy went on for months. But Masson could leave the gloomy cell. He could return to the comforts of his own home, perhaps family, friends. Tyndale could not. Tyndale had no more flight in him. Part of the inquisitor's strategy was the clock, the slow drip and waste of time. Isolation. Confinement.

There was no light. Tyndale had no books, no evidence of his former life. Mozley summarized:

> Latomus' [Masson's] hard and fast reasoning, his appeals to logic or authority, had nothing in them to still the cries of distress and rebellion that were arising from the hearts of thousands, who beheld the fair image of the church defaced, and longed to revive the living spirit that once had dwelt within her, and to call the free energies of all her sons into play. They asked for bread; Latomus and his like offered them a stone.[11]

Maybe it is pure optimism in me, but there is a powerful evangelism at work in Tyndale as he argued his case before Latomus. It lives in his words. His mettle had not wearied under the strain and ignominy. Tapper appears to have bowed out, deferring the bulk of the inquisition to his *good cop*. Tyndale would not fight Tapper's fight. But it is not impossible to imagine Latomus himself experiencing a kind of thaw, a kind of unsettling, as many of them did, particularly in the presence of a man who was more convinced of his faith than he was.

In the end it wasn't enough. Latomus had no turning in him either.

Early in August 1536, the charge of heresy was proven, and some time between 5 and 9 August, an order was given for Tyndale's degradation as a priest, a ceremony that would have meant little to him. He was to be publicly stripped of his priesthood.

O Cursed Judas

The bishops gathered on a high platform and were seated in public view. Again, spectacle was a part of the idiom. Tyndale was then led to the platform before them wearing the vestments of a priest. He was made to kneel. His hands were then scraped with a knife or a piece of glass—anywhere he would have been anointed with oil at his ordination. The office was withdrawn from him, the anointing removed.

The bread and wine of the Mass were placed in his hands then taken away from him, and with a curse. "O cursed Judas, because you have abandoned the counsel of peace and have counseled with the Jews, we take away from you this cup of redemption."[12]

His vestments were then stripped from him one at a time, until all evidence of the priesthood was removed. He then stood before the bishops and the crowd below as a layman, and suffered a final curse. "We commit your soul to the devil."

Tyndale was then handed over to the secular authorities for execution. This, too, was achieved with pronouncement. "We turn him over to the secular court." Dufief answered, "I am the one who wields the temporal sword."[13] Two official conditions were met, the *poena sensus* (pain of sense), and the *poena damni* (pain of loss). The former was the one that was effected by strangulation and burning. The second separated him from God forever, and an eternity in hell.

It is difficult to imagine Tyndale anything but indifferent, even acquiescent. It meant nothing to him.

There was a service book with the odd little ceremony all scripted out.

John Hutton, one of Cromwell's agents in the Low Countries wrote that on 12 August Dufief "certified me that William Tyndale is degraded,

and condemned into the hands of the secular power, so that he is very like
to suffer death this next week."[14]

Tyndale was ultimately condemned for his emphasis on justification
by faith alone and for his attacks on certain doctrine, and "usurpations"
of the papacy. Of course, a whole list of heresies was constructed from
these major elements. It is superfluous to say Tyndale never folded, that
he never recanted, never wavered in those things he had preached and
wrote about since leaving England.

There is one last document I would like to look at.

Come Before Winter

A letter written in Tyndale's own hand was discovered in the middle of the
nineteenth century in Belgium.[15] The date of the letter is uncertain, though
it was written in his cell in Vilvorde. Of all Tyndale's writing, of all he has
bequeathed us outside the Bible itself, for all his mystery, this, for me, is the
most telling—Tyndale at his most human, most vulnerable. His words are
sober, and warm to the touch. Here, at last, Tyndale steps forward into the
soft light, for here at the end he is fully visible in these few words.

> I believe, right worshipful, that you are not unaware of what may have
> been determined concerning me. Wherefore I beg your lordship, and
> that by the Lord Jesus, that if I am to remain here through the winter,
> you will request the commissary to have the kindness to send me, from
> the goods of mine which he has, a warmer cap; for I suffer greatly from
> cold in the head, and am afflicted by a perpetual catarrh [symptoms
> associated with the common cold], which is much increased in this
> cell; a warmer coat also, for this which I have is very thin; a piece of
> cloth too to patch my leggings. My overcoat is worn out; my shirts
> are also worn out. He has a woolen shirt, if he will be good enough to
> send it. I have also with him leggings of thicker cloth to put on above;
> he has also the warmer night-caps. And I ask to be allowed to have a
> lamp in the evening; it is indeed wearisome sitting alone in the dark.
> But most of all I beg and beseech your clemency to be urgent with the

commissary, that he will kindly permit me to have the Hebrew bible, Hebrew grammar, and Hebrew Dictionary, that I may pass the time in study. In return may you obtain what you most desire, so only that it be for the salvation of your soul. But if any other decision has been taken concerning me, to be carried out before winter, I will be patient, abiding the will of God, to the glory of the grace of my Lord Jesus Christ: whose Spirit (I pray) may direct your heart. Amen

W. Tindalus

His words are impossibly gentle. He is not bitter. He is not complaining. It is a simple kindness he asks for. There is nobility in the prose, a highness that cannot be wrested from him whatever despair he might have felt, whatever torments or denials.

A noble dignity and independence breathe through it. There is no touch of flattery, much less of cringing, yet it is perfectly courteous and respectful. Tyndale accepts his present plight with an equal mind, though he will lighten its burden so far as he can. But through it all, his chief thought is for the gospel which is committed to him. A burning love of God fills his heart.[16]

His clothes are ragged, which implies that he has been there some time, perhaps one winter already, and, as his trial drags on, he is anticipating another. Mozley makes a good argument suggesting that Tyndale was anticipating his first winter, the winter of 1535–36. We really don't know. Nor do we know to whom the letter was addressed. The most likely candidate was the Marquis of Bergen, the governor of Vilvorde castle. Thomas Cromwell addressed the petitions for Tyndale's release to the marquis, so this is probable.

It is not known whether or not any of Tyndale's requests were granted. Though tradition suggests that they were, that, too, is doubtful. And he is only asking for that which was his already, confiscated when he was first arrested. It is thought by some that he was given the books he requested and from his cell translated the Old Testament books of Joshua to 2

Chronicles. (The image of the indefatigable translator laboring in love and against time.) But this is pure optimism. And fable.

His most urgent plea was for his books, but it is unlikely that he would have been allowed them. Part of his crime was his translation. It is difficult to imagine, in spite of the tenderness, that he would be allowed to continue anything so unlawful. Even study would be suspect.

When John Frith was in the Tower of London he was allowed guests, and his friends brought him books. The same is true of Thomas More in his captivity. But the state prison at Vilvorde was a different animal. The letter implies conditions that were severe, punitive. Tyndale was allowed no guests.

The Strong Good Medicine Of Death

The date of William Tyndale's execution was 6 October 1536. Because of his distinction as a scholar, he was to be strangled first, then burned at the stake. The only documentation of the event is from Foxe.

> At last, after much reasoning, when no reason would serve, although he deserved no death, he was condemned by virtue of the emperor's decree . . . and, upon the same, brought forth to the place of execution, was there tied to the stake, and then strangled first by the hangman, and afterwards with fire consumed, in the morning at the town of Vilvorde, A. D. 1536: crying thus at the stake with a fervent zeal, and a loud voice, "Lord! open the king of England's eyes."[17]

Though not all biographers are convinced that there were any last words, we may just as well give Foxe his due. Whether the king of England's eyes were ever opened is a matter of debate. For in many ways Henry VIII was the most blind of men. Still, an English Bible would indeed have royal blessing within months of Tyndale's death.

From an account of two executions identical to Tyndale's in Brussels and Louvain, we can clarify the image. A circle was enclosed within a barricade, through which no one could pass except the guards, the executioner, and the condemned. Inside the circle, two beams were set up in the shape of a cross, which would project from the ground to a man's height. At the top of this structure were iron chains. Brushwood, straw, and logs were packed tightly around the upright beam in a kind of hut. The prisoner was brought in and given a last chance to recant. His feet were then bound to the stake. Gunpowder was added to the brush for the quick burn.

Two months after Tyndale's execution, Hutton wrote again to Cromwell, saying: "They speak much of the patient sufferance of Master Tyndale at the time of his execution."[18] I am not sure what else we might have expected. As Mozley said aptly, Tyndale "did not disgrace the faith that was in him."

The flames did not kill William Tyndale, nor did he feel any heat. His body was consumed, certainly, but as he had long trained himself, as he did in Cologne with his precious cargo, he made his way out just in time.

A rope was fitted through a hole in the upright beam and curled around his neck. At the urging of the magistrate, and just before the flame was lit, with all the necessary parties

> *When thou walkest through the fire, thou shalt not be burned; neither shall the flame kindle upon thee.*
>
> – ISAIAH 43:2

present, the rope was pulled with sufficient force to end his life.* No symbol went unused. By strangling Tyndale, the Church thought to silence him forever.

They were wrong.

---

* It has been suggested that the executioner botched the job and Tyndale regained consciousness just before the flames were lit. While this is unlikely, it deserves a footnote. Not to defile the earth with his remains, his ashes would have been cast in the nearby River Zenne. This was the usual practice with the burning of a former priest. That Tyndale's ashes were dispersed creates a useful metaphor for his lasting presence in English letters, and as a world-changer.

Epilogue

ELEGY

But the melodies of the poet ascend and leap and
pierce into the deeps of infinite time.

— Ralph Waldo Emerson, *"The Poet"*

IN A SPEECH AT THE STERLING MEMORIAL LIBRARY AT YALE
University in May 2008 entitled "Reading History and Writing Fiction:
A Life In Books," exploring the library as a metaphor for memory, writer
Penelope Lively described an idle fantasy of hers. In this fantasy, she
imagines a time many years into the future. Human life has long been
extinguished, and into the library comes the advance guard of an alien race.

> Crack teams of scholars are set to work to decode this mystifying
> depository. Everything coexists here. Several task forces penetrate
> the inner reaches of the library and inspect the Lindesfarne Gospels
> alongside a set of eighteenth century sermons, Handel's manuscripts
> in conjunction with studies in accountancy. The works of Dickens in

association with Bee-keeping for Beginners. "What were the priorities of this culture?" they will all wonder.

They will become aware of linguistic diversity, and above all of interconnection. The study group assigned to the Tyndale Bible will be able to announce after several decades that echoes of this apparently unremarkable little work appear in such a range of other material that it's clear that a primitive virus has been identified.[1]

In 1550, Roger Ascham—the renowned and brilliant tutor of the Princess Elizabeth, the future queen of England—passed through Vilvorde. "At the town's end," he wrote later, "is a notable solemn place of execution, where worthy William Tyndale was unworthily put to death."[2] A memorial was placed in the same spot in 1913. There is a William Tyndale Museum in Vilvorde as well. In London, a statue of Tyndale was erected in 1884. A stone monument overlooks the town of North Nibley, Gloucestershire, and he has been given a day of recognition by the Anglican Church. The collect proper (prayer) for 6 October reads:

> Lord, give your people grace to hear and keep your word that, after the example of your servant William Tyndale, we may not only profess your gospel but also be ready to suffer and die for it, to the honour of your name.

William Tyndale certainly deserves the honors, but for his contribution to the English language, to English thought and piety, he has been given what amounts to a formal nod, a gold watch, and a citation for his service.

Uncelebrated as he is, and as he will probably remain, I find myself asking the oddest question. *Would he have wanted it this way?* For all the trumpeting I had intended, the large parade of accomplishments and praises that might epilogue this book, I find that the exclamation point I had considered just won't do. A soft period works fine. It is punctuation enough. It was Tyndale's way.

And I concede.

A more accurate justice, therefore, may be in a quieter end.

I have spun out all my superlatives. I have made my arguments. Compared to English writers of greater name but much less weight per pound, he is magnificently underprized, and thus remains in a kind of exile. Yet, of all the influences that have effected growth, change, aesthetics, motion, sound, of all the Darwinian states that have kept English alive and moving forward into time, William Tyndale will continue to be that primitive virus, that unseen ground and father of our prose, all because of his unremarkable little book. He is, as More prophesied, everywhere and nowhere.

The irony is delicious.

A final word, therefore, I leave to Tyndale himself. With the above preamble in mind, when I read the following excerpt,[3] I realize, and by a warm recognition, if not with some reluctance to say more, that Tyndale has become clearer to me now. It is a matter of trust, I think. He would have willingly spoken these words to Thomas More, to Henry the King, even to his betrayer, Harry Phillips. To understand *that* is at last to understand William Tyndale. And what more fitting epitaph could our little history ask?

> Christ is the cause why I love thee, why I am ready to do the uttermost of my power for thee, and why I pray for thee. And as long as the cause abideth, so long lasteth the effect; even as it is always day so long as the sun shineth. Do therefore the worst thou canst unto me, take away my goods, take away my good name; yet as long as Christ remaineth in my heart, so long I love thee not a whit less, and so long art thou as dear unto me as mine own soul, and so long am I ready to do thee good for thine evil and so long I pray for thee with all my heart: for Christ desireth it of me, and hath deserved it of me. Thine unkindness compared unto his kindness is nothing at all; yet, it is swallowed up as a little smoke of a mighty wind, and is no more seen or thought upon. Moreover that evil which thou doest to me, I receive not of thine hand, but of the hand of God, and as God's scourge to teach me patience and to nurture me. And therefore have no cause to be angry with thee more

than the child hath to be angry with his father's rod or a sick man with a sore or bitter medicine that healeth him, or a prisoner with his fetters or he that is punished lawfully with the officer that punished him.

Thus is Christ all and the whole cause why I love thee, and to all can nought be added.

—William Tyndale

Appendix A

1491–1495   William Tyndale born in Gloucestershire "around the border of Wales." (1494 is widely accepted.)

1508   Attends Oxford University (Magdalen).

1509   Henry VIII becomes King of England.

1512   Receives BA degree.

1515   Receives MA degree. Cardinal Wolsey is appointed chancellor of England.

1516   Desiderius Erasmus publishes his Greek New Testament.

1517   Martin Luther nails his 95 Theses to the church door at Wittenburg, Germany.

Tyndale goes to Cambridge (or so it is thought).

1519   Family of six is burned at the stake for teaching children the Lord's Prayer in English. (Coventry)

1520   Pope Leo X issues a bull, *Exsurge Domine*, 15 June, decreeing that Martin Luther's books were to be sought, confiscated, and destroyed (burned).

1521   Cardinal Wolsey has public burning of Lutheran books at St. Paul's Cross.

Tyndale leaves Cambridge and returns to Gloucestershire and lives at Little Sodbury Manor with Sir John Walsh and his family.

1523 Leaves Gloucestershire for London.

1524 Lives in the home of Henry Monmouth.

Meets with Cuthbert Tunstall, asks permission to translate the Bible into English, and is refused.

Leaves England forever.

Arrives in Hamburg, Germany, early in May.

Leaves Hamburg for Wittenburg, 27 May.

1525 Goes back to Hamburg, proceeds to Cologne, Germany.

Begins printing the New Testament in Cologne.

Has to flee Cologne with only part of the translation printed (the prologue to the Epistle of Paul to the Romans and Matthew 1–22).

1526 Completes first edition of his New Testament at Worms, Germany.

By March copies of the New Testament reach England.

On 24 October, Cuthbert Tunstall attacks NT in a sermon. Claims 2000 errors.

1527 Bishop of Norwich claimed to confiscate all English New Testaments arriving from overseas. Cost him £66 9s. 4d. Encouraged other bishops to do likewise.

1528 Tyndale's friend and patron, Humphrey Monmouth, is questioned, and his house searched, by Sir Thomas More and Sir William Kingston. Monmouth is committed to the Tower on suspicion of heresy and possessing heretical books by Luther and others.

On 7 March Tunstall commissions Sir Thomas More to reply to Lutheran threat, to show the commoner "the crafty malice of the heretics."

Tunstall allows More to read Tyndale's writing, thus beginning a literary feud between Tyndale and More.

The Parable of the Wicked Mammon

The Obedience of a Christian Man

1529 Thomas More becomes chancellor of England. More publishes his *Dialogue Concerning Heresies*, attacking Tyndale.

Tyndale possibly suffers a shipwreck, losing books and his translation.

1530 John Stokesley becomes becomes bishop of London.

Pentateuch

Practice of Prelates

A Pathway to the Holy Scripture

1531 Thomas Bilney and Richard Bayfield are burned at the stake.

Stephen Vaughn promises Tyndale safe passage to England. Tyndale refuses.

An Answer to Sir Thomas More's Dialogue

The Exposition of the First Epistle of St. John

Books of Joshua through 2 Chronicles and the Book of Jonas (Jonah)

1532 James Bainham is burned at the stake.

Thomas More writes *Confutation*.

1533 Thomas Cranmer is appointed archbishop of Canterbury.

Anne Boleyn marries Henry VIII and is crowned queen of England.

John Frith is burned at the stake.

An Exposition upon the VI, VI, VII Chapters of Matthew

1534 Tyndale publishes his revised New Testament.

Tyndale moves into the English House in Antwerp.

1535 Tyndale is betrayed by Henry Phillips and arrested.

Tyndale is imprisoned at Vilvorde Castle.

Myles Coverdale publishes the entire Bible in English.

Sir Thomas More is beheaded for high treason 6 July.

1536 William Tyndale is strangled to death and burned at the stake 6 October.

1537 John Rogers publishes *The Matthew's Bible, the first "authorized" English Bible.*

Anne Boleyn is executed for high treason 19 May.

Appendix B

FIRST USAGE OF WORDS BY WILLIAM TYNDALE

THE FOLLOWING LIST INCLUDES THE FIRST APPEARANCES OF WORDS introduced into the English language by William Tyndale as documented in the *Oxford English Dictionary*. This list, however, is incomplete. Many of the words introduced by Tyndale have been credited to other authors (most particularly Myles Coverdale [The Coverdale Bible, 1535], but also William Shakespeare, the King James Bible, and others). One example of this oversight is the word *behold*, which is credited to the Coverdale Bible for first usage (Mal. 3:1). Yet this same word appears in Tyndale's 1526 New Testament (Matt. 1:20; 7:4; 8:29; 12:49; 18:10; 26:65; John 11:3, Rev. 21:5).

Here is a small sample of familiar words, also miscredited, that have their start in Tyndale: *fig leaves* (Gen. 3), *birthright* (Gen. 25), *ingathering* (Ex. 34), *whoring* (Ex. 34), *sin offering* (Lev. 4), *morning watch* (1 Sam. 2), *handbreadth* (1 Kings 7), *spoiler* (2 Kings 17), *swaddling clothes* (Luke 2), *slaughter* (Acts 9, Heb. 7, James 5), *ministering* (Heb. 1).

William Shakespeare is credited for the word *circumcised* (*Othello*, 1616), and yet it first appears in Tyndale's Genesis 17. The word *dedicating* is credited to the Coverdale Bible (Dan. 3) and to the King James Version (Num. 7), with no mention of Tyndale who introduced the word (Num. 7).

At present, the Coverdale Bible is the 67th most frequently quoted source in the *OED*, with a total of 4,317 actual quotes. As we might guess, this number is grossly inaccurate. The William Tyndale New Testament is currently the 196th most frequently quoted source, with a total of 1,933 quotations (about 0.06 percent of all *OED* quotations).

This first list includes the words found (first usage) in the William Tyndale New Testament (1526–1534). The second list includes the words found in Tyndale's nontranslation works.

Abib

achange

a-doors

agreeing

anathema

anathema maranatha

apostleship

athenian

baning

beggarly

betrayer

bolden

bondmaid

broken-hearted

brotherly

bruterer

busybody

castaway

castor

chasten

chastening

childishness

complainer

Corinthian

daughter-law

deceivableness

divider

dividing

divorcement

excommunicate

excommunicate [trans]

eye-service

fatling

fellow-soldier

finisher

fisherman

godly

God-speed

grossly

guest-chamber

harborous

hard by

heave-offering

heave shoulder

here-hence

holy place

house-top

housewifely

ignorancy

incomer

incorruption

inexcusable

intend

intercession

Jehovah

jesting

jot

judgement-seat

justifier

live

log

longed

long-suffering

lost

lowth

Mercy-seat

mocking-stock

mother-law

network

Nicolaitan

nurse-fellow

offscouring

oiled

open door

ourselves

particolourd

passover

peace offering

persecuter

Philippian

pose

prison fellow

refused

rose-coloured

royetous

sanctifying

scapegoat

sea-shore

shewbread

silvering

silver plate

singleness

sorcerer

stiff-necked

stumbling-block

surfeiting

surmising

sycamine

Syrtis

taskmaster

temperancy

thank-offering

tribute-money

two-edged

unbeliever

uncircumcision

uncondemned

undergird

unghostly

ungodliness

ungodly [n]

ungodly [adv]

unleavened

unprofitableness

untoward

uproar

viper

wave

weakling

whereinsoever

whoremonger

wine-press

wine-vat

wreathed

writing-table

yoke-fellow

Zamsummim

zealous

William Tyndale (1494–1536) is the 618th most frequently quoted source in the *OED*, with a total of 728 quotations (about 0.02 percent of all *OED* quotations). The following are found in all the nontranslation works of Tyndale.

afterwitted

a-good

allegorical

anagogical

ancientness

annunciate

antiquate

apparitor

appropriate

augmenting

beggaring

blazing

bloodshedder

bo-peep

brotherliness

cardinalship
churlishness
clear-eyed
converter
creating

deaconess
declarative
deponent
devilishly
dimensioned
disconsent
disgraduate
disgress
dispicience
dispraiser
dotehead
dunce

earthish
endote
evangelical

fainty
fratry

Galatian
gerah
German
gleering
godless
godliness

hyperdulia
hypocritish

impure
incarnate
infatuate
intemperancy
inunvariable
iterate

knavery

landlady
leaner

metaphysic
miswoman
Moses
mumpsimus

over-roast

patcher
pattering
peace-breaker
pediary
pestilently
petitio pricipii
philautia
pick-quarrel
pilpate
poddish
poetess

pope-holiness
popishness
pottering
priestdom

respondent
ribaldish
Robin Goodfellow
Romish

satisfactory
school doctor
Scotist
self-minded
servant
simular
slibber-sauce
slime-pit
sniveled
snork
snout-fair
sodomitry
splaying
studied
suspension
swash
swinge

thanksgiving
Thomist
toy
transubstantiate
trope

tropological
turnagain

unblameable
unbrought

Appendix C

WILLIAM TYNDALE'S LETTERS TO JOHN FRITH WHILE FRITH WAS CONFINED IN THE TOWER

Letter 1

The grace of our Saviour Jesus Christ, his patience, meekness, humbleness, circumspection, and wisdom, be with your heart. Amen.

Dearly beloved brother Jacob, mine heart's desire in our Saviour Jesus is, that you arm yourself with patience, and be cold, sober, wise, and circumspect: and that you keep a-low by the ground, avoiding high questions that pass the common capacity. But expound the law truly, and open the vail of Moses, to condemn all flesh, and prove all men sinners, and all deeds under the law, before mercy have taken away the condemnation thereof, to be sin and damnable: and then, as a faithful minister, set abroach the mercy of our Lord Jesus, and let the wounded consciences drink of the water of him. And then shall your preaching be with power, and not as the doctrine of the hypocrites; and the spirit of God shall work with you, and all consciences shall bear record unto you, and feel that it is so. And all doctrine that casteth a mist on those two, to shadow and hide them (I mean the law of God and mercy of Christ) that resist you with all your power. Sacraments without signification refuse. If they put significations to them, receive them, if you see it may help, though it be not necessary.

Of the presence of Christ's body in the sacrament meddle as little as you can, that there appear no division among us . . . My mind is that nothing be put forth, till we hear how you shall have sped. I would have the right use preached, and the presence to be an indifferent thing, till the matter might be reasoned in peace a leisure of both parties. If you be required, show the phrases of the scripture, and let them talk what they will. For as to believe that God is everywhere, hurteth no man that worshippeth him nowhere but within in the heart, in spirit and verity, even so to believe that the body of Christ is everywhere, though it cannot be proved, hurteth no man that worshippeth him nowhere save in the faith of his gospel. You perceive my mind: howbeit, if God show you otherwise, it is free for you to do as he moveth you.

I guessed long ago that God would send a dazing into the head of the spirituality, to catch themselves in their own subtlety: and I trust it is come to pass. And now methinketh I smell a counsel to be taken, little for the profits in time to come. But you must understand that it is not of a pure heart, and for love of the truth; but to avenge themselves, and to eat the whore's flesh, and to suck the marrow of her bones. Wherefore cleave fast to the rock of the help of God, and commit the end of all things to him: and if God shall call you, that you may then use the wisdom of the worldly, as far as you perceive the glory of God may come thereof, refuse it not: and ever among thrust in, that the scripture may be in the mother tongue, and learning set up in the universities. But and if aught be required contrary to the glory of God and his Christ, then stand fast, and commit yourself to God; and be not overcome with men's persuasions, which haply shall say, we see no other way to bring in the truth.

Brother Jacob, beloved in my heart, there liveth not in whom I have so good hope and trust, and in whom mine heart rejoiceth, and my soul comforteth herself, as in you, not the thousand part so much of your learning and what other gifts else you have, as that you will creep a-low by the ground, and walk in those things that the conscience may feel, and not in the imaginations of the brain; in fear, and not in boldness; in open necessary things, and not to pronounce or define of hid secrets, or things that neither help nor hinder, whether they be so or no; in unity, and not in seditious opinions; insomuch that if you be sure you know, yet in things that may abide leisure, you will defer, or say (till other agree with you), "Methink the text requireth this sense or understanding:" yea, and that if you be sure that your part be good, and another hold the contrary, yet if it be a thing that maketh no matter, you will laugh and let it pass, and refer the thing to other men, and stick you stiffly and stubbornly in earnest and necessary things. And I trust you be persuaded even so of me. I call God to record, against the day we shall appear before our Lord Jesus to give a reckoning of our doings, that I never altered one syllable of God's word against my conscience, nor would do this day, if all that is in the earth, whether it be honour, pleasure, or riches, might be given me. Moreover, I take God to record to my conscience, that I desire of God to myself, in this world, no more than that without which I cannot keep his laws.

Finally, if there were in me any gift that could help at hand, and aid you if need required, I promise you I would not be far off, and commit the end to God: my soul is not faint, though my body be weary. But God hath made me ill-favoured in this world, and without grace in the sight of men, speechless and rude, dull and slow-witted. Your part shall be to supply that lacketh in me; remembering that, as lowliness of heart shall make you high with God, even so meekness of words shall make you sink in the hearts of men. Nature giveth age authority; but meekness is the glory of youth, and giveth them honour. Abundance of love maketh me exceed in babbling.

Sir, as concerning purgatory, and many other things, if you be demanded, you may say, if you err, the spirituality hath so led you; and that they have taught you to believe as you do. For they preached you all such things out of God's word, and alleged a thousand texts; by reason of which texts you believed as they taught you. But now you find them liars, and that the text means no such things, and therefore you can believe them no longer; but are as ye were before they taught you, and believe no such thing; howbeit you are ready to believe, if they have any other way to prove it; for without proof you cannot believe them, when you have found them with so many lies, etc. If you perceive wherein we may help, either in being still, or doing somewhat, let us have word, and I will do mine uttermost.

My lord of London hath a servant called John Tisen, with a red beard, and a black reddish head, and was once my scholar; he was seen in Antwerp, but came not among the Englishmen: wither he is gone, an embassador secret, I wot not.

The mighty God of Jacob be with you to supplant his enemies, and give you the favour of Joseph; and the wisdom and the spirit of Stephen be with your heart and with your mouth, and teach your lips what they shall say, and how to answer to all things. He is our God, if we despair in ourelves, and trust in him; and his is the glory. Amen.

WILLIAM TYNDALE
I hope our redemption is nigh.

Letter 2

The grace and peace of God our Father, and of Jesus Christ our Lord, be with you. Amen.

Dearly beloved brother John. I have heard say that the hypocrites, now they have overcome that great business which letted them, or that now they have at least way brought it at a stay, they return to their old nature again. The will of God be fulfilled, and that he hath ordained to be ere the world was made, that come, and his glory reign over all.

Dearly beloved, howsoever the matter be, commit yourself wholly and only unto your most loving Father and most kind Lord, and fear not men that threaten, nor trust men that speak fair: but trust him that is true of promise, and able to make his word good. Your cause is Christ's gospel, a light that must be fed with the blood of faith. The lamp must be dressed and snuffed daily, and that oil poured in every evening and morning, that the light go not out. Though we be sinners, yet is the cause right. If when we be buffeted for well-doing, we suffer patiently and endure, that is thankful with God; "for to that end we are called. For Christ also suffered for us, leaving us an example that we should follow his steps, who did no sin. Hereby have we perceived love that he laid down his life for us: there we ought also to lay down our lives for the brethren. Rejoice and be glad, for great is your reward in heaven. For we suffer with him, that we may also be glorified: who shall change our vile body, that it may be fashioned like unto his glorious body, according to the working whereby he is able even to subject all things unto him.

Dearly beloved, be of good courage, and comfort your soul with the hope of this high reward, and bear the image of Christ in your mortal body, that it may at his coming be made like to his, immortal: and follow the example of all your other dear brethren, which chose to suffer in hope of a better resurrection. Keep your conscience pure and undefiled, and say against that nothing. Stick at necessary things; and remember the blasphemies of the enemies of Christ, "They find none but that will abjure rather than suffer the extremity." Moreover, the death of them that come again after they have once denied, though it be accepted with God and all that believe, yet is it not glorious; for the hypocrites say, "He must needs die; denying helpeth not: but might it have holpen, they would have denied five hundred times: but seeing it would not help them, therefore of pure pride and mere malice together, they speak with their mouths that their conscience knoweth false." If you give yourself, cast yourself, yield yourself, commit yourself wholly and only to your loving Father; then shall this power be in you and make you strong, and that so strong that you shall feel no pain: and that shall be to another present death: and his Spirit shall speak in you, and teach you what to answer, according to his promise. He shall set out his truth by you wonderfully, and work for you above all that your heart can imagine. Yea, and you are not yet dead; though the hypocrites all, with all they can make, have sworn your death. *Una salus victus nullam sperare salutem* [The only safety for the conquered is to expect no safety]. To look for no man's help bringeth the help of God to them that seem to be overcome in the eyes of the hypocrites: yea, it shall make God to carry you through thick and thin for his truth's sake, in spite of all the enemies of his truth. There falleth not a hair till his hour be come: and when his hour is come, necessity carrieth us hence, though we be not willing. But if we be willing, then have we a reward and thanks.

Fear not threatening, therefore, neither be overcome of sweet words; with which twain the hypocrites shall assail you. Neither let the persuasions of worldly wisdom bear rule in your heart; no, though they be your friends that counsel. Let Bilney be a warning to you. Let not their visor beguile your eyes. Let not your body faint. "He that endureth to the end shall be saved." If the pain be above your strength, remember: "Whatsoever ye shall ask in my name, I will give it you." And pray to your Father in that name, and he will ease your pain, or shorten it. The Lord of Peace, of hope, and of faith, be with you. Amen.

WILLIAM TYNDALE.

Notes

Prologue

1. G. M. Trevelyan, *England in the Age of Wycliffe*, 104.
2. Barbara Tuchman, *A Distant Mirror*, 32.
3. Ibid., 32.
4. Benson Bobrick, *Wide As the Waters*, 36.
5. Quoted in John Richard Green, *England*, vol. I, 412.
6. Tuchman, *A Distant Mirror*, 304.
7. Quoted from *De Hæretico Comburendo, 1401* (Regarding the Burning of Heretics).
8. Excerpt from the Statutes of the Realm (Henry IV) *De Hæretico Comburendo, 1401* (Regarding the Burning of Heretics).
9. C. H. Williams, *William Tyndale*, xiii.
10. David Teems, *To Love Is Christ*, 166.
11. David Teems, *Majestie: The King Behind the King James Bible*, 251.
12. John Frith (1503–1533) in response to Thomas More.
13. Quoted in David Daniell, *The William Tyndale New Testament*, viii.
14. Daniell, ed., from the introduction to *The William Tyndale New Testament*, xxiv.
15. Letter from William Tyndale to John Frith when Frith was in the Tower. See complete letter in appendix C.
16. William Tyndale, *The Obedience of a Christian Man*, 151.
17. Quoted in Daniell, *The Bible in English*, 772.
18. Daniell, *William Tyndale: A Biography*, 116.
19. *The Works of Thomas More* (ed. Schuster et al), 8: 1.212.
20. J. F. Mozley, *William Tyndale*, 93.
21. Ibid., 188–189.

Chapter 1

1. William Tyndale, *Doctrinal Treatises and Introductions to Different Portions of the Holy Scriptures*, ed. by Rev. Henry Walter (Parker Society), 32.

2. Williams, *William Tyndale*, 1.

3. Richard Marius, *Thomas More*, 317.

4. Mozley, *William Tyndale*, 10.

5. Tyndale, *Obedience of a Christian Man*, 131.

6. Ibid., 170.

7. Mozley, *William Tyndale*, 1.

8. David Rollison, *The local origins of modern society: Gloucestershire 1500–1800*, quoted in Levine review of Rollison's "Local Origins," *Social History*, vol. 19, no. 1, 100.

9. Mozley, *William Tyndale*, 4.

10. Ibid.

11. Ibid.

12. Rawdon Brown, ed., "Venice: December 1530," Calendar of State Papers Relating to English Affairs in the Archives of Venice, Volume 4: 1527–1533, 265–273.

13. Mozley and others suggested that Tyndale may have meant Alfred the Great, 849–899.

14. Quoted in Daniell, *William Tyndale: A Biography*, 12.

15. Mozley, *William Tyndale*, 9.

16. Glenn S. Sunshine, *Reformation for Armchair Theologians*, 2.

17. Tuchman, *A Distant Mirror*, 304.

18. Ibid., 288.

19. From the *Oxford English Dictionary*, lollard.

20. Williams, *William Tyndale*, xiii.

21. C. S. Lewis, *The Literary Impact of the Authorized Version*, 27.

22. Gwyneth Lewis, Welsh poet laureate, in an interview with Robert Harrison (*Entitled Opinions* broadcast, Stanford University, 16 February 2010).

23. William Shakespeare, *Henry IV, Part One*, III, i, 202–208.

24. John Foxe, *Actes and Monuments of the Church*, 542.

25. Jerry Brotton, *The Renaissance*, 3.

26. Quoted in the *OED* under the heading "Renaissance," from W. K. Ferguson, *Renaissance in Historical Thought*.

27. Brotton, *The Renaissance*, 39.

28. Ibid., 40.

29. Ibid., 10.

30. Ibid., 11.

31. William Tyndale, *Answer to Thomas More*, 75–76.

32. Brian Moynahan, *God's Bestseller*, 7.

33. Ibid., 9.

34. Mozley, *William Tyndale*, 14.

35. Ibid.

36. G. E. Duffield, ed., *The Works of William Tyndale*, xv, (quoted from *Practice of Prelates*).

Chapter 2

1. Hebrew had an even slower start than Greek. Though some Hebrew grammar books and a lexicon arrived in the first decade of the 16th century, the first Regius

(royal) professorship at Cambridge wasn't established until 1540, and at Oxford in 1546—both founded by Henry VIII. The universities of Paris, Wittenberg, and Louvain established the same professorial seats around the same time.

2. C. S. Lewis, *English Literature in the Sixteenth Century*, 175.

3. William S. Bishop, "Erasmus," *The Sewanee Review* (1906), 130.

4. Ibid.

5. William Manchester, *A World Lit Only by Fire*, 183.

6. Bishop, "Erasmus," *The Sewanee Review*, 9.

7. Bishop ("Erasmus," *The Sewanee Review*, 1906) tells the story of Gerard and Margaret (Erasmus's mother), a tale spun together both with legend and bits of truth. Gerard and Margaret were in love, but the families objected. As young couples often do when faced with hostility and forbidden love, they continued their relationship. Impossibility and passion always make a great tale. Margaret got pregnant. Gerard was called to Rome on some mission and had planned to return and marry Margaret, but he was detained. He was then told that Margaret had died. It was then he became a priest. When he found out the truth, it was too late to wed. Bishop says the story is probably a lie anyway, or partly a lie. Considering the deeper meaning of Erasmus's name, it seemed to beg a note.

8. *Oxford English Dictionary—desiderium*, etymology: Latin = longing, sense of want, desire <stem of *desiderare*> (author's emphasis).

9. Charles Nauert, "Desiderius Erasmus," *Stanford Encyclopedia of Philosophy*.

10. Richard Marius, *Martin Luther*, 247.

11. Desiderius Erasmus, from the prologue of his Greek New Testament.

12. Benson Bobrick, *As Wide as the Waters*, 111.

13. Desiderius Erasmus, *Paraclesis*, (the introduction to the Greek New Testament).

14. Bishop, "Erasmus," *The Sewanee Review*, 140.

15. *In Praise of Folly* (Erasmus) quoted in Manchester, *A World Lit Only by Fire*, 123.

16. Patrick Collinson, *The Reformation*, 39.

17. Bobrick, *As Wide as the Waters*, 89–90.

18. Bart Ehrman, *Misquoting Jesus*, 79.

19. From a sermon Martin Luther preached in 1522, quoted in Patrick Collinson, *The Reformation*, 33.

20. Daniell, *William Tyndale*, 49.

21. W. E. Campbell, *Erasmus, Tyndale, and More*, 23.

22. Ibid., 25.

23. Ibid., 25–26.

24. Daniell, *William Tyndale*, 33.

25. Ibid., 36.

26. Bishop, "Erasmus," *The Sewanee Review*, 136.

27. Anonymous, quoted in Manchester, 183.

28. Mozley, *William Tyndale*, 236–7.

29. William Tyndale, "W. T. unto the Reader," *Prologue to the Pentateuch*, 5.

30. Mozley, *William Tyndale*, 21.

31. Moynahan, *God's Bestseller*, 22.

Chapter 3

1. Quoted in Mozley, *William Tyndale*, 26.
2. Daniell, *William Tyndale: A Biography*, 63.
3. Mozley, *William Tyndale*, 29.
4. Foxe, *Actes and Monuments (1563)*, 513–14.
5. Tyndale, *Answer to Sir Thomas More's Dialogue*, 57.
6. Tyndale, "W. T. unto the Reader" (excerpt from the preface to the Pentateuch).
7. Foxe, *Actes and Monuments*, 542.
8. Greenblatt, *Renaissance Self Fashioning*, 107.
9. Ibid.
10. Tyndale, "W. T. Unto the Reader" (preface to the Pentateuch), 3.
11. Ibid., 4.
12. Daniell, *William Tyndale: A Biography*, 84.
13. "We therefore command and ordain that henceforth no one translate on his own authority any text of Holy Scripture into English . . . and that no one read anything of this kind lately made in the time of the said John Wycliffe . . . either publicly or privately, whole or in part" unless it was first "approved and allowed" by the local bishop of the diocese.—From the *Constitutions of Oxford*
14. Tyndale, "W. T. unto the Reader" (preface to the Pentateuch), 4.
15. Bobrick, *Wide as the Waters*, 96.
16. Even Monmouth's name smacked of home, of the western midlands. Though he had no tie to such a place, Monmouth is a town in south Wales, and his name suggests a western origin. Like Sir John Walsh, Monmouth had done business with Edward Tyndale who was said to be "the most powerful man in the vale" (Bobrick, *Wide as the Waters*, 98).
17. Bobrick, *Wide as the Waters*, 97.

Chapter 4

1. Thomas More, *A Dialogue Concerning Heresies* quoted in Brian Moynahan, *God's Bestseller*, 55.
2. Daniell, *William Tyndale*, 299.
3. Mozley, *William Tyndale*, 53.
4. Moynahan, *God's Bestseller*, 64.
5. *Author* is not a term that would have been recognized in 1525. Only later in the sixteenth century did the word begin to have the meaning that we associate it with today. The person who originates or gives existence to anything—an inventor, instructor, or founder. "He who gives rise to or causes an action, event, circumstance, state, or condition of things. One who sets forth written statements; the composer or writer of a treatise or book" (*Oxford English Dictionary*).
6. Moynahan, *God's Bestseller*, 71.
7. Mozley, *William Tyndale*, 57.
8. Ibid., 59.
9. Ibid.

10. Ibid.

11. Daniell, *William Tyndale: A Biography*, 110.

12. Mozley, *William Tyndale*, 60.

13. Moynahan, *God's Bestseller*, 75.

14. *Doctrinal treatises and introductions to different portions of the Holy Scripture*, Rev. Henry Walter, ed., (The Parker Society, 1847), 7.

15. Daniell, *William Tyndale*, 121.

16. Elizabeth Nugent, *The thought & culture of the English Renaissance: an anthology of Tudor prose 1481–1555*, 417.

17. "The gift of God" is found in John 4:10, Acts 8:20, Romans 6:23, I Corinthians 7:7, Ephesians 2:8, and 2 Timothy 1:6. "Walk in darkness" is found in John 8:12 and I John 1:6. "Spirit of meekness" is found in I Corinthians 4:21 and Galatians 6:1.

18. Patrick Collinson, *The Reformation: A History*, 63.

19. De Lamar Jensen, *Confrontation at Worms: Martin Luther and the Diet of Worms*, 101.

20. "And the Lord said, I am Jesus whom thou persecutest, it shall be hard for thee to kick against the pricks" (Acts 9:5 TNT).

21. I Timothy 6:19 TNT.

Chapter 5

1. Moynahan, *God's Bestseller*, 83.

2. Ackroyd, *Albion*, 307.

3. Scruton, *England: An Elegy*, 99.

4. Conroy, *My Reading Life*, 253.

5. Daniell, *William Tyndale*.

6. Bobrick, *Wide as the Waters*, 105.

7. Tyndale, *Parable of the Wicked Mammon*, 126.

8. Robert Alter, *Genesis: Translation and Commentary* (excerpt from the *Preface to the Reader*).

9. The same may be said for clarity and the mere appearance of clarity. They are not the same thing. The trick, perhaps, is to be able to recognize one from the other. In his book, *Pen of Iron*, Robert Alter suggests that the decline in the role of the King James Bible (which implies Tyndale's translation) is due to a "general erosion of a sense of literary language . . . Americans read less, and read with less comprehension; hours once devoted to books from childhood on are more likely to be spent in front of a television or a computer screen." Alter is not shy with his assessments. "Obviously, there are still people in the culture, including young people, who have a rich and subtle sense of language, but they are an embattled minority in a society where tonedeafness to style is increasingly prevalent."

10. Harold Bloom, *Jesus and Yahweh*, 47.

11. Greenblatt, *Renaissance Self Fashioning*, 107.

12. Daniell, *Word, Church, and State*, 10.

13. Lewis, *Literary Impact of the Authorized Version*, 14.

14. Robert Pinsky, *Democracy, Culture, and the Voice of Poetry*, audio book.

15. Jill Krementz, *The Writer's Desk*, xi.

16. Lewis, *Literary Impact of the Authorized Version*, 34.
17. Peter Auksi, *Journal of Medieval and Renaissance Studies*, vol. 8–9, (Duke University Press), 256.
18. Ibid.
19. J. F. Davis, *Heresy and Reformation in the South East of England*, 1520–1559, 23.
20. Walt Whitman, *Leaves of Grass* (1855 edition), 12–13.
21. Ibid., excerpt from the prologue, 13.
22. Tyndale, *The Parable of the Wicked Mammon*, 130.
23. John Newton's classic hymn "Amazing Grace" is based on Luke 15:32 and John 9:25, which in Tyndale's New Testament are translated (respectively), "For this thy brother was dead, and is alive again: and was lost, and is found." and "One thing I am sure of, that I was blind, and now I see."

Chapter 6

1. Robert Demaus, *William Tyndale: A Biography*, 149.
2. Moynahan, *God's Bestseller*, 101.
3. Tyndale, *W. T. to the Reader* (introduction to the Pentateuch), 3.
4. William Tyndale, *Practice of Prelates* (from *The Works of the English Reformers*, Thomas Russell, ed.), 482.
5. Demaus, *William Tyndale: A Biography*, 151.
6. Patrick Collinson, *The Reformation: A History*, 61.
7. Foxe, *Actes and Monuments*, 545.
8. Quoted in Moynahan, *God's Bestseller*, 102.
9. Quoted in Mozley, *William Tyndale*, 226.
10. Halle, *Edward Halle's Chronicle*, 762.
11. Mozley, *William Tyndale*, 147.
12. Ibid., (quoting from Edward Halle's Chronicles), 148.
13. Ibid., 147.
14. Lewis, *English Literature in the Sixteenth Century*, 34.
15. "The voice of a cryar in the wilderness," from the Tyndale New Testament became "the voice of one crying in the wilderness" in the King James Bible.
16. Foxe, *Foxe's Book of Martyrs*, 176.
17. Tyndale, excerpt from the *Preface to the Five Books of Moses*.
18. Williams, *William Tyndale*, 30.
19. Moynahan, *God's Bestseller*, 133.
20. Ibid., 313.
21. Foxe quoted in Moynahan, *God's Bestseller*, 316.
22. Demaus, *William Tyndale: A Biography*, 352.
23. Though some Hebrew grammar books and a lexicon arrived in the first decade of the sixteenth century, the first Regius (royal) professorship at Cambridge wasn't established until 1540, and at Oxford in 1546—both founded by Henry VIII. The universities of Paris, Wittenberg, and Louvain established the same professorial seats and around the same time.
24. Foxe, *Actes and Monuments*, 395.

Chapter 7

1. Thomas Wolfe, *The Story of a Novel*, 28–29.
2. Alighieri, *The Inferno*, 95.
3. Quoted by William Merwyn in *Ideas* with Paul Kennedy, "Dante: the Poet of the Impossible."
4. Alighieri, *Convivio* (trans. by Richard Lansing), 9.
5. From *Ideas* CBC Radio broadcast with Paul Kennedy, "Dante: the Poet of the Impossible."
6. Giusseppe Mazzota, "Dante, the Poet of the Impossible," *Ideas with Paul Kennedy* (podcast).
7. Vladimir Nabokov, *Lectures on Literature*, 10.
8. There is another parallel to consider between Dante and Tyndale, which is also germane to Renaissance studies, particularly the origin of Renaissance Humanism. Dante wrote his *Divine Comedy* in the vernacular, which was unheard of at the time. Dante was the first to introduce a vernacular literature, anticipating both Luther and Tyndale (and Wycliffe) in the act. It was Dante who first gave permission. Concerning the great thaw we refer to as the Renaissance (Western culture slowly liberated of its ancient bonds), it was Dante perhaps, a generation before John Wycliffe, who suggested not only a vernacular literature, but also a dependence on the classics (remembering that it was the Roman poet Virgil who guided Dante, the pilgrim of eternity, through the Inferno). Dante, as the suggestion implies, was the true father of Renaissance Humanism.
9. Mislosz, *Notes on Exile*, "*To Begin Where I Am: Selected Essays*," 19.
10. Wolfe, *Story of a Novel*, 29.
11. Maeera Y. Schreiber, "The End of Exile: Jewish Identity and Its Diasporic Poetics" (*PMLA*, March 1998).
12. Daniell, *William Tyndale: A Biography*, 213. William Tyndale to Stephen Vaughn.
13. From the *Online Bible Greek Transliterator with Strong's Concordance*. Romans 8:35.
14. Tyndale, *Parable of the Wicked Mammon*, 152.
15. Foxe, *Actes and Monuments*, 545.
16. Walt Whitman, from the preface to his 1855 edition of *Leaves Of Grass*.
17. Paraphrased from Genesis 3:24.
18. I Corinthians 15:45 TNT.
19. Wolfe, *The Story of a Novel*, 32.
20. Psalm 22:1 is another William Tyndale translation (Matthew 27:46 as translated in the 1526 NT) Myles Coverdale used Tyndale's translation for his Psalm 22:1: "My God, my God, why hast thou forsaken me?"
21. *Israel* [larsy] means "you have struggled with God and with men and have overcome."
22. Acts 13:22 TNT.
23. Wolfe, *Story of a Novel*, 33–34.

Chapter 8

1. Foxe, *Actes and Monuments*, vol. 7, 288.
2. Tyndale, *Parable of the Wicked Mammon* (in *Works of the English Reformers*, vol. I), 77.

3. Ibid., 77–78.

4. Daniell, *William Tyndale*, 144.

5. Tyndale, *Parable of the Wicked Mammon* (preface to the reader).

6. Ibid., 79.

7. Quoted in Daniell, *William Tyndale*, 143.

8. Ibid., 76.

9. Ibid., 134.

10. Ibid., 98

11. Ibid., (marginal note).

12. Ibid., 106.

13. Ibid.

14. *The Oxford English Dictionary* credits Myles Coverdale for the introduction of *evangelion* in 1542. "This is the first promes and the first sure Euangelion." Tyndale, who has hundreds of attributions in the OED is not mentioned with regard to this word. However, in his *Prologue to the Epistle of Paul to the Romans* it is found in the first sentence. Coverdale used Tyndale's construction.

15. *William Tyndale New Testament*, "A Prologue to the Epistle of Paul to the Romans," 207.

16. Tyndale, *Parable of the Wicked Mammon*, 88.

17. Ibid., 111.

18. Ibid., 94.

19. Ibid., 95

20. *William Tyndale New Testament*, "The Prologue Upon the Epistles of Saints James and Judas," 361.

21. Tyndale, *Parable of the Wicked Mammon*, 99.

22. Ibid., 103.

23. *Neighbor* is an important word in the Tyndale lexicon. In *The Parable of the Wicked Mammon* he explores its etymology. "Neighbor is a word of love, and signifieth that a man should be even nigh and at hand, and ready to help in time of need." *The Oxford English Dictionary* [etymology] the Germanic base of *nigh* [Denoting proximity, nearness] *adj.* + the Germanic base of *boor* [countryman] *n.*

24. Ibid., 138.

25. Ibid., 92.

26. Ibid., 143.

27. Ibid., 121.

28. Ibid., 104.

29. Ibid., 131.

30. Ibid., 120.

31. Bernard of Clairvaux, *On Loving God* (audio).

Chapter 9

1. Joanna Denny, *Anne Boleyn*, 18.

2. Quoted in Denny, *Anne Boleyn*, 20.

3. Denny, *Anne Boleyn*, 132.

4. D' Aubigny, *Letters and Papers, Foreign and Domestic of the Reign of Henry VIII*, 367.

5. Quoted in Moynahan, *God's Bestseller*, 163.

6. Tyndale, *Doctrinal Treatises and Introductions to Different Portions of the Holy Scriptures*, ed. by Rev. Henry Walter (Parker Society), 130.

7. Foxe, as quoted in Mozley, *William Tyndale*, 143.

8. Tyndale, *Obedience of a Christian Man*, 39.

9. Daniell, *William Tyndale: A Biography*, 246.

10. Tyndale, *Obedience of a Christian Man*, 3.

11. Ibid., (section titled "Antichrist"), 107.

12. Ibid., 65.

13. Martin Luther quoted in William Manchester, *A World Lit Only by Fire*, 141.

14. Lewis, *English Literature in the Sixteenth Century*, 189.

15. William Tyndale, *The Works of the English Reformers*, vol. 2: "Answer to Sir Thomas More," 48.

16. Tyndale, *Obedience of a Christian Man*, 170–171.

17. Ibid., 149.

18. Ibid., 31.

19. Ginsberg, "Ploughboys Versus Prelates," 48.

20. Ackroyd, *Albion*, 134.

21. Tyndale, *Obedience of a Christian Man*, 149–150.

Chapter 10

1. According to the *Oxford English Dictionary*, More is credited with first usage of *paradox* in 1533. (T. More, 2nd Pt., *Confutacion Tyndals Answere* iv. cii, "To proue vs thys wonderfull straunge paradox, thys opynyon inopinable.")

2. Quoted in James Wood, *The Broken Estate: Essays on Literature and Belief*, 3–15.

3. Denny, *Anne Boleyn*, 171.

4. Quoted in Mozley, *William Tyndale*, 216.

5. In John F. Davis, "The Trials of Thomas Bilney and the English Reformation," *The Historical Journal*, 784.

6. Manchester, *World Lit Only by Fire*, 109.

7. Quoted in Denny, *Anne Boleyn*, 161.

8. Wilcox, *Fire in the Bones*, 115.

9. George Cavendish, *Thomas Wolsey, The Late Cardinal: His Life and Death*, (audio).

10. Marius, *Thomas More*, 338.

11. John F. Davis, *The Historical Journal*, vol. 24, no. 4 (Dec. 1981), "The Trials of Thomas Bylney and the English Reformation," 775.

12. Foxe, *Actes and Monuments*, vol. 6, 130.

13. John Wycliffe, Walter Brute, William Thorpe, Sir John Oldcastle, Reynold Pecock (Bishop of Chichester), Walter Hilton, Thomas Bilney, *Writings of the Reverend and learned John Wickliff*, 267.

14. Moynahan, *God's Bestseller*, 251.

15. Foxe, *Actes and Monuments*, 513.
16. Edward Arber, ed., *Supplication of the Beggars* (1529), xi.
17. M. A. Tierney, *Dodd's Church history of England, from the commencement of the sixteenth century to the Revolution in 1688*, 419.
18. Quoted in Moynahan, *God's Bestseller*, 130.
19. Simon Fish, *Supplication of Beggars*, quoted in Foxe, *Actes and Monuments*, 516.
20. Simon Fish, *Supplication of the Beggars*, xv.
21. Foxe, *Actes and Monuments* (1563), vol. 7, 194.
22. Quoted in *Foxes Book of Martyrs*, 329.
23. Foxe, *Actes and Monuments*, 196.
24. Ibid., 330.
25. Ibid., 702.
26. Ibid., 705.
27. Foxe, *Actes and Monuments*, 183.
28. Ibid.
29. Moynahan, *God's Bestseller*, 261.

Chapter 11

1. Quoted in Moynahan, *God's Bestseller*, 124.
2. Foxe, *Actes and Monuments*, 4.
3. Essay by John T. Day, "Tyndale and Frith on Tracy's Will and Justification," *Word, Church, and State*, 162.
4. John Frith, *Answer Unto Sir Thomas More Book II*, (in *Works of the English Reformers*), 146.
5. Mozley, *William Tyndale*, 251.
6. Frith, *Disputation of Purgatory*, (from *The Works of the English Reformers: William Tyndale and John Frith*), 83–84.
7. Ibid., 76.
8. Ibid., 322
9. Quoted in Mozley, *William Tyndale*, 247.
10. Foxe, *Actes and Monuments*, 545.
11. Ibid., 130.
12. Mozley, *William Tyndale*, 252.
13. Ibid.
14. Demaus, *William Tyndale*, 347.
15. Sir Thomas More, *Letter against Frith* (from *Yale Complete Works*, 7).
16. From "The Story, Life, and Martyrdom of John Frith" (in *The Works of the English Reformers*, 1833), 79.
17. Foxe, *Actes and Monuments*, 3.
18. Ibid., 17–18.
19. Ibid., 528.
20. Mozley, *William Tyndale*, 260.

Chapter 12

1. Tyndale, *Obedience of a Christian Man*, 138.
2. Moynahan, *God's Bestseller*, 54.
3. Tyndale, *Obedience of a Christian Man*, 126.
4. Tyndale New Testament (1534) "W. T. unto the Reader."
5. Mozley, *William Tyndale*, 225.
6. Ramius, *Thomas More*, 317.
7. Tyndale, *Obedience of a Christian Man*, 123.
8. Ramius, *Thomas More*, 317.
9. Demaus, *William Tyndale: A Biography* (1886), 445.
10. Demosthenes (384–322 BC) was an Athenian orator, a gifted rhetorician. He wrote speeches and was well adept at legal argument. His defense of his city against Alexander the Great followed the tone of More's defense of his Catholicism. The reference would be well received by More.
11. Mozley, *William Tyndale*, 212–213. (Letter from Cuthbert Tunstall to Sir Thomas More, 7 March 1528).
12. Lewis, *English Literature in the Sixteenth Century*, 171.
13. Ibid.
14. Ibid.
15. Quoted in Ackroyd, *The Life of Thomas More*, 279.
16. *The Works of Thomas More*, (Yale Edition), vol. 8, 479.
17. Ackroyd, *Life of Thomas More*, 311.
18. Williams, *William Tyndale*, 77.
19. Daniell, *The Bible in English*, 149.
20. The actual quote is from William Tyndale's, *An Answer to Sir Thomas More's Dialogue*. "Covetousness maketh many, whom the truth pleaseth at the beginning, to cast it up again, and to be afterward the most cruel enemies thereof, after the ensample of Simon Magus; yea, and after the ensample of Sir Thomas More, knight, which knew the truth, and for covetousness forsook it again . . . Covetousness blinded the eyes of that gleering fox more and more, and hardened his heart against the truth, with the confidence of his painted poetry, babbling eloquence, and juggling arguments of subtle sophistry, grounded on his unwritten verities, as true and authentic as his story of Utopia."
21. *The Works of the English Reformers*, 15.
22. Ibid., 243.
23. Daniell, *Tyndale New Testament*, ix.

Chapter 13

1. Ackroyd, *Thomas More*, 307.
2. More, *Responsio ad Lutherum*, 17 (*Works*).
3. Ackroyd, *Thomas More*, 227.
4. Ibid.
5. *The Works of Thomas More*, vol. 5, part I, 17–21 (*Responsio ad Lutherum*).

6. More, *Responsio ad Lutherum* (The complete works of St. Thomas More, vol. 5, pt. I), 77.

7. Marius, *Thomas More*, 282.

8. Lewis, *English Literature in the Sixteenth Century*, 175.

9. Ackroyd, *Albion*, 323.

10. More, *Responsio ad Lutherum* (Yale modern translation).

11. Lewis, *English Literature in the Sixteenth Century*, 167.

12. Ibid., 169.

13. Lewis, *English Literature in the Sixteenth Century*, 175.

14. Ramius, *Thomas More*, 98.

15. Sir Thomas More, *History of King Richard III*, 9.

16. Ibid., 8.

17. Daniell, *William Tyndale*, 262 (English Historical Documents 5, 828–9).

18. Mozley, *William Tyndale*, 215.

19. Lewis, *English Literature in the Sixteenth Century*, 166.

20. Daniell, *William Tyndale*, 265.

21. Ibid.

22. Robert Bolt, *A Man For All Seasons*, vii.

23. Karlin, *Thomas More Studies*, 3 (2008), "More's Dialogue Concerning Heresies and the Idea of the Church," 32.

24. Ibid., 33.

25. *The works of the English reformers: William Tyndale and John Frith*, vol. 2 *(Answer to Sir Thomas More's Dialogue)*, 26.

Chapter 14

1. Denny, *Anne Boleyn*, 102.

2. Tyndale, *Answer to Sir Thomas More's Dialogue*, 11.

3. Ibid.

4. Tyndale, *Answer Unto Sir Thomas More's Dialogue*, 8 (preface).

5. Ibid., 13.

6. Ibid.

7. *ecclesia*—OLB Greek Transliterator.

8. Tyndale, *Answer to Sir Thomas More's Dialogue*, 14.

9. Tyndale, *The Practice of Prelates*, 281.

10. Tyndale, *An Answer to Sir Thomas More's Dialogue*, 14 (quoting More's *Dialogue Concerning Heresies*).

11. Ibid., 16.

12. Quoted in Bobrick, *Wide as the Waters*, 114.

13. Mozley, *William Tyndale*, 233.

14. Tyndale, *Obedience of a Christian Man*, 11.

15. Ibid., 115.

16. Quote from Thomas More, *Confutation* in Christopher Anderson, *Annals of the English Bible*, 337.

17. Daniell, *Let There Be Light*, 26.
18. Lewis, *English Literature in the Sixteenth Century*, 180.
19. Ibid.
20. Ibid., 173.
21. Ibid., 175.
22. Tyndale, *An Answer*, (ed. H. Walter), 151.
23. Lewis, *English Literature in the Sixteenth Century*, 192.
24. Ibid., 164.
25. Quoted in Ackroyd, *The Life of Thomas More* (quoting Edward Hall, *Chronicles*), 406.

Chapter 15

1. Daniell, ed., *Tyndale's New Testament*, 1534, xxix.
2. Foxe, *Acts and Monuments*, 395.
3. Mozley, *William Tyndale*, 287.
4. Tyndale, *Obedience of a Christian Man*, 19.
5. Daniell, *William Tyndale New Testament*, xxviii.
6. Ibid., 13.
7. Ibid., 14.
8. Ibid., 13.
9. Ibid., 18.
10. Mozley, *William Tyndale*, 182–183.
11. Quoted in Mozley, *William Tyndale* (from Edward Halle, *Hall's Chronicles*), 179–180.
12. Tyndale, *Prologue upon the First Epistle of St. Paul to the Corinthians*, 243.
13. Tyndale, *Prologue to the Prophet Jonas*, Tyndale OT, ed. David Daniell, ed., 629.
14. Tyndale, excerpt from *Exodus 15*, 109–110.
15. Bloom, *The Shadow of a Great Rock: A Literary Appreciation of the King James Bible*, 19.
16. Ibid., 5.
17. Ibid., 15.
18. From *The Prologue to the Prophet Jonas*.
19. Tyndale, *Prologue Showing Us the Use of Scripture*.
20. *Oxford English Dictionary*.
21. Tyndale, *Prologue into the Second Book of Moses Called Exodus*.
22. Tyndale, *Wicked Mammon*, 115.
23. Tyndale, *Prologue Showing the Use of the Scripture*.
24. Tyndale, *The Book of Jonas*, 628.
25. Tyndale, *Prologue to the Book of Jonas*, 635.
26. Ibid.
27. Quoted in Moynahan, *God's Bestseller*, 234.
28. Tyndale, *Prologue to the Book of Jonas*, 638–639.

Chapter 16

1. Tyndale, *Answer to Sir Thomas More's Dialogue*.
2. Tyndale, *Practice of Prelates*.

3. Tyndale, *Practice of Prelates* (excerpt from subheading "Of the Divorcement").

4. Moynahan, *God's Bestseller*, 221.

5. Quoted in Daniell, *William Tyndale*, 213.

6. Ibid.

7. Ibid., 214.

8. Demaus, *William Tyndale*, 281.

9. Ibid., 284.

10. Ibid., 308.

11. C. H. Williams, *William Tyndale*, 42.

12. Demaus, *William Tyndale*, 290.

13. "Unless I am proved wrong by the testimony of Scriptures or by evident reason, I am bound in conscience and held fast to the Word of God" (Spoken by Martin Luther at the Diet of Worms, 1521).

14. Marius, *Thomas More*, 363.

15. Quoted in Moynahan, *God's Bestseller*, 256.

16. Ibid.

17. Richard Marius, *Thomas More*, 404.

18. Moynahan, *God's Bestseller*, 258.

19. Stephen Vaughn in a letter written to Thomas Cromwell.

20. Daniell, *William Tyndale*, 185.

21. Foxe, *Actes and Monuments*, vol. 6, 182.

22. Quoted in C. H. Williams, *William Tyndale*, 43.

23. Demaus, *William Tyndale*, 319.

24. Tyndale, *An Exposition upon the Fifth, Sixth, and Seventh Chapters of Matthew*.

Chapter 17

1. Quoted in Moynahan, *God's Bestseller*, 326.

2. Ibid.

3. Daniell, *William Tyndale*, 361.

4. Quoted in Mozley, 307. Letter was from George Collins to unknown recipient.

5. Moynahan, *God's Bestseller*, 315.

6. Foxe, *Actes and Monuments*, 396.

7. Christopher Anderson, *Annals*, 418.

8. Mozley, *William Tyndale*, 301.

9. Foxe, *Foxe's Book of Martyrs*, ed. William Byron Forbush, 183.

10. Foxe, *Actes and Monuments*, 397.

11. Ibid.

12. Foxe, *Foxe's Book of Martyrs*, ed. William Byron Forbush, 183.

13. Ibid.

14. Quoted in Mozley, *William Tyndale*, 301.

15. Demaus, *William Tyndale*, 398.

16. Mozley, *William Tyndale*, 305.

17. Ibid., 309–311.

18. Ibid., 311.
19. Ibid., 316.
20. Ibid., 319.
21. Ibid., 320.
22. Mozley, *William Tyndale*, 320.
23. Foxe, *Actes and Monuments*, 311.

Chapter 18

1. First use of *inquisition* was the Wycliffe Bible 1382, *Oxford English Dictionary*.
2. Quoted in Daniell, *William Tyndale*, 371.
3. Foxe, *Actes and Monuments*, 544.
4. Ibid., 128.
5. Quoted in Williams, *William Tyndale*, 57.
6. Quoted in Mozley, *William Tyndale*, 329.
7. Mozley, *William Tyndale*, 329.
8. Ibid., 330
9. Ibid., 331.
10. Ibid., 331–332.
11. Ibid., 332.
12. Quoted in Moynahan, *God's Bestseller*, 376.
13. Ibid., 376.
14. Ibid., 338.
15. Mozley, *William Tyndale*, 333.
16. Ibid., 335–336.
17. Foxe, *Actes and Monuments*, 544.
18. Quoted in Mozley, *William Tyndale*, 342.

Epilogue

1. Speech by Penelope Lively at the Sterling Memorial Library at Yale University, May 9, 2008, entitled "Reading History and Writing Fiction: A Life In Books" (Yale University Netcast).
2. Quoted in Daniell, *The Bible in English*, 156.
3. William Tyndale, *Obedience of a Christian Man*, 150–151.

Bibliography

Ackroyd, Peter. *The Life of Thomas More*. New York: Nan Talese (Doubleday), 1998.

———. *Albion: The Origins of the English Imagination*. London: Nan Talese (Doubleday), 2003.

———. *Chaucer (Ackroyd Brief Lives)*. New York: Nan Talese (Doubleday), 2004.

———. *The Life of Thomas More*. New York: Nan Talese (Doubleday), 1998.

Alighieri, Dante. *The Divine Comedy*. Translated by Mark Musa. New York: Penguin, 1995.

———. *La Vita Nuova*. Translated by Mark Musa. Oxford: Oxford University Press, 1992.

———. *Convivio*. Translated by Richard Lansing. *Digital Dante* (web), Columbia University.

Alter, Robert. *Pen of Iron: American Prose and the King James Bible*. Princeton: Princeton University Press, 2010.

———. *Genesis: Translation and Commentary*. New York: W. W. Norton and Company, 1996.

Avis, Paul. *God and the Creative Imagination*. London and New York: Routledge, 1999.

Anderson, Christopher. *The Annals of the English Bible*, vol. I. London: Pickering. 1845.

Bloom, Harold. *Genius: A Mosaic of One Hundred Exemplary Creative Minds*. New York: Warner Books, 2002.

———. *Hamlet: Poem Unlimited*. New York: Riverhead Books (Penguin Putnam), 2003.

———. *Jesus and Yahweh*. New York: Riverhead Books, 2005.

———. *The Shadow Of A Great Rock: A Literary Appreciation of the King James Bible*. New Haven: Yale University Press, 2011.

———. *Shakespeare: The Invention of the Human*. New York: Riverhead Books (Penguin Putnam), 1998.

———. "Dante Alighieri." *Bloom's Modern Critical Views*. Broomall, PA: Chelsea House Publishers, 2004.

Boccaccio, Giovanni. 2002. *Life of Dante*. Translated by J. G. Nichols. London: Hesperus Press Limited. (Orig. pub. 1374?).

Bolt, Robert. *A Man For All Seasons*. New York: Vintage International (Vintage), 1960.

Bobrick, Benson. *Wide as the Waters*. New York: Simon and Schuster, 2001.

Brotton, Jerry. *The Renaissance: A Very Short Introduction*. Oxford: Oxford University Press, 2006.

Brown, Rawdon, ed. "Venice: December 1530." *Calendar of State Papers Relating to English Affairs in the Archives of Venice*, Volume 4: 1527–1533.

Campbell. W. E. *Erasmus, Tyndale, and More*. Milwaukee: The Bruce Publishing Company, 1949.

Cavendish, George. 2010. *Thomas Wolsey, the Late Cardinal: His Life and Death*. Blackstone Audio. (Orig. pub. 1554).

Collinson, Patrick. *The Reformation: A History*. New York: Modern Library, 2004.

Collis, Louise. 1983. *Memoirs of a Medieval Woman*. New York: Harper Colophon. (Orig. pub. 1964).

Conrad, Joseph. 1999. *Heart of Darkness*. New York: Penguin. (Orig. pub. 1903).

———. *A Personal Record*. New York: Doubleday, Page, and Company, 1912.

Conroy, Pat. *My Reading Life*. New York: Nan A. Talese (Doubleday), 2010.

Coulton, G. G. *Chaucer and His England*. London: Bracken Books, 1993 (1st ed. 1908).

Creighton, Mandell. *Cardinal Wolsey*. London: Macmillan and Co., 1891.

Crystal, David. *English: The Global Language*. Project sponsored by the U. S. English Foundation, 1996.

Daniell, David. *William Tyndale: A Biography*. New Haven and London: Yale University Press, 1994.

———. *Let There Be Light: William Tyndale and the Making of the English Bible*. London: The British Library, 1994.

———. *The Bible in English*. London: Yale University Press, 2003.

Demaus, Rev. R. *William Tyndale: A Biography*. London: The Religious Tract Society, 1886.

Denny, Joanna. *Anne Boleyn: A New Life of England's Tragic Queen*. London: De Capo Press (mem. Perseus Books Group), 2004.

Dodd, Charles. Tierney, M. A. *Dodd's Church history of England, from the commencement of the sixteenth century to the Revolution in 1688*. London: New Bond Street. 1839.

Dods, Marcus. *Erasmus and Other Essays*. London: Hodder and Stoughton, 1891.

Duffield, G. E., ed. *The Work of William Tyndale*. Philadelphia: Fortress Press, 1965.

Emerson, Ralph Waldo. "The Poet." *Selected Writings of Ralph Waldo Emerson*. Edited by Brooks Atkinson. New York: Modern Library, 1950.

Ehrman, Bart D. *Misquoting Jesus*. San Franciso: HarperCollins, 2005.

Fish, Simon. *A Supplication of the Beggars*. (Spring of 1529). Edited by Edward Arber. Westminster: Archibald Constable and Co., 1895.

Foxe, John. *Foxe's Book of Martyrs*. Edited by William Byron.

———. *Actes and Monuments of the Church: Containing the History and Sufferings of the Martyrs*. Edited by Rev. M. Hobart Seymour. New York: Robert Carter & Bro., 1855.

Forbush. Grand Rapids: Clarion Classics (Zondervan House), 1967 (First English ed. 1563).

———. *Actes and Monuments*. Volumes I–VII.

Fuller, Thomas, DD. *Church History of Britain: from the Birth of Jesus Christ until the Year MDCXLVIII*. Oxford: Oxford University Press, 1845.

Green, John Richard. *England*. Volumes 1-4. New York: Peter, Fenelon, Collier. 1893.

Greenblatt, Stephen. *Renaissance Self-Fashioning*. Chicago: University of Chicago Press, 1980.

Halle, Edward. *Hall's Chronicle: Containing the History of England During the Reign of Henry the Fourth and the Succeeding Monarchs, to the End of the Reign of Henry the Eighth, in Which are Particularly Described the Manners and Customs of Those Periods. Carefully Collated with the Editions of 1548 and 1550.* London: Printed for J. Johnson, et al, 1809. (Original 1548 title: *The vnion At the Two noble and illustre famelies Lancastre & yorke, Beetno long ih, With ail the Actes done in bothe the tymes of the princes, Eothe of the one linage and of the other, Beginnyng at the tyme of kyng henry the fowerth, The first aucthor of this deuision, And so successiuely proceadvno to the reigne of the high and prudent prince Kyng henry the eight, The vndubitate flower and very heire of both the sayd linages,* 1548.)

Hoffman, Eva. *Lost in Translation.* London: Random House, 1989.

Hudson, William Henry. *The Story of the Renaissance.* London: Cassell and Company, 1912.

Huizinga, Johan. *Erasmus and the Age of Reformation.* New York: Harper (Torchbooks), 1957.

Jensen, De Lamar. *Confrontation at Worms: Martin Luther and the Diet of Worms.* Brigham Young University Press, 1973.

John of the Cross (San Juan de la Cruz). *The Ascent of Mount Carmel.* Trans. and ed. by Allison Peers. Ligouri, MO: Triumph Books, 1991.

Joseph, Sister Miriam. *The Trivium: The Liberal Arts of Logic, Grammar, and Rhetoric.* Paul Dry Books, 2002.

Kingsley-Smith, Jane. *Shakespeare's Drama of Exile.* New York: Palgrave Macmillan, 2003.

Krementz, Jill. *The Writer's Desk.* New York: Random House, 1996.

Lewis, C. S. *English Literature in the Sixteenth Century.* Oxford: Clarendon Press, 1954.

———. *The Literary Impact of the Authorized Version.* London: Fortress Press, 1963.

Lively, Penelope. "Reading History and Writing Fiction: A life in Books." Speech given at the Sterling Memorial Library at Yale University, May 9, 2008. Yale University Podcast.

Long, John D. *The Bible in English: John Wycliffe and William Tyndale.* New York: University Press of America, 1998.

Marius, Richard. *Thomas More.* New York: Alfred A. Knopf, 1984.

———. *Martin Luther: The Christian Between God and Death.* Cambridge: Harvard University Press, 1999.

Maugham, Somerset. 1946. *The Summing Up.* New York: Mentor Books (New American Library of World Literature). (Orig. pub. 1938).

McCrum, Robert, William Cran, and Robert MacNeil. *The Story of English.* New York: Viking Penguin, 1986.

McCrum, Robert. *Globish: How the English Language Became the World's Language.* New York: W. W. Norton and Company, 2010.

McGrath, Alister. *In the Beginning.* New York: Anchor Books, 2002.

Merton, Thomas. *The New Man.* New York: The Noonday Press, 1961.

Meyer, G. J. *The Tudors: The Complete Story of England's Most Notorious Dynasty.*

Milbauer, Asher Z. *Transcending Exile.* Miami: Florida International University Press, 1985.

Milosz, Czeslaw. *To Begin Where I Am: Selected Essays.* New York: Farrar, Straus and Giroux, 2002.

More, Thomas. *The Complete Works of St. Thomas More.* vol. I–12. Yale Edition. New
   Haven and London: Yale University Press, 1969.

——. *The History of King Richard III and Selections from the English and Latin Poems.* Edited by
   Richard S. Sylvester. Yale University Press, 1976.

Mozley, J. F. *William Tyndale.* New York: The Macmillan Company, 1937.

Nabokov, Vladimir. *Lectures on Literature.* New York: Harcourt (A Harvest Book), 1980.

——. *Verses and Versions: Three Centuries of Russian Poetry—Selected and Translated by
   Vladimir Nabokov.* Eds. Brian Boyd and Stanislav Shrabin. New York: Harcourt,
   2008.

Nicolson, Adam. *God's Secretaries.* London: Harper Collins Publishers, 2003.

Norton, David. *A History of the English Bible As Literature.* Cambridge: Cambridge
   University Press, 2000.

Nugent, Elizabeth. *The Thought and Culture of the English Renaissance: an anthology of Tudor prose
   1481–1555.* Cambridge: Cambridge University Press, 1956.

Offor, George. *The New Testament of our Lord and Saviour Jesus Christ Published in 1526 from
   the Greek into English, by that Eminent Scholar and Martyr, William Tyndale. Reprinted verbatim:
   With a Memoir of his Life and Writings.* London: Paternoster Row, 1836.

Pinsky, Robert. *Democracy, Culture, and the Voice of Poetry.* Princeton: Princeton University
   Press, 2002.

Pollard, Alfred W. *Records of the English Bible: The Documents Relating to the Translation and
   Publication of the Bible in English.* London: Oxford University Press, 1911.

Rollison, David. *The Local Origins of Modern Society: Gloucestershire 1500–1800.* London:
   Routledge, 1992.

Roper, William. *The Life of Sir Thomas More.* Edited by S. W. Singer. London:
   Whittingham Press (Bond Street), 1822. University of Oxford English Faculty
   Library.

Rubin, Harriet. *Dante in Love.* New York: Simon and Schuster, 2004.

Rubin, Miri. *The Hollow Crown: A History of Britain in the Late Middle Ages.* New York:
   Penguin, 2005.

Russell, Thomas (ed.). *The Works of the English Reformers: William Tyndale and John Frith in
   Three Volumes.* London: Paternoster Row, 1831.

Scruton, Roger. *England: An Elegy.* London: Chatto and Windus, 2000.

Shuger, Deborah Kuller, *The Renaissance Bible: Scholarship, Sacrifice, and Subjectivity.* Berkeley:
   University of California Press, 1994.

Shutt, Timothy. *The Modern Scholar: Dante and His Divine Comedy.* Recorded Books, LLC,
   2008.

——. *The Modern Scholar: Masterpieces of Medieval Literature.* Recorded Books, LLC, 2005.

Starkey, David. *Monarchy: From the Middle Ages to Modernity.* New York: Harper Collins,
   2000.

Storr, Vernon F. *The English Bible: Essays by Various Writers.* London: Methuen and Co,
   Ltd., 1938.

Sunshine, Glen. *The Reformation for Armchair Theologians.* Louisville: Westminster John
   Knox Press, 2005.

Teems, David. *And Thereby Hangs a Tale.* Eugene: Harvest House Publishers, 2010.

———. *Majestie: The King Behind the King James Bible*. Nashville: Thomas Nelson Publishers, 2010.

Teresa of Avila. *The Complete Works of St. Teresa*, Volume One. Edited by Alison Peers. London: Sheed and Ward, 1972.

Therese of Lisieux. *Story of a Soul* (Autobiography). Washington: ICS Publications, 1972.

Trevelyan, G. M. 1963. *England in the Age of Wycliffe 1368–1520*. New York: Harper Torchbooks. (Orig. pub. 1899).

Tyndale, William. *The Obedience of a Christian Man*. Edited by David Daniell. New York: Penguin Classics, 2000 (Orig. pub. 1528).

———. *The New Testament* (1534). Edited by David Daniell. New Haven and London: Yale University Press, 1995.

———. *The Old Testament* (1534). Edited by David Daniell. New Haven and London: Yale University Press, 1992.

———. *The Lord's Supper*. New York: Penguin Classics.

———. *The Parable of the Wicked Mammon* (1528). In *The Works of the English Reformers: William Tyndale and John Frith*, vol. 1. Edited by Thomas Russell. London: Ebenezer Palmer, 18, Paternoster Row, 1831. Harvard College Library.

———. *Answer to Sir Thomas More's Dialogue* (1531). In *The Works of the English Reformers: William Tyndale and John Frith*, vol. 2. Edited by Thomas Russell. London: Ebenezer Palmer, 18, Paternoster Row, 1831. Harvard College Library.

———. *Doctrinal Treatises*. Edited by Walter Henry (1785–1859). Cambridge: Cambridge University Press, 1848.

———. *The Practice of Prelates* (1530). In *The Works of the English Reformers: William Tyndale and John Frith*, vol. 1. Edited by Thomas Russell. London: Ebenezer Palmer, 18, Paternoster Row, 1831. Harvard College Library.

———. *A Pathway to Scripture* (1530). In *The Works of the English Reformers: William Tyndale and John Frith*, vol. 2. Edited by Thomas Russell. London: Ebenezer Palmer, 18, Paternoster Row, 1831. Harvard College Library.

———. *An Exposition upon the Fifth, Sixth, and Seventh Chapters of Matthew* (1531). In *The Works of the English Reformers: William Tyndale and John Frith*, vol. 2. Edited by Thomas Russell. London: Ebenezer Palmer, 18, Paternoster Row, 1831. Harvard College Library.

———. *An Exposition upon the First Epistle of John* (1531). In *The Works of the English Reformers: William Tyndale and John Frith*, vol. 2. Edited by Thomas Russell. London: Ebenezer Palmer, 18, Paternoster Row, 1831. Harvard College Library.

———. *The Testament of Master Tracie, Esquire* (1535). New York: Penguin Classics.

———. *Erasmus's Enchiridion* (1533). New York: Penguin Classics.

Weber, Max. *From Max Weber: Essays in Sociology*. Translated and edited by H. H. Gerth and C. Wright Mills. New York: Oxford University Press, 1946.

Weir, Alison. *Henry VIII: The King and His Court*. New York: Ballantine, 2001.

Westcott, Brooke Foss. *A General View of the History of the English Bible*. 3rd ed. Rev. W. A. Wright, 1905.

Whitman, Walt. *Leaves of Grass* (1855 edition). Edited by Malcolm Cowley. New York: Penguin, 1959.

———. *Leaves of Grass* (1892 final edition). Copyrights 1891 by Walt Whitman. Copyright 1897 by literary executors of Walt Whitman. Entered as Stationer's Hall.

Wilcox, S. Michael. *Fire in the Bones: William Tyndale—Martyr, Father of the English Bible*. Salt Lake: Desert Book, 2004.

Williams, C. H. *William Tyndale*. London: Thomas Nelson and Sons LTD, 1969.

Williams, Rowan. *Christian Imagination in Poetry and Polity*. Oxford: SLG Press, 2004.

Willson, David. *A History of England*. Hinsdale, IL: The Dryden Press (Holt, Rinehart, and Winston), 1972.

Wilson, Edmund. *A Piece of My Mind*. Garden City: Doubleday Anchor Books, 1958.

Wolfe, Thomas. *The Autobiography of an American Novelist*. Edited by Leslie Field. Cambridge, MA: Harvard University Press, 1983.

Wood, Anthony. *Athenae Oxoniensis: An Exact History of all the Writers and Bishops Who Have Had Their Education in the University of Oxford*. Edited by P. Bliss. London, 1815.

Wycliffe, John, and Walter Brute, William Thorpe, Sir John Oldcastle, Reynold Pecock (Bishop of Chichester), Walter Hilton, Thomas Bilney. *Writings of the Reverend and learned John Wickliff*. London: The Religious Tract Society, 1831.

Yeats, William Butler. *The Collected Poems of William Butler Yeats*. Hertfordshire: Wordsworth Edition, 2000.

Articles

Adams, Robert P. "Designs by More and Erasmus for a New Social Order." *Studies in Philology*, vol. 42, no. 2 (April 1945).

Bartlett, I. Ross. "John Foxe As Hagiographer: The Question Revisited." *The Sixteenth Century Journal*, vol. 26, no. 4 (Winter 1995).

Bennett, Joseph. "The Poetic Basis of Music." *The Musical Times and Singing Class Circular*, vol.16, no. 373 (March 1874).

Bishop, William S. "Erasmus." *The Sewanee Review*, vol. 14, no. 2 (April 1906).

Clark, James Andrew. "More and Tyndale as Prose Stylists." *Moreanna*, vol. 21, no. 82 (June 1984).

Clebsch, William A. "The Earliest Translations of Luther into English." *The Harvard Theological Review*, vol. 56, no. 1 (January 1963).

Collinson, Patrick. "The Apostle of England." Trinity College, Cambridge.

Davis, John F. "The Trials of Thomas Bylney and the English Reformation," *The Historical Journal*, vol. 24, no. 4 (December 1981): 775–790.

———. "Heresy and Reformation in the South-East of England, 1520–1559." *Royal Historical Society Studies in History*. Series no. 34. (1983).

Ewert, A. "Dante's Theory of Language," *The Modern Language Review*, vol. 35, no. 3 (July 1940): 355–366.

Ginsberg, David. "Ploughboys Versus Prelates: Tyndale and More and the Politics of Biblical Translation." *The Sixteenth Century Journal*, vol. 19, no. 1 (Spring 1988): 45–61.

Hardin, Richard F. "Caricature in More's *Confutation*." *Moreanna*, vol. 93 (February 1987).

Hecht, Jamey. "Limitations of Textuality in Thomas More's Confutation of Tyndale's Answer." *The Sixteenth Century Journal*, vol. 26, no. 4 (Winter 1995).

King, John. "The Light of Printing: William Tyndale, John Foxe, John Day, and Early Modern Print Culture." *Renaissance Quarterly*. vol. 54, no. 1 (Spring 2001). University of Chicago Press.

Knappen, M. M. "William Tyndale: First English Puritan." *Church History*. vol. 5, no. 3 (September 1936). Cambridge University Press.

Levine, David. *Social History*, vol. 19, no. 1 (January 1994). Review of "*The local origins of modern society: Gloucestershire 1500–1800*," by David Rollison.

Maveety, Stanley R. "Doctrine in Tyndale's New Testament: Translation as a Tendentious Art." *Studies in English Literature, 1500–1900, Volume 6, No. 1, The English Renaissance* (Winter 1966): 151–158.

Mozley, J. F. "Notes and Queries." *The Oxford Journals* (June 1946).

Nelson, William. "The Teaching of English in Tudor Grammar Schools." *Studies in Philology*, vol. 49, no. 2 (April 1952).

Nauert, Charles. "Desiderius Erasmus." *Stanford Encyclopedia of Philosophy*, 2008.

Patterson, W. Brown. "Englishing the Scriptures." *The Sewanee Review*, vol. 105, no. 1 (Winter 1997). The Johns Hopkins University Press.

Peritz, Ismar J. "Tyndale's Monument." *Journal of Bible and Religion*, vol. 7, no. 2 (May 1939).

Price, F. D. *The English Historical Review*, vol. 86, no. 341 (October 1971). "Review of C. H. Williams, *William Tyndale*" (London: Thomas Nelson, 1969).

Rex, Richard. "The Crisis of Obedience: God's Word and Henry's Reformation." *The Historical Journal*, vol. 39, no. 4 (December 1996).

Rollison, David. "Discourse and Class Struggle: The Politics of Industry in Early Modern England." *Social History*, vol. 26, no. 2 (May 2001).

———. "Property, Ideology and Popular Culture in a Gloucestershire Village 1660-1740." *Past & Present*, no. 93 (November 1981).

———. "The Bourgeois Soul of John Smyth of Nibley." *Social History*, vol. 12, no. 3 (October 1987).

Scarisbruck, J. J. "Thomas More: A Model for Us All." *Moreanna*, vol. 22 (November 1985).

Shreiber, Maeera Y. "The End of the Exile: Jewish Identity and Its Diasporic Poetics." *PMLA*, vol. 113, no. 2 (March 1998).

Schwartz, Delmore. "The Isolation of Modern Poetry." *The Kenyon Review*. vol. 3, no. 2 (Spring 1941).

Trinterud, L. J. "A Reappraisal of William Tyndale's Debt to Martin Luther." *Church History*, vol. 31, no. 1 (March 1962). Cambridge University Press.

Reference

The Catholic Encyclopedia: An International Work of Reference on the Constitution, Doctrine, Discipline, and History of the Catholic Church, vol. 3, no. 15. Edited by Charles G. Herbermann. New York: The Universal Knowledge Foundation, 1912.

Oxford English Dictionary. Oxford University Press. Internet edition.

Acknowledgments

M y first and most gracious thanks to my editor Janene MacIvor, for her generosity, her knowledge, and for her effectiveness in her craft. To Merry MacIvor, for her quick mind, her sharp eye, and her mother's gift of editorial diplomacy and persuasion. To my wife, Benita, who took care of things at home while I worked in Georgia and in Florida for months at a time, writing on the run to get a hint of what Tyndale was up against. And at last, to my dog, Sophie, my beloved Dalmatian who we lost while I was away from home. Sorrow and homesickness played a necessary role in the making of this book.

About the Author

David Teems is the author of *To Love Is Christ* (Nelson, 2005), *And Thereby Hangs a Tale* (Harvest House, 2010), *Majestie: The King Behind the King James Bible* (Nelson, 2010), and *Discovering Your Spiritual Center* (Leafwood, 2011). David and his wife, Benita, live in Franklin, Tennessee, near their sons, Adam and Shad. Adam and his wife, Katie, have three children: Julian, Evie, and Audrey Gray.

More from David Teems

In the beginning, James.

Orphaned, bullied, lonely, and unloved as a boy, in time the young King of Scots overcame his troubled beginnings to ascend the English throne at the height of England's Golden Age. In an effort to pacify rising tensions in the Anglican Church, and to reflect the majesty of his new reign, he spearheaded the most important literary undertaking in Western history—the translation of the Bible into a beautiful, lyrical, and accessible English.

David Teems's narrative crackles with wit, using a thoroughly modern tongue to reanimate the life of this seventeenth-century king—a man at the intersection of political, literary, and religious thought, yet a man of contrasts, dubbed by one French king as "the wisest fool in Christendom."

Warm, insightful, even at times amusing, Teems's description of King James has all the elements of a grand tale—conspiracy, kidnapping, witchcraft, murder, love, despair, loss. *Majestie* offers an engaging new look at the world's most cherished, revered, and influential translation of Sacred Writ and the king behind it.

> { "Engrossing and entertaining . . . a delightful read in every way." }
>
> — *Publishers Weekly*